GIVE ME LIBERTY!

Also by Gerry Spence

O.J.: The Last Word
The Making of a Country Lawyer
How to Argue and Win Every Time
From Freedom to Slavery
Gunning for Justice
Of Murder and Madness
Trial by Fire
With Justice for None

GIVE ME LIBERTY!

Freeing Ourselves

in the

Twenty-first Century

GERRY SPENCE

ST. MARTIN'S GRIFFIN NEW YORK

Photo on p. xvi: "Edith in Texas Cotton Field, 1913" by Lewis Hine. Courtesy of the Library of Congress.
Photo on p. 110: Cowboy on horseback. Courtesy of Corbis-Bettmann.
"It's Alright Ma, I'm Only Bleeding" by Bob Dylan. Copyright © 1965 by Warner Bros., Inc. Copyright renewed 1993 by Special Rider Music. All rights reserved. International copyright secured. Reprinted by permission.
Photo on p. 200: Selma to Montgomery, Alabama, march. Courtesy of UPI/Corbis-Bettmann.
"Dream Deferred," from *Collected Poems* by Langston Hughes. Copyright © 1951 by Langston Hughes. Reprinted by permission of Alfred A. Knopf, Inc.

Production Editor: David Stanford Burr

Gerry Spence's Web site: www.givemeliberty.com

Library of Congress Cataloging-in-Publication Data

Spence, Gerry.
    Give me liberty : freeing ourselves in the twenty-first century / Gerry Spence.
            p.   cm.
    Includes index.
    ISBN 0-312-19267-3 (hc)
    ISBN 0-312-24563-7 (pbk)
    1. Liberty. 2. United States—Politics and government. 3. United States—Social conditions. I. Title.
JC599.U633   1998
306'.0973—dc21   98-25899
                                                                       CIP

First St. Martin's Griffin Edition: October 1999

10 9 8 7 6 5 4 3 2 1

To Robert R. Rose, Jr., my dear friend.
He taught the power of love.

CONTENTS

⋅•⋅

PART I

We, the People, the New American Slaves

PART II

Freeing the Self

PART III
Freeing the Nation

A CONTENTS OF DREAMS

·—·

TWENTY-SIX DREAMS TO LIBERTY

The following is a list of twenty-six steps that we can take to reclaim our society. They are described at length in Part III of the book.

OUR CRY FOR LIBERTY

I ask you: Are you free?

I say we are slaves. All of us.

I ask you: Are you different from the many who secretly feel like slaves—slaves to their jobs from which they cannot escape, slaves to a government that no longer serves them but to which they have become hopelessly indentured, slaves to a life that is beyond their control as the stick thrown into the stream is enslaved to the rushing current?

"Are you free?" I asked a woman pounding at her computer. She was one of hundreds who occupied those small cubicles that covered five floors, each floor larger than a gymnasium, acres of humans each at a small desk. She didn't look up when I spoke to her.

"I haven't got time to talk to you," she said, still fixed on her screen. "This computer records everything I do. If I stop, it tells on me. If I slow down, it squeals on me. If I go to the bathroom, it makes a record of it. If I don't make my quota for the day, my name goes into the red zone. If it stays there a couple of days, someone else will be sitting here instead of me. I got kids. Am I free? Go away," she said. Then, as I left, she hollered after me. "Everybody in this country is free but me."

"Are you free?" I recently asked a secretary working for the local telephone company.

"I hate my job," she said. "Since the big downsizing, I'm doing the work of seven. Whatever anyone asks me to do I have to do, and I have to do it *now*, even if I am days behind in my regular work. Sometimes I'm so tired I want to fold up on the floor and cry."

"Why don't you quit?" I asked. "This is a free country."

"I can't quit," she said. "I only have seven years to retirement. And they can even fire you before your pension vests. Last week they laid off Melinda, who had worked for the company two years longer than me, and yesterday they hired a young girl right out of junior college to take her place." Then she said, as if she had said something wrong, "But this is the best country in the world."

"Are you free?" I asked a worker at the cement plant. He shook the cement dust off his coveralls and pushed up his goggles. "Yeah," he said, "I'm free. But we haven't had a pay increase in four years. Working longer for less. Hard times in good times," he said.

"Why don't you quit?"

"Can't," he said. "We got our home here. Couldn't get our money out of it. Used to be a good town, but now it's gone to hell. Kids are in school. They don't want to leave. Wife's got a job. We probably couldn't find better jobs anywhere else. Besides, this is all I know." Then he pulled his goggles down and picked up his shovel.

"Are you free?" I asked the manager of the hotel.

He looked surprised. "What do you mean?" he asked. Then he said, "I like my work. Only thing is, I get moved around a lot. Last year they sold the company again, and I was sold along with it. Been in three cities in the last four years."

"Must be hard on you," I said.

"You get used to it," he said. "A person shouldn't complain. But it's hard on my wife. And the kids are always being yanked up by their roots."

"Why don't you refuse to move? You're free, aren't you?"

"I'm just another piece of furniture. I get sold with the hotel, the beds, the linens." He shook his head. "But I like my work."

"Are you free?" I asked a government social worker. She wanted to make things better for the poor, and she wanted security for herself.

"I'm as free as you," she said. She was spunky. "But we have to follow the regulations. Sometimes I feel like a robot. No room for spontaneity. And they're always cutting budgets. And besides that, we have a new director about every other year, and they are only interested in politics. Politics. Politics. It's disgusting. But one thing: I have security."

"So does the polar bear in the zoo."

"Don't be funny," she said. Then she looked at me strangely for longer than was comfortable. Suddenly she said, "I feel like the polar bear."

"Are you free?" I asked a college student who was taking a course in business.

"Sure," he said. "I take whatever classes I want. I'm free to choose my own career."

"Why are you taking business?" I asked.

"Business is the thing nowadays. Good market for business majors in the corporate sector."

"Does that mean you are preparing a product that you can sell on the open market?"

"A product?"

"Yes. *You* are the product. Do you think you will enjoy working for a corporation?"

"I think so," he said. "They have a lot of benefits, and I'd like to run a big corporation someday." He cocked his head from side to side. "I want to be a big shot." Then he put his hands in his pockets and strode away in long bouncy steps.

"Are you free?" I finally asked the CEO of a large food-store chain. He was on the board of directors of three other major corporations.

"Since you mentioned it, freedom at the top is bullshit," he said. "The people who work here think I can do whatever I please. But I have shareholders to please. I have Wall Street to please. I have the fuckin' media to please. If they get on your case they can drive your stock to hell, and you go with it.

"If I fire an incompetent worker, the government is on my ass for discrimination. If I fire some old bastards who have lost all incentive to do an honest day's work, I'm charged with age discrimination. You can't close the door in your office while your secretary's in there for fear you'll end up being hit with a sexual harassment suit. I have an open-door policy: Open door whenever there's a female around." He laughed. "Yes, I'm a slave—the biggest fuckin' slave in the company."

I say we are slaves. All of us. And in bewildering ways, our bondage is more pernicious than the slavery of old, for the New American Slave embraces the myth of his freedom as he would a dead puppy and, with all affection, speaks to it as if it were alive.

Our nation was built on slavery, a house torn down by the great Civil War. But this new house, a house of mirrors, of secret rooms, of hidden passages—indeed, a vastly more subtle and deluding structure—has been built on the same malignant foundation. And today we live in this house, and we are all still slaves. Hear Goethe's warning: "No one is as hopelessly enslaved as the person who thinks he is free."

And if we are the New American Slaves, who is our master? The New Master is an entanglement of megacorporations on the one hand and an omnipowerful national government on the other, each stuck to the other like a pair of copulating dogs, each unable to move without dragging the other behind it, each dependent upon the other, hating the other, but welded to the other in a dissolute enterprise.

The New Master, a political and economic hybrid that was not invented to serve a free people, is driven by a gluttony unparalleled in human history. The power it produces is incalculable. Utterly fabricated to generate profit, it feeds off the people, digests the people, and excretes the people in a game of world domination in which profit is virtue and money is god. The New Master is mad.

Like any unabashed heretic, I have an agenda. As I see it, we are in this together. I wish us all to be freed. But before we can free each other, we must first free ourselves. And how?

In this book I offer recipes for our personal freedom that can invest each of us with the power to break out of the zoo. We shall discover how the mind constructs the cage but also opens the gate. We shall discover how, experiencing our new liberty, we can never be defeated. And we shall discover how to create a new paradigm for success, so that success is based not on the accumulation of great wealth, but on the acquisition of great personhood.

But to free ourselves is not enough. I propose radical reform to reclaim America: We must take back the airways, the voice of the people, and create a new constitution for the twenty-first century. I propose a revolutionary method to finance elections. And, to save ourselves from the lies, the cheating, the unholy sellouts of self-seeking candidates, I propose the eventual abolishment of elections altogether. To replace them, I outline a means by which we can draft our representatives by lot, and by which we can create a Senate composed of the nation's finest minds and most evolved citizens, a pristine government to lead us at last to the promised land.

I shall show how, in the New Free America, we can convert our corporate master to our willing slave. At the same time we shall discover how to retrain our lawyers to serve the people and how to select our judges so that they are no longer beholden to those who have elevated them.

In the latter pages of the book, we shall revisit the looming threat of a new fascism, the eerie shadow of which already darkens this great land. Yet, aware of that danger, and having been empowered to free ourselves, the cry of Martin Luther King, Jr., can still become our cry: "Thank God Almighty, we are free at last!"

What I have to say will surely anger many. Indeed, within these pages one should find something to anger everyone, else I shall have failed. But my intent has not been to anger. My intent is to tell the truth as I know it, realizing that what is true for me may be blasphemy for others.

This book, then, is a manual for freeing the self, and an invitation to join with one another in creating a new free nation for the twenty-first century. It is a cry exhaled out of love for the walking dead. It is a battle plan for a nation anesthetized under promises long ago proven fraudulent, a call to Americans to awaken and rise up from under the decaying shrouds of myth and to one day inhale the bright, brisk air of liberty.

—GERRY SPENCE
Jackson Hole, Wyoming

PART I

We, the People,
the New American Slaves

Overture

I am aware that many object to the severity of my language; but is there not cause for severity? I will be as harsh as truth, and as uncompromising as justice. On this subject, I do not wish to think, or speak, or write with moderation. No! No! Tell a man whose house is on fire to give a moderate alarm; tell him to moderately rescue his wife from the hands of the ravisher; tell the mother to gradually extricate her babe from the fire into which it has fallen; but urge me not to use moderation in a cause like the present. I am in earnest—I will not equivocate—I will not excuse. I will not retreat a single inch—and I will be heard.

—WILLIAM LLOYD GARRISON, ABOLITIONIST LEADER,
ON SLAVERY IN AMERICA, 1831

ONE

...

We, the People,
the New American Slaves

———— • ————

To speak of atrocious crimes in mild language is treason to virtue.
—EDMUND BURKE,
BRITISH STATESMAN

Man is born free, yet he is everywhere in chains.
—JEAN JACQUES ROUSSEAU,
FRENCH PHILOSOPHER,
OPENING SENTENCE OF
THE SOCIAL CONTRACT, 1762

—THE PICNIC—

On the broad park lawn on the Fourth of July you can hear the people talking. The American dream is vanishing. They say it like this:

"Things ain't like they used to be." It's the old boy in the straw cowboy hat and the five-dollar sunglasses talking; Alabama, they call him. He was laid off when the company was downsized.

"Yeah," Mac, the guy in the Nike baseball cap, says. And then he says nothing more.

Sometimes a sense of helplessness oozes up from the under-mind, and we put it down in the same way we fight nausea. Although we should be in perpetual genuflection before the gods because we are the fortunate citizens of this blessed land, still, without the power to manage our lives and to alter the course of our nation, we are not free.

On the eve of this new century, we wonder what has happened to the glory and the dream. To be sure, we have come far. African-Americans no longer sit in the back of the bus. Women have realized their power and exhumed their rights. We change parties every four years or eight, and quit our jobs as we please, all of which argues for our freedom.

How can we be slaves if we can quit General Motors and go to work for General Dynamics, or General Foods, or General Electric? Still, when we lose our twenty-year middle-management employment, will we find a similar job elsewhere? Or will we end up where millions have—first on the unemployment rolls, and later working as a security guard or a salesclerk at the local shopping mall, or even at both jobs, for little more than minimum wage?

Alabama is talking to his friend. "I tol' the boss when he give me the pink slip, 'Listen, pal, I was looking for a job when I found this one. So shove it.'" Then Alabama pops another Bud.

But the right to come and go in and out of one's employment imposes upon the New American Slave the often impossible task of marketing himself. He has become the "loose slave," a slave without a master, one who, in this new-age servitude, faces the risk of perishing in the wilderness of unemployment.

Yet if we can exercise all of the amenities of freedom—if we can quit our jobs, holler at our bosses, and say what we wish if we have the nerve to say it; if Alabama can call the president "a dirty two-bag pile of shit"; if we can burn the flag and worship whatever god we please; if the brownshirts must knock politely with a warrant in their hands before they can drag us off to frightening places—are we not free?

That we can travel in the country wherever we please and sleep at night without extreme fear of the police at the door—does this not mean that we enjoy as much freedom as do any civilized people in a complex society? And if not, do we wish to know?

What favor do we provide the polar bear born in the zoo by returning him to the harsh frozen tundra of the northland? What service does some country lawyer, some late American heretic, perform in printing these impieties? LOVE IT OR LEAVE IT, the bumper stickers on the cars of patriots used to read during the Vietnam War. GET WITH IT OR GET OUT.

But I thought then, as I do now, that the true test of liberty is the right to test it, the right to question it, the right to speak to my neighbors, to grab them by the shoulders and look into their eyes and ask, "Are we free?" I have thought that if we are free, the answer cannot hurt us. And if we are not, must we not hear the answer?

What if we have never known freedom and have been taught to embrace our bondage, to fight for it, even to worship it?

What if we have been born in a cage like the polar bear at the San Diego Zoo, and having known nothing else, we accept the cage as freedom?

What if our minds have been captured and played with, our minds molded as a child molds clay, our minds formed from birth to fit within the skull of the New American Slave?

What if our minds have been soaked in the brine of television, the voice of the corporate state that speaks to us for an average of more than four hours every day from cradle to grave and converts us into that great amorphous glob called the American consumer?

What if we are taught in school the state religion called capitalism, a religion that condemns as heresy all that interferes with the monied class extracting yet more money from those least able to protect themselves? What if the state's religion is the religion of the dollar, a faith based on a sort of economic Darwinism?

What if a form of subtle slavery has been taught to us, made acceptable to us, made to appear even as freedom itself? What if we are not free, but instead are taught the *faith of freedom,* as Muslims and Christians and Buddists are taught their faiths?

—What I Mean by "Slavery"—

By slavery—the old or the new—I mean *that state in which the person has no effective control over the course of his or her life.* Despite his freedom to jump from job to job or junket by jet from beach to beach, if no matter how he schemes or toils he cannot explore his boundless uniqueness, *if he has lost his only power, the power of the self, he is enslaved.*

In the same way, *the people of a nation are enslaved when, together, they are helpless to institute effective change,* when the people serve the government more than the government serves them.

When the course of government, like a descending glacier, cannot be altered by any action, by any petition, by any protest, by any desperate striking out, the nation is enslaved.

When the people have at last discovered that it makes no palpable difference to their well-being which party takes power and, in despair, display the pain of their impotence by shunning the polls on election day, the people are enslaved.

When the voice of the people has been silenced, and with straining ears they can hear only the shrieking of the New Master selling its trinkets over the people's airways, the people are enslaved.

At last, when the same smiling politicians plunder the nation, their hands in the pockets of the corporations, and the people cannot prevent it, the people are enslaved.

The slavery of which I speak lurks in the memories of unjust laws we call precedents. The slavery of which I speak reveals itself in our social values, in our apathetic, often unconscious acceptance of *the way of things.*

To be sure, there have been changes, but the changes have occurred within the same historical structure of servitude. The structure does not change. The sense of class does not change. The notion that the few of power are endowed with the right to dominate the many who are weak does not change. The right to use up human beings for profit, to toss them out when they grow old, the right to downsize, to take away their work, to belittle the poor, to see laboring men and women and, yes, even children as the mere cost of labor—as numbers—none of this changes.

Such are the remnants of the slave state that preceded us. We have been saturated with it under different labels, perhaps better labels: "the free market," we call it, or "free enterprise." Easy words. Words we accept at the Fourth of July picnic along with the fried chicken and apple pie while the band plays "America the Beautiful."

If we are to test our freedom, we must be willing to reexamine our birth as a nation, for from the seed comes the flower. Those who boast that their ancestors came over on the *Mayflower* or took part in the American Revolution must remember that the progenitors of black America arrived on slave ships, in spaces no larger than small coffins. Chained together by neck and leg, they lay in the dark, choking from the stench of their own excrement. An observer claimed that the deck of one slave ship was "so covered with blood and mucus that it resembled a slaughter house." Some killed others in desperate attempts to breathe. By 1800, 10 to 15 million Africans had been transported to America as slaves, and some have estimated that two out of three captured Africans died before they were successfully installed as slaves in "the land of the free."

—As the Sapling, So Grows the Tree—

Can we not see them—Thomas Jefferson, James Madison, and the others—waving the Declaration of Independence in the face of King George III, crying that, as a self-evident truth, "all men are created equal"? And in George Washington's slave quarters, when the light of liberty penetrated the fog of hypocrisy, three hundred African men and women huddled half naked and half starved, their backs bearing the scars of the overseer's whip.

Our failing memories serve our servitude. We have sorted out the ugly, and in only a few generations we have frilled them at the edges with such images as the benevolent master who loved his slaves in much the same way as the Park Avenue dowager loves her poodle. At school our children are provided but a romantic trot across the infamous centuries of slavery that lie at our foundation. But the stench of the old slave state has permeated every pore of the grand enterprise.

America was founded on slavery and prospered from the sweat and misery of black slaves for nearly two hundred years before the Civil War. In the four years of that slaughter, a war that produced as a by-product the emancipation of 4 million black slaves, 620,000 Americans died. In that terrible war, 360,000 Yankees were sacrificed, and at least 260,000 Rebels—in the end, over clashing notions of freedom. More Americans were lost in that infamous conflagration than the total casualties incurred in all of our country's other wars through Vietnam.

And now, less than a century and a half later, do we think that terrible war purified the nation? We have fought other wars for freedom, and masses of our young have died in them as well. We have marched. We have beseeched the courts. We have put our faces into the faces of the politicians, those unctuous devils of slick words. But white and black alike, whatever the color of the hide, when we test it, are we free?

The struggle between the opposing forces of liberty and slavery has always raged in America, even from the beginning. Perhaps that has been the defining energy of the nation. The Pilgrims, too, were at the feeding roots of the nation. One sees them in the mind's eye, all severely stated in their black and white, the tall Pilgrim's hat, the prim bonnets, the people stern and smileless, devoted to the virtue of work, of prudence and brotherly love.

We see John Winthrop, a Puritan, standing in 1630 on the deck of the flagship *Arbella* as it lumbers in the middle of the stormy Atlantic. He is a founder of the Massachusetts Bay Colony and is addressing the simple, anxious flock who have come with him, these Puritans who have lately escaped the religious persecution of the English. Turning a profit, although an acceptable goal, was not the dominant theme. "Man," he proclaims, "is commanded to love his neighbour as himself. Upon this ground stands all the precepts of the moral law, which concerns our dealings with men."

He holds on to the mast in the rolling seas. "This law," he admonishes, "requires two things. First, that every man afford his help to another in every want or distress. Secondly, that he perform this out of the same affection which makes him careful of his own goods. . . . We must be knit together, in this work, as one man," he warns. The Puritans stressed community. "We must entertain each other in brotherly affection," says Winthrop. "We must be willing to abridge ourselves of our superfluities, for the supply of others' necessities. We must uphold a familiar commerce together in all meekness, gentleness, patience and liberality. We must delight in each other; make others' conditions our own; rejoice together, mourn together, labour and suffer together, always having before our eyes our commission and community in the work, as members of the same body."

At opposition to the forces of slavery was the man whose body would soon be moldering in the grave. Abolitionist John Brown, echoing the sermons of the Puritans of two centuries before, spoke of the Scriptures, saying that "it teaches me further to remember them that are in bonds as bound with them. Now if it is deemed necessary that I should forfeit my life for the furtherance of the ends of justice, and mingle my blood with the blood of my children and with the blood of millions in this slave country whose rights are disregarded by wicked, cruel and unjust enactments, I say, let it be done."

And it was done, his body, sprung from the hangman's trap, hanging by the noose, swinging in soft, silent cadence to the marchers on each side who soon would clash in support of the opposing forces surrounding the issue of slavery.

A network of abolitionists—many of them black—known as the Underground Railroad proved once more that eternal paradox—that law and morality are often at irreconcilable odds. The Fugitive Slave Law of 1850 made it unlawful for any citizen to engage in the moral act of helping fugitive slaves escape. Yet the Underground Railroad, begun in the 1780s under Quaker auspices, had long since provided freedom for countless escaped slaves who traveled by night and who, during the day, were hidden by sympathetic whites and free blacks. At the borders, "conductors" met the fugitives and guided them safely into Canada. Harriet Tubman, sometimes called the Moses of the blacks, and Levi Coffin, a Cincinnati Quaker, were famous for their rescues. The great freedom fighters of the nineteenth century, among them William Lloyd Garrison and Wendell Phillips, fought the mobs and endured the jails of petty politicians on behalf of the African slave. Indeed, the enmity created over the unlawful aid given runaway slaves and the heroic accounts of their escapes fueled the flames between North and South that would eventually excite the states into civil war.

But the underlying conflict of that great war has not been put to rest. The struggle between the opposing forces of freedom and slavery rages on; it has only gone once again underground, where it smolders and occasionally erupts into violence. But mostly we trudge on, unaware of its pernicious presence, accepting its grasp on us as *the way of things*.

That many of the Founding Fathers—including Washington, Madison, and Jefferson—were slave owners is seen as but a fascinating contradiction. We have grown used to contradictions and accept them. Democracy and the corporate ownership of our politicians is a contradiction. Free speech and the control of the airways by the corporate few is a contradiction. Free enterprise and vast numbers of the population who are so poor they cannot begin to rise up from the pit of poverty is a contradiction. That the Founders made their fervid entreaties for liberty while they laid their whips to the backs of their slaves was a contradiction explainable, we say, by the fact that slavery was an accepted institution, acceptable because that abomination had become *the way of things*.

Had these courageous writers of the Declaration of Independence, those humane Founding Fathers who built "that new refuge for humanity" upon the backs of black slaves, so cultured the virulent germ of slavery that, by the time of the Revolution, the germ had taken an irrevocable hold in America as *the way of things*? Indeed, has the germ of slavery, mutated to its present form, proven to be indestructible?

The first slave ship bearing twenty African slaves docked in Jamestown, Virginia, in 1619. And the curse spread. By the time of the American Revolution, the prevailing religion in America was profit, a religion demanding freedom for those with the power to pursue it and slavery for the helpless whose labor produced it. Slavery could be immensely profitable. James Madison told a visitor shortly after the American Revolution that he could make $257 a year on every Negro, and that the cost to him for the poor wretch's keep was in the neighborhood of but $12 or $13 annually.

By 1776 slaves were at ignoble toil in all of the thirteen colonies. Slaves constituted 14 percent of the population in New York, 7.5 percent in New Jersey, and 10 percent in Rhode Island. As early as 1700,

6,000 slaves—one-twelfth of Virginia's population—were held in bond-age in that state. By 1763, 170,000 slaves—about half the same state's population—labored for their white masters. King George III's crime was, of course, that he dared collect taxes without representation. But before "the shot heard 'round the world" was fired, the colonists had pressed into labor for their own profit over a million black human beings who, without tolerable food, clothing, and shelter, and without hope, toiled under lash and torture.

But by the time of the Revolution, the ominous power structure of the nation had already been established. Five of the first seven presi-dents of the new union were slave masters. For fifty of the first sixty-four years of our nation's history, our presidents were slave masters. The Speaker of the House was a slave master for twenty-eight of the nation's first thirty-five years. The president pro tem of the Senate was most often a slave master. Chief Justice Roger Taney of the United States Supreme Court, himself a former slave master, held in the infamous Dred Scott decision of 1857 that Scott, a slave, was mere property even though he had been transported from a slave state to a free state. Taney had been appointed by the slave-master president Andrew Jackson to take the seat of the slave-master chief justice John Marshall.

As late as 1835, eleven states in the Union—nearly half—had econ-omies dependent upon the ignoble labor of slaves. Indeed, the govern-ment of the United States had been dominated by the slave-owning states for nearly a hundred years before the great Civil War.

In 1798 Julian Niemcewicz, a Polish poet, spent two weeks at Mount Vernon. He claimed that the slaves' huts were far inferior to the poorest cottages of Polish peasants. "The husband and wife sleep on a miserable bed, the children on the floor." The slaves were per-mitted a few chickens, but no pigs or ducks. "They receive a peck of Indian corn every week, and half of it is for the children, besides twenty herrings in a month. They receive a cotton jacket and a pair of breeches yearly."

The slave quarters at Mount Vernon were said to be without floors or windows, the latter being totally unnecessary since the cracks be-tween the logs admitted sufficient light (not to mention the cold and the rain as well). "Our beds," reported one of the slaves, "were collections of straw and old rags, thrown down in the corners and boxed in with boards, a single blanket the only covering." At the same time, at Monticello, Jefferson's two hundred slaves, while better fitted, were nothing more than disposable property, although some were direct blood relations of the president himself.

Let us look again at the Founders without the glare of their halos. They were never the champions of the struggling masses. In the colonies, they occupied the high ground of power and enlisted powerless poor whites to support them. Possessing power, they exercised it for themselves. Can we not see slave owner Patrick Henry in his wig standing at the precipice of the Revolution, stabbing his fist in the direction of the throne, the great defender of the rights of men, ensconcing his immortal words into the wet cement of history? "I know not what course others may take, but as for me, *give me liberty or give me death!*"

But who spoke for the slaves in the squalid quarters within earshot of Patrick Henry? And for the free women? And, at last, the poor? And in this weary, repetitive drama, who now speaks for the great masses of the powerless in America, both the rich and the poor, who have abdicated their right to govern to the corporate oligarchy?

By 1836, 2.6 million slaves toiled in bondage in the United States, annually increasing their numbers at the rate of 60,000 a year. At one point before the nation exploded into civil war, Abraham Lincoln began to contemplate how the enormous value of the nation's slaves as property had influenced the moral judgment of the men owning such property. He told a favorite story about two preachers, one who believed the word of God would always prevail, the other arguing instead for the power of money. To support his point, the first preacher opened the Bible and, pointing to the word of God, asked, "Do you not see the word?"

"Yes, of course," the second preacher replied. Then the second preacher put a gold coin over the word. "Now," the second preacher asked in return, "do you see the word?"

Acknowledging that America's slaves were valued at $2 billion *in nineteenth-century dollars,* Lincoln argued that the power of such wealth in human flesh rendered it impossible for the South's slave owners to comprehend the staggering immorality of converting human beings to property. It was not for him to judge, he said, but "[t]wo thousand million dollars, is a pretty thick coating." Then he added, "The mind cannot grasp it at once, this immense pecuniary interest—it has its influence upon the mind."

We remember, of course, that the Constitution was void of any specific reference to "slave" or "slavery," "Negro" or "African," which patent omission was not lost in Lincoln's 1858 debates with Stephen A. Douglas. That Lincoln should include blacks among those who were "created equal" was a "monstrous heresy," cried Douglas. "The signers of the Declaration had no reference to the negro . . . or any other inferior and degraded race, when they spoke of the equality of men." Then Douglas demanded of his audience: Did Thomas Jefferson "intend to say in that Declaration that his negro slaves, which he held and treated as property, were created his equals by Divine law, and that he was violating the law of God every day of his life by holding them as slaves?"

During one of the debates, Douglas shouted, "If you, Black Republicans, think that the negro ought to be on a social equality with your wives and daughters, whilst you drive the team, you have a perfect right to do so. . . . Those of you who believe that the negro is your equal . . . of course will vote for Mr. Lincoln."

The issue of slavery, said Lincoln in the last debate, "is the eternal struggle between these two principles—right and wrong. . . . No matter in what shape it comes, whether from a king who seeks to bestride the people of his own nation and live by the fruit of their labor, or from one race of men as an apology for enslaving another race, it is the same tyrannical principle."

Although slavery was never mentioned within the four corners of the Constitution, the Founders, sensing the underlying hypocrisy of their preachments, nevertheless, with the addition of the Ten Amendments, immortalized the spirit of liberty in that document. And Washington and Jefferson both publicly and privately spoke of their hatred of slavery. Jefferson, in his *Notes on the State of Virginia*, wrote in 1781, "The whole commerce between master and slave is a perpetual exercise of the most boisterous passions, the most unremitting despotism on the one part, and degrading submissions on the other. Our children see this, and learn to imitate it." More recently, Jefferson has been seen as a theoretical abolitionist. But it would require the most heinous war in our history to put meaning to the rhetoric that "all men are created equal." And still we struggle with these words.

—THE HYPOCRITES' DREAM—

The hypocrisy of the Founders did not prevent their dreaming, as shall I within these pages. Washington wrote, "I am principled against selling negroes, as you would do cattle at a market," and in his will he ordered all of his slaves freed upon his wife's death. Old slaves or children without parents would "be comfortably cloathed and fed by my heirs"; the children should be taught to read and write and "be brought up to some useful occupation . . . a regular permanent fund should be set up" instead of "trusting to the uncertain provision" of individuals. And no slave should be sold "under any pretext whatsoever."

Washington went on to write in his will, "I . . . most pointedly, and most solemnly enjoin it upon my Executors . . . to see that *this* clause respecting Slaves, and every part thereof be religiously fulfilled at the Epoch at which it is directed to take place, without evasion, neglect or delay." After Washington died in 1799, his wife, Martha, released his slaves in December 1800, a year and a half before she died herself. The estate supported pensioners until 1833, but one must not assume that Martha's heirs did not once more, and until the Civil War itself, wield the cudgel and the whip against the black man.

—ALABAMA'S SPEECH—

Once more we can see the people gathered at the park on the Fourth of July, the band playing, the old folks sitting stiffly in their white plastic chairs tapping their feet, the grease of fried chicken smeared at the corners of their mouths. We see and hear the children laughing, running through the sprinklers on the broad lawn, the firecrackers popping in the distance, explosions at the hands of children as idiotic as the gunfire of war at the hands of their parents. On this birthday of America, we are proud.

The wretched pound at our borders to get in. They swim the rivers, pile like rats into treacherous old tubs, and fight the storms to gain asylum. America is the land of the free, and with the exception of the early Greek democracies, some claim it is the greatest civilized nation ever to grace the face of the earth. And perhaps that is the simple truth of it.

But through the rolling notes of the John Philip Sousa march, through the grinding voice of the old veteran standing at the podium recounting the dead heroes who laid down their lives for our liberty at Guadalcanal, we can hear the sound of muffled voices.

Alabama wants to climb up on the podium and grab the microphone from the speaker. He wants to holler to the people tapping their feet to the band music and munching their chips, "I worked twenty-five years in the boiler room for the fuckin' company. I give somethin' too. Company said I was gonna get a good retirement and . . ." And then in his fantasy he stops, because nobody cares what the company said and nobody cares about Alabama.

Now we can hear the band playing "The Star-Spangled Banner," and we see the Stars and Stripes floating in the high mountain air in that small town beyond the din and dirt of the cities, beyond the concrete and the madness where the people merge with each other as endless blades of grass make up the lawn. Small communities are still sprinkled across this country. Many thrive like villages within great cities. People still gather together. They assemble in their churches and hold meetings in the school gyms, and they exercise their rights.

Then Mac, sitting on the other side of the big cottonwood tree, laughs and says, "I voted for old Bill. Some stud, old Bill."

"Yeah. They oughta retire him to the stud farm," Alabama says back.

"Don't make any difference who you vote for these days. None of 'em any good. Don't vote anymore," Mac says.

The music has stopped. The old boy in his American Legion cap is getting helped off the platform. The people clap. "Look who we have to vote for," Alabama says. "The good ones don't run. Too smart to run. The smart ones are making all the bucks. Just the sleazebags run. You vote for your sleazebag and I'll vote for mine." Today, less than half of the eligible voters in the country trudge to the polls, most having come to realize that how they vote will have little to do with their betterment or the enlightened evolution of the nation. "Why bother?" is the universal refrain. "It makes no difference anymore" has become the accepted liturgy of our times.

At last the New American Slave has come to realize that to rise up and speak out will only prove that which is worse than being struck down: *to be ignored as irrelevant*. Under the skin of the mule and the hide of the elephant, Democrats and Republicans are identical: They have become the bought-out, sold-out servants of the New Master. When the rhetoric fades, the same old hacks, themselves the most piteous of all slaves—slaves who have been purchased and sold to the highest bidder—occupy the same moldering seats of Congress and the same monument to hypocrisy called the White House. In passing, one thinks of Richard Nixon, who, accepting his nomination in 1968, said, 'Let us begin by committing ourselves to the truth—to see it like it is, and tell it like it is—to find the truth, to speak the truth, and to live the truth."

Then the band starts playing "America," and the mayor hops up to the podium. Now he leads the people in the Pledge of Allegiance, the crowd quiet except for the children laughing in the distance. We see the people with their hands over their hearts standing obediently before the flag, muttering at the end of it, "with liberty and justice for all." After that the high school band marches off the field and the people go back to their talking, the boys throwing Frisbees, the dogs chasing after them, barking, the children screaming on the merry-go-round.

Alabama sits on the lawn and leans back against the old cottonwood tree, the trunk as rough as rocks. He begins to sing, off-key, of course. The Bud. He sings in a half-gurgle. After his twenty-five years in the boiler room, should we expect his song to come ringing out in the clear, joyous notes of the choirboy? The singing of the crowd is over. But

Alabama warbles on. No one pays any attention to him. It is as if he is expelling heavy words that make his breath come hard. "O'er the land of the free, and the home of the brave," he sings. And then he doesn't sing anymore.

TWO

·◆·

Man, the Enslaving Mammal

―――――・◆・―――――

Make yourself sheep and the wolves will eat you.
—BENJAMIN FRANKLIN

When the foreman dropped the pink slip on Alabama, the noise in the boiler room faded away into a silence between the two men. The men called the foreman "the weasel" because he was a small, skinny, thin-faced man with a sharp nose and small eyes that were too close together. The weasel usually didn't look at you when he talked to you.

"What's this here?" Alabama asked as he leaned the shovel up against the boiler, pulled the glove off of his right hand, and took the slip.

"Sorry," the weasel said.

"What's this here?" Alabama asked again. Already he knew what it was. Then he said, "Why, I been here twenty-five years."

"I know," the weasel said. "Sorry. They're cutting all across the board. Annie up in the office got hers too."

"Annie come here the spring afore I did," Alabama said. Then the silence, and then he said, "I done my work good."

"Yeah," the weasel said. "You always done your work good."

"I was always here," Alabama said.

"Yeah," the weasel said. Then he said, "They give you two weeks' severance."

"I been here twenty-five years. I was gonna retire in four." Alabama turned his long face from the weasel. His face was covered with sweat and boiler soot. The weasel wasn't looking at Alabama. He was looking down.

"Gotta go," the weasel said. He had some other pink slips in his hand.

"They'll get you too," Alabama said after him. The weasel didn't say anything back, just sort of slipped away with his head down like he always did. Then Alabama walked to the lunchroom and opened his locker, and he felt empty. He left the locker door open when he walked out with his lunch pail and his dirty coveralls. Then suddenly Alabama was free. But he did not know he was free. And he did not like his freedom. He felt like he had been killed but he was still walking.

—MAN, THE ENSLAVING BRUTE—

Man is the only mammal that enslaves his own. The human species is not to be esteemed as the thinking animal, but adjudged as the enslaving beast. The recorded history of the species is almost entirely devoted to wars surrounding the issue of liberty—man's striving to gain his freedom on the one hand and endeavoring to enslave members of his own species on the other.

And man survives at the extremes. He lives at the equator and the poles. He adopts religions that promise eternal joy or everlasting pain. He is more likely to see things as black and white rather than in tones of gray. In the same way that he is either powerful or weak, aggressive or passive, he is likely either to accept slavery docilely or to revolt against it without quarter.

But like a demon looking for a wretch, slavery has always sought to impose itself upon the people. It is a free-floating force readily invited into the self—often by the self—or it may loom as an indomitable exterior force over which we have had no more control than the black slave had over the overseer's whip. It is as immortal as the cholera germ, and as ubiquitous as the virus that brings on the common cold.

The English gorged on the profits of slavery long before the first slaves were transported to America. In 1563 the English navigator John Hawkins captured a Portuguese ship carrying African slaves to Brazil, took aboard the three hundred slaves, and traded them for ginger, pearls, and sugar at an immense profit. Queen Elizabeth had previously denounced the practice of slavery, saying with all due piety, "It [the slave trade] would be detestable and call down the vengeance of Heaven upon the undertaking." But she soon took shares in John Hawkins's second slave-running venture and loaned him one of her ships, her avarice having overwhelmed the wrath she had expressed against it the year before.

In a similar surrender to greed, the descendants of the pious Puritans were by 1733 operating over sixty distilleries in Massachusetts that produced "demon rum" made from molasses supplied by slave traders who in turn sold the molasses for the capital needed to buy African natives, who at last were sold to West Indian sugar planters at great profit. So long as there was money in it, slavery was to endure, no matter the noisy protests against it.

Today the insatiable quest for profit promotes the new slavery. In bewildering ways, the new is more pernicious than the old, for the New American Slave is told he is free, and he clings to that myth as if his life depended upon it, a suspicion that cannot be totally ignored.

Considering how the institution of slavery has settled upon us, I think of the stories of two black slaves, one named Lavinia Bell, who was fearless, heroic, and relentless in her search for freedom, and one named Charley, who loved his servitude and who fantasized heaven as being an extension of his slavery on earth. Both stories illustrate the same proposition: that the slave microbe infects individuals in different ways, and that those stories resonate in profound ways today. In the story of Lavinia Bell, we shall see her awesome struggle against it, and the spirit she symbolizes will reappear in modern times in many cases close and dear to us. Out of deep respect for her courage and her hunger for freedom, and to bring us closer to our history, I'll tell her story.

—LAVINIA BELL—

Lavinia Bell was born in Washington, D.C., of free parents, perhaps in the late 1830s or early 1840s. From them she had acquired the unquenchable thirst for freedom. But when she was a child, a man named Tom Watson stole her, as thieves steal dogs. She thought she was past ten when she was taken, and along with two or three black men and about forty head of cattle, she was transported to Galveston,

Texas. There Lavinia, a comely girl with straight legs and a good back, was sold. Her master was a man known as William Whirl.

Because of Lavinia's long legs and pretty face, Whirl brought her up as a showgirl. She also had an independent air about her that provided a lively and pleasing personality, the sort observed in the precocious child performer. She was taught to charm her audience by singing and dancing. So perfectly could she cackle like a hen and crow like a rooster that people couldn't tell whether it was the child or the barnyard fowl, and she could act in various other ways so that her master was able to attract a crowd from the surrounding country to be entertained by his trick slave.

When she was a few years older, perhaps fourteen, and her crowing proved no longer so amusing, she was sent into the cotton fields to labor with the other hands. Under the overseer, her treatment was cruel. The slaves wore no clothes, for they had none, except for some old ragged shirts owned by a few of them; but even they were not permitted to wear the shirts as the overseer attempted to force a sort of iniquitous equality among the workers.

Whether they worked or not, scarcely a day passed that the slaves were not rendered fifty lashes. Lavinia later told how some were put down on their knees like small horses, harnessed to plow up the land, and, with boys for riders, whipped when they flagged in their struggle. At times, with the whip over their backs, and for punishing small offenses, she and the other slaves were compelled to walk on their bare feet over the hackles (the metal teeth used for dressing flax), and the hackles punctured their feet, and their feet bled and were marred by many scars from such brutality.

But Lavinia Bell was a woman who had been born free, and to her, that made the difference. Over and over she tried to escape, but she had no knowledge of the way to freedom, and each time she was readily apprehended and brought back, and often beaten to unconsciousness. On one occasion, she and the man she called her husband attempted an escape. For two years the man had been fitted with leg irons, which had grown into his flesh. The irons, of course, slowed him in his flight, and again they were captured, beaten so viciously and, as her interviewer said, so "otherwise cruelly ill-used," that he died.

Lavinia Bell's mistress, Polly Whirl, was a Dutch woman who had always taken kindly to Lavinia. One night she taught Lavinia to recognize the North Star so that she might follow it to Canada, where black fugitives could be free. Then, once more, utterly naked and only at night, Lavinia began her journey. She lived on herbs and nuts and grubs, and was parched with thirst and pregnant. Finally she reached a place in Mississippi called the Shades of Death. There in the bushes she gave birth to twins, one of them dead. She gave the live child to a woman to keep for her, though the circumstances were not recorded. But while at the Shades of Death she was discovered, arrested, and thrown in jail as an escaped slave, after which her master, Whirl, came up from Galveston to claim her. This was in the month of March in the year 1858.

Whirl had difficulty convincing the authorities that Lavinia Bell was his property, and he swore he would never again be bothered with proving the identity of the wench. Upon her return to the slave quarters at Galveston, he slit both of her tiny ears and branded her on the back of her left hand with a hot iron. Then he cut off the little finger of her right hand with an ax, searing the wound with a hot iron, and as if that were not enough, he branded her on the stomach as well, as any calf in the barnyard is branded. The whole of this account was reported in a feature published in the Montreal *Gazette,* on January 31, 1861, the story setting forth the actual words of Lavinia Bell from an interview.

There came a time following her recapture when Whirl believed that Lavinia Bell was inciting other slaves to escape and head north. Whirl promised not to whip her if she would identify who had provided her the information on how to reach Canada. But she refused. Those who recorded her testimony claimed she was born a martyr, but I think not. She was, instead, a child born free, and that continued to define her difference.

To force her to identify her benefactor (who was, of course, his own wife), Whirl fixed Lavinia in a buck, one of the most fiendish torture devices of all. She was doubled in two so that her legs were passed over her head, where they were held in place with a stout stick passed across the back of her neck. While she was in this position, several panels of fence board were removed, a notch cut in the boards, and her neck placed in the notch. She was then whipped. And the whipping by Whirl was so fierce, the lashes so unrelenting on her helpless body, that but for the interference of the overseer, who quietly stepped in, she would have been murdered.

The open and bleeding wounds that crossed her body in every direction were rubbed with salt and pepper to keep away the green flies. Later Whirl struck her on the head with a hoe handle a number of times and fractured her skull. She testified that a silver plate had to be installed by the doctor, and that afterward Whirl cursed her, often saying she had a dollar in her head to pay her way to purgatory.

In an attempt to break her will, Whirl left Lavinia Bell for days at a time with nothing to eat or drink. I have seen stupid men treat wild horses like that, and for the same reason: to starve them into submission. One time, she later reported, in punishment for some disobedience, she was hoisted into a tree, a chain locked around her neck and her wrists handcuffed (the marks were said to be still visible to the reporter at the time of the original article). There she was left to hang for two days and nights with nothing to eat while Whirl taunted her, asking her if she would like something, but not once, she said, did she satisfy him by uttering a word in response.

On still another occasion, several of her teeth were knocked out by Whirl's hammer after she had bitten off part of his nose, and yet another time she was knocked down with the butt of a whip, leaving a scar of more than three inches in length across her cheek.

She had remained imprisoned in Whirl's slave quarters for more than a year when once more she escaped. Still naked, she somehow sneaked aboard a steamer and hid in its hold among some barrels, but she was discovered by a crew member and taken before the captain, who interrogated her. She answered him in unintelligible gibberish. When the boat arrived in Louisiana, she ran ashore and there again began her long trek northward. One time she was chased, but she plunged into a river and swam underwater and was able to elude her pursuers. From there she again headed north toward the Shades of Death, where she was able to retrieve her child, and then, traveling by the beacon of the North Star, she reached Warren County, Illinois, where she was at last on free soil. Yet her misery was not over.

Printed in the want ads of the standard newspapers in the South were an assortment of slave-related notices. They were published as openly and shamelessly as if the advertiser were seeking a lost cat. Here are a few such advertisements as they were republished by William Lloyd Garrison in *The Liberator* to acquaint the world with the evil they revealed:

The subscriber's servant has run away. He had one ear cropped off and his back was badly cut up.

$50 reward. Ran away from the subscriber, his negro man Paul. I understand Gen. R. Y. Hayne has purchased his wife and children and has them on this estate where, no doubt, the fellow is frequently lurking.

The undersigned, having bought the entire pack of negro dogs, now proposes to catch runaway negroes. His charge will be $3 per day for hunting and $15 for catching a runaway.

In the meantime, in Illinois, Lavinia Bell was captured and sold to a resident of Natchez for $250, but she was soon able to escape, after which she wandered to Richmond, Virginia, where again she was arrested as a runaway and thrown in the local jail. From this jail she escaped as well, and she got as far as Cumberland, where yet again she was arrested and jailed. But this time she was given aid by a sympathetic citizen, escaped, and trudged on to Louisville, Kentucky, where once more she was arrested, and where once more she broke jail, and thereafter traveled to Boydstown. At Boydstown she was captured, and her child, whom she amazingly had managed to carry with her, was taken away.

At Boydstown she was hired out while awaiting someone to claim her, but she escaped once more, crossed the Ohio River, and got as far as Zanesville, Ohio, this area being a stronghold of abolitionist sympathy. In Zanesville she was captured and hauled back to Boydstown under the Fugitive Slave Law. (One can by this time readily understand why Ralph Waldo Emerson, with a copy of the Fugitive Slave Law in his pocket, wrote in his journal in 1850: "This filthy enactment was made in the nineteenth century—I will not obey it—by God!")

But Lavinia Bell was never to be contained in captivity. She escaped from Boydstown, traveling always on foot through Ohio to New York State, later mentioning Watertown and Whitehall as towns through which she had passed. Finally, near Rouse's Point, a charitable man paid her way to Montreal by railroad. She arrived there on the Monday evening before her story was first published. The story in the Montreal *Gazette* ends with these bleak words:

[She] was brought to the house of a man of her own race, Mr. Cook, No. 13, St. Urbain Street, where she now is in a state of perfect destitution received from the brutal Whirl. Her object now is, if possible, to earn money to support herself, and raise enough to purchase the freedom of her child, the property of Ann Choil, Boydstown, Kentucky: 250 dollars is the amount necessary to restore the child to his mother. Need we commend the poor woman to the citizens of Montreal for their practical aid, after the history we have given of her? We feel that there will be an immediate response from all.

Ought we not cherish Lavinia Bell? Her story marks the long road we have already traveled toward liberty. Today we stand in the middle of the road, while the traffic hurls by dangerously in both directions. We can see where we have come from—out of the struggles of nearly forgotten heroes such as Lavinia Bell. And we can see the long road ahead until it disappears into the fog from our view. The spirit of Lavinia Bell is immortal. It lives on in today's well-generated women's movement. As the germ of slavery is immortal, so the spirit of liberty is contagious. It has carried women from the days of Lavinia Bell—and of her mistress, a more comfortable slave—toward these times when women still struggle to occupy a higher slope on freedom's mountain.

In our times, we have witnessed our own who have laid it all down in the struggle for freedom. I think of Karen Silkwood, whose surviving children I represented in their suit against Kerr-McGee. Silkwood saw the innocent faces of young workers exposed to the deadly radiation of plutonium. I can still hear her voice as she spoke to Steve Wodka, a union representative: "Steve, they are just kids. They do not understand what is happening to them." She believed they were dying, as perhaps she was dying. Her heroism emerged when, facing that peril and compelled by her knowledge of it, she took action to expose the company—with fatal consequences. But her death resulted in litigation that examined the hazardous conditions under which her fellow workers toiled—another form of slavery, one brought on by their ignorance of the danger imposed upon them in the name of profit.

—THE OTHER SIDE: THE STORY OF OLD CHARLEY—

But in the days of overt slavery we would have also encountered those who appeared to be happy slaves, or those who, by the adaptability of the species, were able to adjust to that malignant condition. Ought those who are content in their servitude be free of our meddling? Does not freedom include the freedom to deal with our servitude as we please? They who stand easy in their harnesses, who find fulfillment in their labor and bear their pain through less sensitive hides—ought they not be let alone? Perhaps they are the fortunate ones. Their masters claim to love them, and they their masters. By what right, then, do we impose upon them the pain of liberty? By what right do we dare enslave them with freedom?

I think of the former slave Charley Williams. He was freed by Yankee soldiers. But he stayed on with the "Old Master," as many did. Charley told his story in his last days, when the master was long dead and Charley was living in his small, rickety cabin. Life was different after the war. He said in his shaky old voice, "All you got to have is a silver dime to lay down for everything you want, and I don't git de dime very often.

"But I ain't give up!" Charley said. "Nothing like dat! On de days when I don't feel so feeble and trembly, I just keep patching around de place. I got to keep patching so as to keep it whar it will hold de winter out, in case I git to see another winter.

"Iffen I don't, it don't grieve me none, 'cause I wants to see Old Master again anyways. I reckon maybe I'll jest go up and ask him what he wants me to do, and he'll tell me, and iffen I don't know how, he'll show me how, and I'll try to do it to please him.

"And when I git it done, I wants to hear him grumble like he used to and say, 'Charley, you ain't got no sense, but you is a good boy. Dis here ain't very good, but it'll do, I reckon. Git yourself a little piece o' dat brown sugar, but don't let no niggers see you eating it; if you do, I'll whump your black behind.'

"Dat ain't de way it gonna be in heaven, I reckon, but I can't set here on dis old rotteny gallery and think of no way I better like to have it. . . ."

Charley tells us that when the Old Master was on his deathbed, he asked for his former slaves to come to him, and in the Master's last delirious moments he believed his slaves were out in the rain working. When they came to the door of the Master's room, Charley says, "we hear Old Master say, 'Dat's all right, Simmons [the overseer]. I don't want my niggers working in de rain. Go down to de quarters and see dey all dried off good. Dey ain't got no sense but dey all good niggers.' Everybody around de bed was crying and we all was crying, too."

About his own death Charley says, "I don't care about staying no longer, only I hates to leave Mathilda. But any time de Lord want me I'm ready, and I likes to think when He ready He going tell Old Master to ring de bell for me to come on in."

From the beginning we have heard these sweet stories, the stories, too, of "black mammies" who were loved like mothers and the "Uncle Toms" who were adored. We have heard the stories of how black servants in the South were treated as members of the family, although they rarely inherited from their employers and were never invited to the country club, and certainly no one allowed his daughter to marry one of them. I believe such stories, for the human species is as good as it is bad. But the state of slavery in its most benevolent form is evil. And holding up the more fortunate accounts of it only serves to apologize for the evil, to mask it as good, and to invite the innocent to enter the trap.

When I think of Charley's master, I think of the many good employers, of corporations managed by people who impose a conscience on that otherwise amoral entity. And the workforce of the nation also includes many who, like Charley, are content, and who want to be told, who want to please the employer, and who want little else, except a pat on the back and, as it were, a small pinch of brown sugar.

—THE BARGAIN OF SLAVERY—

Yet if today we look, we can see the slave ghoul lurking, always searching for the new master and the new slave. It pokes its countenance into every workplace. As in any relationship, a bargain is struck, impersonal as it may be. The worker at the large corporation may never have laid eyes on the CEO, or the CEO on his worker. But as we shall later examine in greater depth, as in any bargain, the bargain of slavery demands *permission* by both worker and employer.

The worker who bargains his life away at the workplace often becomes mere property that can be discarded or sold. Almost daily I encounter people who sit at the same desk but who, during a few short years, have been employed by one corporation after another, corporations that have purchased not only the physical plant but the employees who go along with it, like a farmer who buys the farm along with the horses who plow the fields—businesses fully equipped, slaves and all.

The fortune of such human property depends upon little more than the fountain pen of a selling board of directors or of an executive bent on downsizing. In critical ways, such workers may be no less the slave than old Charley, and should they dare cry out, their voices will likely be absorbed in the deadly roar of the master's profit machinery.

Many have in various ways longed for the gift of freedom. But often their desires have been heard as the demands of the ingrate worker, of the unreasonable union activist, of the troublemaker. Their cries have been heard as the sour grapes of those who have failed to work hard enough and long enough, the jeremiad of those who have not been smart enough or prudent enough. In the old slavery, one slave master— although he may have been more benevolent than another—was still a slave master. Modern slavery provides choices, but the choices must be exercised within the structure of the New Slavery. The next job, in a different place with different faces, will prove in essential ways to be the same. As was the fate of Lavinia Bell, the system is designed to catch us and return us to the master.

THREE

·—•—·

Recognizing the New American Slave

——·—•—·——

*I am sorry to disturb anyone, but the slave holders have so many friends!
I must be the friend of the slaves.*
—WILLIAM LLOYD GARRISON, CIRCA 1831

Alabama stops at the bar on his way home. "Gimme a Bud," he says to
the bartender.

"Little early today, ain't you, Alabama?" the bartender says back.

When Alabama gets home, it is past midnight and his wife, Louella,
is waiting for him. She lets him fumble with his key at the lock for a
while before she finally takes pity and opens the door. She is angry.

"You ain't pulled a trick like this since Elmo was born. What'sa matter with you?"

He barges on past her like a fullback hitting the line and lands on
the floor. He lies there, facedown, Louella standing over him with her
hands on her hips, her blue flannel nightgown to her ankles.

"What'sa matter with you?" she asks again, peering down at the man.
On the floor he looks very small. And when he doesn't say anything,
she stoops down to check him out. He is drunk, all right. Then she
sees it clutched in his hand. She takes the pink slip from him.

"You musta give the boss cause," she says.

"I al'ays done my work," Alabama mumbles.

—RECOGNIZING THE SLAVE—

The Wealthy Slave

A person's status, slave or free, is not established by the extent of his wealth. Although some slaves have hoarded large quantities of money and property, such wealth itself does not afford freedom. The wealthy slave may be all the more subservient to the master. Since most wealthy slaves have elevated material riches above all other virtues and have dedicated their lives to their acquisition, in so doing they have had to pay a higher cost in liberty. Some say the wealthier the slave, the more likely his insanity, for how could any possessed of his senses put money above all other human values, above love and mercy, above charity and honesty, above freedom itself? How could any but the mad praise avarice as the ultimate virtue of the species?

Although the evidence is compelling that America has become a highly sophisticated, socially refined and integrated slave state, we view this as the natural consequence of an acceptable Darwinian game in which there must always be the poor to be devoured, and the rich to devour them. Few have understood that being rich or being poor is, in most ways, irrelevant to the state of slavery.

In the paneled boardrooms, arrogant men look down on the multitudes and perceive them as ants—indeed, as less than ants. Without ever having met him, they decide the fate of old Alabama in the boiler room after his twenty-five years of loyal service. They set the wages and the hours for Sarah, who drops dead-tired in her bed at night because she cannot make enough in her daytime job to pay the bills. But even these corporate overseers in those high caves—perhaps *especially* they— are slaves. Henry David Thoreau proclaimed, "[T]he rich man . . . is always sold to the institution which makes him rich."

Wealth is usually paid for in freedom. The chief executive officer, fighting to maintain the viability of his company's stock—not to mention his own stock options—is likely more a slave than the janitor mopping up spatters around the CEO's private latrine. That the corporate executive may, at the flick of a pen, alter the company's bottom line by laying off seventy thousand workers—usually at Christmastime—does not argue that his power to destroy the lives of his workers elevates him from slave to master. He is but an overseer, often all the more indentured, for he must always answer to the master, not in words but in profit—quick profit, quarterly profit, never-ending profit. He can never provide the master enough profit. He is confronted by four ghastly quarters every year, year after year, until he falls in his traces. And if the CEO fails, he will be replaced with no more concern from the corporation than the changing of a flat tire.

For nine months, John Walter, hired as president of AT&T to be groomed as the megacorporation's new CEO, was preparing to fill that slot. Forty-eight hours before his resignation, he claimed his relationship with Robert Allen, the retiring CEO, was solid. But the board and Allen thought otherwise and asked Walter to resign, one director claiming that Walter lacked the "intellectual leadership" to run the business. In the time that it takes for board members to raise their hands to vote, the career of the overseer can be destroyed. One day the CEO can be the powerful head of a megacorporation; the next, a member of the jobless masses. High-priced slaves are as easily dumped as the worker in the cutthroat, cost-cutting ravages of downsizing.

The CEO's life is reduced to one of perpetual fear—fear of the board, the stockholders, and Wall Street. His belly is churned into bleeding hamburger. He must be charming. He must be right. He must constantly possess the elusive and illusive graces of the politician. He must be wise and display the immaculate qualities of leadership. Yet he cannot lead the corporation, because it cannot be turned in one direction or another without risking serious damage to its structure, for which he surely would be blamed. He cannot sleep at night. He is friendless. He is hated by those who covet his job. He is hated by those who labor under his management. He is lonely.

He cannot raise a single libidinous salute without worrying about his fragile position on his lofty perch. His phone rings at all hours. He cannot escape, not for a moment. He is so constrained by the corporation that his every breath belongs to the company. In the meantime, the janitor cleaning up around the CEO's toilet bowl, has, on rare occasion, at least been heard to sing in the shower.

The Administrator and Politician as Slave

Before delivering a Law Day speech at a Western university, I attended a reception with its president. By the time the evening was over, the poor man had osculated the hindquarters of every dowager and shaky old fossil who might die in the near term and leave the school even a pittance. His nose, brown as a little acorn, had been worn smooth from a lifetime of toadying and truckling. He knew all the politicians within three hundred miles of the campus by their first names, as well as the names of their spouses, their lovers, and their children, all of whom he mentioned with the most exuberant affection, but whom, in his heart, he must have despised.

The president told me he had answered forty-three phone calls between his arrival from work and when he left home to have dinner with several of his board members. He had recently suffered heart bypass surgery, though he was quick to advise me that he was in the best of health. He could not afford to be seen as ill, old, or tired. His belly hung over his belt like bread dough over a pan, but he passed it off as a temporary condition he was happily rectifying on his treadmill. His eyes were puffy, his skin as pallid as old newspapers. When he walked into the reception, without missing a beat, without forgetting a name, he sucked up to every professor, every assistant, every spouse of every secretary—indeed, at last to everyone, for he could afford no enemies. Not one.

Although this man had the power to fire half the house in attendance that evening, to maintain his position at the top of the heap he had to be allied with everyone. And thus he lacked the liberty to take a stand on any issue. He could not permit himself to lead, to create controversy, to be brave. As the time for my speech approached, he began to fret at the thought that I might say something offensive to the audience (as I have been known to do), because, ostensibly, I was speaking under his auspices.

In the end, few likely respected him at all. I thought him one of the most wretched men I had ever met, the quintessential organizational slave who is cloned in nearly every politician, administrator, corporate minion, and public servant.

The Worker as Slave

From the master's point of view, the slave is primarily the property of the master. The slave's will is subjugated to the will of the master. The slave is but the cost of labor, a digit lost in the endless numbers set out in neat columns on the financial sheet. Slaves do not have many rights. Today, in the master's workplace, many of the slave's crucial constitutional rights are suspended.

When Alabama first went to work for the company, he was an apprentice in the boiler room. He cleaned up. They used to say you could eat off of Alabama's floors, even when the boiler was coal-fired. But Alabama didn't like the boss much. "Sneaky little bastard," he said. "I got a mind to tell him. He don't need to come sneakin' up here watchin' me. I don't need nobody watchin' me. I do my job."

"Well, I wouldn't be givin' anybody a piece of my mind," the boiler tender said. "I wouldn't be sayin' nothin' or you'll be lookin' for another job."

"I got a right to speak," Alabama said. "An' I don't give a hoot in hell. I was lookin' for a job when I found this'n," which was what he always said. But Alabama didn't say anything to the boss, not then, and not later when the company broke the workers' strike with some thugs from Chicago. Then Alabama fantasized another of his speeches. He saw himself walking up to the president of the company and saying, "You are a no-good sonofabitch, treating your good men like that who ain't had a raise in ten years. An' the likes o' you wouldn't know, but a pound o' hamburger is costin' double what it was two years ago. Louella knows. But you wouldn't know 'cause you are a no-good sonofabitch." But Alabama knew better than to exercise his right of free speech.

"You don't even know where ol' Henry Horn's office is," Mac said.

"Why, it's back East somewheres—in Chicago, I reckon," Alabama said. "But that don't make no difference. The old sonofabitch don't know where I'm workin' either." And then they both laughed and started shoveling.

In substantial ways, the worker's constitutional rights are forfeited when he enters the workplace. The company can search the worker's locker as it chooses and can require the worker to give up his blood to be tested for drugs. Under certain circumstances, it can record the worker's conversations, and where no union protects the workers, it can usually fire a person without a hearing or even without any cause at all.

"Look at the boss cross-eyed, and the sonofabitch can fire you," Mac said. "They can tell you who you can talk to and when you can talk to 'em, an' they can tell you when to eat and when to take a leak. They can tell you when to go and when to come back. They can tell you when you're gonna work and when you ain't." Mac was on a roll. "Why, they try to tell you how to think and who to vote for. Old Jimmy Hamm was in here the last election—he's the superintendent—and tells us if we knowed which side our bread was buttered on we better vote for his man. I tol' him I sure as shit would. But I never voted. Fuck him. What's the use anyways?"

No longer legally owned by the master, the modern slave owns himself, and sees himself as a salable commodity. Whereas the old slave was sold at the master's whim, the new slave must sell himself. By means of the fictions of both time and money, he cuts his life into segments called hours, months, or years and sells these precisely measured slices of human life for dollars. The English author John Ruskin said, "The distinguishing sign of slavery is to have a price, and to be bought for it."

I have a young friend who is a marvel with a brush. I see the stuff of Picasso and Chagall in the boy, the creative genius that occasionally exposes itself and causes us wonder and joy. He told me he was about to enter a well-known university, one not, however, noted for its fine arts department.

"What are you going to study there?" I asked.

"Going to take either advertising or veterinary medicine."

"You mean you are either going to sell dog food or cut off the appendages of puppies?" I asked, surprised.

"Well, yes. Why not?" he asked.

"Why?" I asked.

"Because," he said as if I should have understood in the first place, "there's a market in both fields."

Today, if the slave is unable to sell himself to a master, he is judged as a worthless drudge living off the leavings of the national plantation—one of those "welfare leeches." Although we may encounter happy slaves, many loathe their work, live only for the weekends, and, because of the financial burdens they have assumed, remain helpless to escape. As in the slavery of the old South, even the children of the New American Slave do not belong to him, but are bred and educated by him as replacement parts for the master's relentless machinery, one child selling himself to Boeing as a draftsman in Seattle, another to Toyota on the assembly line in Tennessee.

The Unchosen—the Free

Some Americans are free. But most are free because they were not chosen. Most of the great artists and poets were not chosen. The homeless are free in ways that we are not. They pay no taxes, water no lawns, and suffer no leaking roofs or dripping faucets. They waste none of their lives earning money to pay off small loans with staggering interest to the banks. They own nothing, and therefore are free of anything owning them. They assume no obligation to family and accept no demands on them from society. Some are content to be who they are. They are free from the whip and prod of goals that demand they become someone they are not. They do not know where their next meal is coming from, but neither did the hunters and gatherers who are said to have lived in primordial bliss.

The homeless do not grow soft lolling on feather beds. They do not grow weak gorging themselves to death on fatty foods. And so, is it not true that the only difference between the homeless, who wander the pavement, and idyllic prehistoric man, who wandered in the Garden, is that the former roam in concrete jungles to the cacophony of the maddening city jangle while the latter traipsed over the unsullied earth to the song of the ethereal warblers?

Mildred, the old woman who pushes her shopping cart along the street with her curled toes sticking out of the holes in her worn canvas shoes, was not chosen. You've seen her kind: the vacant look in the eyes, the hands gray with dirt, the lumbering in slow, painful steps, the cart filled with piteous possessions, perhaps a ragged blanket, some cans she will sell for pennies, some stale food she picked out of the garbage. She is free. Free to starve, free to be judged as untouchable, free to be shunned as one to whom we would not dare speak, as one for whom we would not spare even a quick smile. But she is free.

Yet I do not argue that to enjoy freedom we must be free of our jobs, free of possessions, free of a boss, free of the moral imperatives set upon us by the community, free of our parents, free of friends and the incidental obligations of friendship—at last, free of any attachment that makes any demand upon us. To be sure, Cassidy Jones, who sleeps on the steps of city hall in Santa Barbara, enjoys no such lofty freedom. He often sleeps during the day to protect himself from the crimes of those who rob him of even his scant belongings—his dirty sleeping bag, his pocket knife, his raincoat, his wool cap.

Cassidy Jones has friends. He is a member of a society of the homeless. Together they wield a certain power in the city—mostly by their annoying presence, their constant reminder of our own servitude to money and possessions, and their quiet pricking of our consciences, which tell us we have too much and yet we seek more.

I have said that by freedom I mean that people are in charge of their lives, that they are free to make the choices that count in their daily reality. Cassidy Jones is free not because he has no possessions or home or job, but because he lives on the streets of Santa Barbara pursuing the lifestyle *he* chose. Most of us would find his choice enslaving. He is enslaved to poverty, enslaved to the limited alternatives he has on a daily basis to express himself, to make his contributions to society, to enrich himself in personal growth.

But no board of directors found Cassidy Jones's leadership "intellectually inadequate." No group passed judgment on him and rejected him. Cassidy Jones rejected the group. In many ways, Cassidy Jones, compared to John Walter of AT&T, is manifoldly more free. Cassidy Jones made the decision where he will sleep at night, albeit on the steps of city hall. A group of businesspersons—mostly men, cold as bottom lines, calculating as machines—made a major life decision for John Walter. The difference is, of course, that Cassidy Jones, when he left his last job, got a few weeks' unemployment. Walter, poor devil, received $3.8 million—which included his signing bonus and severance— plus a $22 million reimbursement for money he left on the table at R. R. Donnelly—all for less than nine months' work. Yet, in the end, freedom cannot be measured in money any more than enslavement can be measured by the lack of it.

—THE CRY AT THE DOOR—

Although, in fact, many suffer in the new bondage, today people have begun to adapt to their slavery, even cherish it. Most yearn for acceptance, struggling for entry into the system—to hold a job with a corporation, to become entwined in the bureaucracies, to make money, to own many things, to be soothed in the soft blanket of security. Many demand the right to become enslaved and cry at the door to be let in, to be locked inside the great cage, to be used and used up.

—Rejecting the Master—

The paradox—and most truths are paradoxes—is that by being rejected we are freed. Today, each of us possesses the power to reject the false goals, the enslaving values, the unjust demands. Every slave has the power to reject the master. In the same manner that the slave was free to run away, we are free to disown that which owns us. But we shall always pay a mighty price for freedom. We may hide in the swamps of scorn. We may skulk about smeared with the mud of the outcast. We may grow used to backs always turned on us, and callused to slights and sneers. We may pretend we are not wounded. But freedom is painful and raw. Sometimes I think freedom is like walking naked into the night with one's hide freshly torn away from one's body. And yet, as we shall see, the skinned self can become the free and the beautiful.

The next morning Louella puts Alabama's usual breakfast on the table, couple of eggs over easy and a side of sausage. Short stack of pancakes. Then she wakes him up.

"Better get up," she says.

He rolls over, his back to her, and pulls the covers over his head. She can hear him under the blankets. "I ain't goin' noplace," he says.

"Better get up anyway. Your eggs'll get cold."

After a while he comes to the breakfast table, his eyes red from the Bud. He breaks an egg yolk and watches the yellow ooze out.

"Better eat," Louella says. "You gotta go look for a job today."

FOUR

·—·

Women in Chains

———— *·—·* ————

The trouble with our people is as soon as they got out of slavery they didn't want to give the white man nothing else. But the fact is, you got to give 'em something. Either your money, your land, your woman or your ass.
—ALICE WALKER, AFRICAN-AMERICAN AUTHOR, *THE COLOR PURPLE*, 1982

—THE NEUROSIS OF A NATION—

While African-Americans were, on paper, freed by the Emancipation Proclamation of 1863, the race riots, the police beatings, and the tumultuous cries of the inner city today echo the lamentations of the African slaves of old. Guilt over the old slavery remains. And the guilt has often turned to prejudice. Agony remains. And the agony has often turned to anger. And when we try to atone for the crimes of our history, nostrums like busing and affirmative action come too little, too late.

In unanticipated ways, the maturing of the national psyche mirrors that of a child becoming an adult. In his adult relationships, the abused child attempts to deal with the pain of his injury by continuing to recreate the same set of anguishing circumstances he once encountered. Freud had a name for it: *repetition compulsion*. He believed it was an impulse to reenact emotional experiences of early life whether any advantage might result from it or not. In much the same way, our nation, suffering from its early psychic damage as a slave state, now, as a mature nation, produces in neurotic repetition, generation after generation, one new form of slavery after another.

I wish to tell you another true story of a slave named Mary Reynolds as it was recounted in the book *Bullwhip Days: The Slaves Remember.*

Although this is the story of but one slave woman, and we cannot make a case from a single story, the narrative has relevance here because it reveals to me that *the underlying structure of slavery*, though not as cruel, persists in its fundamental form today.

—THE STORY OF MARY REYNOLDS, A SLAVE—

Mary's father was a free black who met her mother, a slave, at the plantation of a Dr. Kilpatrick. Her father tried to buy her mother and her three children, but as Mary told her story,

Massa [Dr. Kilpatrick] was never one to sell any but the old niggers who was only part workin' in the field and past their breedin' times. So my paw marries my maw and works the fields, same as any other nigger. They had six gals: Martha and Pamela and Josephine and Ellen and Katherine and me. . . . I was just 'bout big 'nuf to start playin' with a broom, to go 'bout sweepin' up and not even half doin' it, when Massa sold me. . . .

Massa wasn't no piddlin' man. He was a man of plenty. . . . He was a medicine doctor. . . . It would take two days to go over all of the land he owned. He had cattle and stock and sheep and more'n a hundred slaves and more besides. He bought the bes' of niggers near every time the spec'lators come that way. He'd make a swap of the old ones and give money for young ones what could work. He raised corn and cotton and cane and taters and goobers, 'sides the peas and other feedin' for the niggers. . . .

Slavery was the worst days that was ever seed in the world. They was things past tellin', but I got the scars on my old body to show to this day. I seed worse than what happened to me. I seed them put men and women in the stocks with their hands screwed down through holes in the board and they feets tied together and they naked behinds to the world. Solomon, the overseer, beat them with a big whip and Massa look on. The niggers better not stop in the fields when they hear them yellin'. They cut the flesh 'most to the bones, and some they was, when they taken them out of the stock and put them on the beds, they never got up again.

When a nigger died, they let his folks come out the fields to see him afore he died. They buried him the same day—take a big plank and bust it with a ax in the middle 'nuf to bend it back, and put the dead nigger in betwixt it. They'd cart him down to the graveyard on the place and not bury him deep 'nuf that the buzzards wouldn't come circlin' round. Niggers mourns now, but in them days they wasn't no time for mournin'.

—THE STORY OF SARAH, A MODERN SLAVE—

A sharp difference, can, of course, be demonstrated between the overseer who, with whip in hand, extracted the last drop of labor from the slave, and the modern foreman who lays the psychic whip against his workers. But the difference is not in the goal but in the means by which the goal is to be achieved. But in the old slave state and the new alike, the *object* is the same: to permit the master to maximize his profit. And, as if caught in an eternal cycle, such slavery, diluted as it may be, is repeated over and over.

I know a single mother named Sarah. She works two jobs, as a book-keeper by day and a waitress by night. Some days she works fourteen hours. She drops dead-tired into her bed at night. Her three children run wild in the streets. She is too weary to stop them. Too worn to mother them. The costs of day care eat up her savings. Her rent is usually behind. A single paycheck stands between her and welfare. She dare not be ill. She is too tired to cry.

Sarah came to my office one day seeking someone to help her collect her back child support, her husband having disappeared into more furtive breeding pastures. She was a small woman, thin, with the tired eyes of a draft animal. We spent many months search-ing for her husband, only to find him laid out in an alcoholic stupor, a man lost to himself, his family, and society. His history was to labor only long enough to buy one more bottle of cheap wine. Prison was no threat to him, and in fact, prison had often been a welcome relief.

The woman felt trapped. She could not escape her drudgery. She was afraid to let up, even for a moment. Others stood in line for her jobs. One day she will be used up, and one day discarded. And when she dies, she will be buried deep enough that "the buzzards wouldn't come circlin' round."

"What can I do?" she asked me.

"I don't know," I said.

"I guess all I can do is pray." She laughed. And then she left.

No one equates Mary's torture with Sarah's; the difference, indeed, marks the advancement of our civilization. But a comparison is in order. We have been introduced to the new, enlightened age of worker freedom. Sarah is free. She can leave her job if she is fortunate enough to find another. But the new job will be the same: the demands the same, the hours the same, the pay substantially the same. The overseer will have a different hard face, but he will be driven by the same pressure for more production, more profit—the concern being, as always, the bottom line.

Slavery is in the structure. But the bottom line does not reflect the misery or fear of either Mary or Sarah, slave or free. The bottom line does not care for either of them. Slavery has been so seamlessly woven into the fabric of our national character that we no longer recognize that it is, at last, the same cloth.

Mary Reynolds told how the slaves were freed in the Civil War. Dr. Kilpatrick moved to Texas and many of the slaves went with him. Often she worked for other people, and she and her husband "farmed round," as she called it.

I been blind and 'mos' helpless for five year. I'm gittin' mighty enfeeblin', and I ain't walked outside the door for a long time back. . . . I 'members 'bout the days of slavery, and I don't 'lieve they ever gwine have slaves no more on this earth. I think Gawd done took that burden offen his black chillun, and I'm aimin' to praise Him for it to His face in the days of glory what ain't so far off.

—WOMEN, STILL SLAVES IN THE STRUGGLE—

That women were born on this earth as slaves, as breeding animals, has long been the dogma of many of our derivative societies as well as the church, an obscenity already institutionalized in the system when our Founding Fathers failed to grant women equal rights under the Constitution. Against that presumption, modern women have arisen to seek their freedom.

Today, the slavery of women takes on only a slightly more subtle form. Today's woman works harder for less money. Her promotions are often grudgingly given, sometimes with sexual favors demanded, explicitly or implicitly. Today, sexual harassment suits plague the courts not because modern men exercise their power more today than before, but because in the advancement of human rights we have become more aware of the rights of women. Nothing in the structure has changed. We saw it in its harshest form in the world of the old slave Mary Reynolds.

> Us niggers knowed the doctor [her master, Dr. Kilpatrick] took a black woman quick as he did a white, and took any on his place he wanted, and he took 'em often. But mostly the chillun born on the place looked like niggers. Aunt Cheyney allus say four of hers was Massa's, but he didn't give them no mind.
>
> Aunt Cheyney was jus' out of bed with a sucklin' baby one time, and she runs away. Some say that was 'nother baby of Massa's breedin'. She don't come to the house to nurse her baby, so they misses her and old Solomon gits the nigger hounds and takes her trail. They gits near her and she grabs a limb and tried to heist herself in a tree, but them dogs grab her and pull her down. The men hollers them onto her, and the dogs tore her naked and et the breasts plumb off her body. She got well and lived to be a old woman, but 'nother woman has to suck her baby, 'cause she ain't got no sign of breasts no more.

Mary herself was once hired out by Dr. Kilpatrick to "some ornery white trash, name of Kidd." The worker she was with ran away and Kidd thought Mary knew something about it.

> He hanged me by the wrists from a limb on a tree and spraddled my legs round the trunk and tied my feet together. Then he beat me. He beat me worser than I ever been beat before, and I faints dead

away. When I come to, I'm in bed. I didn't care so much iffen I died. . . . Massa looks me over good and says I'll get well, but I'm ruin' for breedin' chillun.

Back in those days, the slave was exhibited on the block, stripped naked in front of the ogling crowd for the slave buyers who bid on the bodies. They bought human beings like breeding cattle, like working horses, like any property that would make money or bring pleasure. Today, with obsequious masks on our faces, we present, instead, our résumés.

Today, we see the modern businesswoman who, fighting for her freedom, has taken on a new master. She lives within the walls of the corporate community. Her life, like that of her male counterpart, is regulated by the demands of the profit machinery. She has become an impersonal cog in the machinery, the difference between her and her black sisters of old being that the old slave wished to be freed of her slavery and prayed, as Mary Reynolds did, "for the end of tribulation," while the modern businesswoman, as does her male rival, struggles with all her energy and commitment to advance within the corporate cage.

We see her like her male counterpart—all straight and tight, her jaw set, hunting and gathering not the fruit and the root but perks and money, competing for status in that insane world where human worth is still lost in the pecuniary pocket.

"Alabama, you gotta go out and find a job. You been moping around the house now for two weeks." She's working two jobs—the ticket cage at the theater a couple of hours every night, except Sundays, for the minimum wage, and cleaning for the old lady down the street who can't take care of her house anymore.

Alabama doesn't say anything. He walks over to the refrigerator and pops a Bud.

"An' drinkin' that beer ain't gonna help any," Louella hollers from the bedroom.

"Little Bud never hurt nobody," Alabama says back. He plops down in front of the television. Oprah is on. She's talking about how some hotshot society dame has a diamond-studded bra. Acts like she thinks it's great. "A man could eat them diamonds," Alabama says.

"You got a dirty mind," Louella says. "You never could get over your dirty mind."

"I don't mean it that way," Alabama says. "You're the one with the dirty mind. Man could buy a hell of a lot of steak and spuds with them diamonds she got hanging there. Pay a lotta rent."

"She's got the money," Louella says.

"Yeah," Alabama says. Then he changes the channel to the Lakers game.

FIVE

·-·

Arguments for Slavery

*In our country the lie has become not just a moral category,
but a pillar of the state.*
—ALEXANDR SOLZHENITSYN, RUSSIAN WRITER AND DISSIDENT

"Can't find no work," Alabama says.

"You ain't been lookin'. I was talkin' to Louella," Mac says.

"I s'pose you got yourself a big-time job," Alabama says. He raises his bottle to his old boiler-room partner to let him know he isn't being mean.

"I'm older'n you," Mac says. "They don't want no old bastards."

"You ain't so fuckin' old. You can still get it up, can't ya?" He laughs.

Mac takes a swig out of his bottle. "Not lately," he says.

"Whatcha gonna do? Unemployment's runnin' out."

"Well, I'll tell you one fuckin' thing. I ain't gonna go on welfare," Mac says.

"Well, hell no. But whatcha gonna do?"

"My brother-in-law's a bricklayer. I been thinkin' about carryin' hod."

"What about your back? I done all the hard work in the boiler room, the liftin' an' the shovelin' an' all—on account o' your back. You can't carry them brick and that hod." Then Alabama adds, "Unless I'm there to carry it for you."

"Well, I'll tell you one thing," Mac says. "When we was workin' for the company we sure had that security."

—THE VIRTUES OF SLAVERY—

The bodies were strewn across the fields and in the trenches like dead fish washed up on the beach, the Gray and Blue rotting and bloating together under the same sun. The wounded, their limbs ripped from them by cannon and sword, were as hapless victims ground up in some monstrous machinery. The soil could absorb only so much of the blood. Otherwise it ran in small streams, creating red gullies where it flowed. The fighting was said to be about slavery.

The South's elite argued that slavery was "a great moral, social and political blessing—a blessing to the slave, and a blessing to the master." As one Southern senator put it, "It has established the foundation for an upper class of gentlemen to cultivate the arts, literature, hospitality and public service. . . . It has created a far superior society to that of the vulgar, contemptible, counter-jumping Yankees." Another Southern senator observed, "There is not a respectable system of civilization known to history whose foundations were not laid on the institution of domestic slavery."

In most of the South, the arguments supporting slavery were accepted as correct. Slavery was claimed to be a virtue since it had "civilized African savages and provided them with cradle-to-grave security that contrasted favorably with the miserable poverty of 'free' labor in Britain and the North." It was *the way of things*. Today we hear similar arguments concerning illegal Mexican immigrants who, to grow our produce, labor in the fields for less than the minimum wage and live in squalor reminiscent of the worst days of slavery. The rationalization is that the workers would be starving in their own country.

We wear clothing and jog in running shoes made by the small hands of Third World children who slave in sweatshops for pennies an hour. The argument is that we provide work for little girls who otherwise would be cast into prostitution. Slavery in one form or another, in one historical era or another, turns to the same worn logic. As James McPherson described the reasoning in his splendid book, *Battle Cry of Freedom,* slavery in the South "elevated white labor and protected it from degrading competition with free Negroes." Slavery was not evil, declared states' rights champion John C. Calhoun, but "a positive good . . . the most safe and stable basis for free institutions in the world."

Politics then as now refused to define the moral issues and instead exploited prejudice. Faced with the conventional warning that their wives and daughters would be raped or married or otherwise taken up by what Stephen Douglas called "thousands of thick-lipped, bullet-headed, degenerate blacks," poor whites in the South joined in support of slavery. As the Democrats cautioned during Lincoln's campaign in 1860 for the presidency, "Free love and free niggers will surely elect Old Abe." A writer in a Texas Methodist weekly believed that the intention of the abolitionists was to force, by poison and fire, the South's "fair daughters into the embrace of buck negroes for wives."

After Lincoln was elected president, an Alabama newspaper declared that the North intended "to free the Negroes and force amalgamation between them and the children of the poor men of the South." And as ever, the church, in support of power, submitted its own divine opinions: "Abolition preachers will be at hand to consummate the marriage of your daughters to black husbands," a Southern preacher bellowed, to gratify "the hellish lust of the Negro!"

During the Civil War, the South's whites, who were nearly as poor as their enslaved black brothers, took up arms by the hundreds of thousands and laid down their lives in vast numbers to preserve the "honor of the South." As long as there were slaves, as poor as the poor whites were, they did not occupy the bottom rung of the social ladder. That disease persists to this day, when the Ku Klux Klan, the church burners of the South, and those who provide the most vociferous racial ruckus are often poor whites whose condition would rarely be the envy of their black neighbors.

Impoverished and illiterate, poor whites were still white. Georgia's Governor Joseph Brown summarized the value of slavery to the poor white by asserting that slavery "is the poor man's best government. Among us the poor white laborer . . . does not belong to the menial class. The Negro is in no sense his equal. . . . He belongs to the only true aristocracy, the race of white men." Hence, it was argued, freedom for the poor white man was not possible without slavery for the black man.

Slavery, like any economic system, like free enterprise itself, had become *the way of things* and was not to be questioned—except, of course, it *was* questioned. For at the margins of every system lurk the radical fringe, the heretics who interminably question *the way of things*, and ask such nonsense as, by what right, other than by force of power or by accident of birth, do some men dominate others?

—THE DIVINE RIGHT OF THE MASTER—

Power is so easily confused with divine selection—the notion that the accident of birth, the draw of propitious genes scooped up from the lottery of life, affirm the nod of God. Indeed, the South's aristocracy saw its right to steal the lives of black slaves as God-given. "Slavery," wrote George Fitzhugh, a member of one of Virginia's first families, "is the natural and normal condition of society." He argued, "The situation of the North is abnormal and anomalous." He thought that to bestow upon men an equality of rights is "but giving license to the strong to oppress the weak," and "that capitalism exercises a more perfect compulsion over free laborers than human masters over slaves, for free laborers must at all times work or starve, and slaves are supported whether they work or not." Fitzhugh thought slavery "the oldest, best and most common form of Socialism," and "the natural and normal condition of laboring men, white or black."

The Muscogee Herald, quoted in the *New York Tribune* on September 10, 1856, was brazen in its distaste for the Northern style of freedom, exposing for all to behold the arrogance of the old South over the helpless slave. "Free Society! We sicken at the name. What is it but a conglomeration of greasy mechanics, filthy operatives, small-fisted farmers, and moon struck theorists. . . . The prevailing class one meets with [in the North] is that of mechanics struggling to be genteel, and small farmers who do their own drudgery, and yet are hardly fit for association with a Southern gentleman's body servant."

In 1858 Representative James Hammond of South Carolina declared, "In all social systems there must be a class to do the menial duties—to perform the drudgery of life. . . . It constitutes the very mudsill of society." Then with loathing, he acknowledged another class. Speaking of the workers of the North, he said, "Your whole hireling class of manual laborers and 'operatives,' as you call them, are essentially slaves."

One thinks of the sordid epidemic of corporate downsizing that has uprooted millions of Americans from their jobs; of the hiring of "contract workers," who earn no benefits, to take their place; of corporations that seek to avoid the cost of retirement for their employees; of corporations that will extract the best of life from their workers and then, when they are old, or when they are sick, abandon them. Loyalty seems to travel in but one direction, the corporation demanding loyalty of its employees but being only too ready to sacrifice them whenever the bottom line suggests it. Thomas B. Labrecque, chief executive of Chase Manhattan Bank, who cut 10,000 jobs, said, "If you're doing what you think is right for everyone involved, then you're fine. So I'm fine." Even the Wyoming cowboy, with love and respect, at last puts his old, faithful horse out to good pasture.

—HONOR AND SLAVERY—

Then as now, in both the North and the South, the mirror of hypocrisy was at full reflection. White men who shamelessly dishonored the rights of blacks habitually proclaimed that any attack upon the institution of slavery was an assault against not the evil but the honor of the slaveholders who practiced it. Honor! Strangely, in defense of that most dishonorable institution, the South cited honor as the most compelling of reasons to resist its abolition. But at the bottom of the South's retaliatory outrage smoldered an awareness that the criticisms against slavery were right, that slavery was contradictory to the freedom that the South itself demanded, leaving the slave owners little else to grasp than their professed "honor."

Then as now, slavery enunciated through the lips of profit had at last become a virtue. John Calhoun heard speeches in the Senate on the subject of abolition with "deep mortification and regret." With full-throated oratory he proclaimed, "We must rise like culprits to defend ourselves." Rather than receive another petition from the North touching on the subject of slavery, Calhoun would rather "have my head disserved from my body." Other Southern members of Congress considered themselves "foully slandered" by "vile insults" whenever the slave issue was raised for consideration.

The plague of slavery created ethical anarchy. Even in Congress, Southerners argued that slavery was not an evil, that the North had misconstrued the institution for its own devious purposes. Calhoun argued that "the African race never existed so comfortably, so respectably, or in such a civilized condition. Both races," he asserted, "thrived under the practical operation of the institution." He soon sprayed his perfumed logic over the putrid issue by asserting that slavery itself was the best protection of democracy. "The defense of human liberty against the aggressions of despotic power," Calhoun declared, had been always the most efficient in states "where domestic slavery was to prevail."

Before the great war, one slave owner wrote, "I have long thought the Southern people were becoming Black Republicanized, to some extent, by a kind of insensible absorption. We are becoming morbidly sensitive on anything pertaining to the 'dear nigger,' " which observation is heard today in a slightly different form among those who complain that America has become too obsessed with racism, too rabid about affirmative action, too softhearted concerning welfare mothers in the projects.

In the pre–Civil War era, Southern members of Congress competed for the highest pedestal of pettifoggery. Congressman Hammond, with unalloyed loyalty to the cause, insisted that "domestic slavery, regulated as ours is, produces the highest toned, the purest, best organization of society that has ever existed on the face of the earth." The South's favorite argument was that the African had been rescued from his savagery. Yet I think of the response to that polemic by W.E.B. Du Bois, the great early-twentieth-century civil rights pioneer, who asked in response:

Is a civilization naturally backward because it is different? Outside of cannibalism, which can be matched in this country, at least, by lynching, there is no vice and no degradation in native African customs which can begin to touch the horrors thrust upon them by white masters. Drunkenness, terrible diseases, immorality, all these things have been gifts of European civilization.

—THE DESPICABLE HELPLESS—

That black slaves in chains could be held in such contempt presents an anomaly of the human spirit. What is it about the helpless that compels us to despise them so? Even the hawk respects the sparrow. We see it still today—the smug affluent looking down in disgust from disdainfully proud places as if the poor below had, by merely existing, somehow violated the rights of the rich to acquire yet more wealth.

Strange, so strange, that we should hate most those we have injured the most. It is as if by hating them more we feel our guilt for the original crime is somehow lessened. The dynamic of which I speak is endemic to the slave state. The old slave master, despite the exceptions thrust in our faces, hated the slave. How could he love the slave who hated him? Is it not he who, by becoming enslaved, enslaves us? And is it not the slave who, standing there as the victim of this most hideous of acts, accurately reflects who we are? How dare he stand there all whipped and hopeless? How dare he remind us of our guilt? How dare he convert us from men to beasts? Whip him more. That is the strange and ghastly way of it.

Why do we so often shun the poor on the streets, despise their innocent children, deprive them of their common entitlements, and lock every door of opportunity against them? There is something in the makeup of the human beast that causes it to scorn those who suffer more than it, to loathe those who have become its victims, to hate the weak. But hatred has its virtues. It often balms the pain of guilt.

—THE HOLY LADDER—

I do not argue for a classless society. None has ever existed. Power derived from fate's lottery always separates us. Some, of course, will always be more gifted with natural talent. Some will always inherit position, power, and prestige. And greed—some call it the acquisitive nature—will likely remain endemic to many of the species who fear for their temporal existence and, in panic, confuse life with things, believing that if they grab enough, steal enough, hoard enough, perhaps they can possess enough to avoid death.

I do not inveigh against the nature of man, although I admit his brain has often gotten in the way. Instead I argue against the arguments for slavery—that so long as there are those who are exploited *more than we,* robbed *more than we,* enslaved and raped *more than we,* the system that permits such inhumanity must be preserved. Since slavery grinds down to the bottom, it serves all who subsist even a step above, and the holy ladder, at all costs, must therefore be preserved.

—THE SAME OLD ARGUMENTS—

In sum: Slavery benefits the slave. If it weren't for the master, the slave would be in the jungle—the savage jungle of Africa or today's psychic jungle of unemployment and rejection. Still, the slave, then or now, is but property. And always, the slavery of the least powerful benefits those slaves just a rung above, so that, in the end, the system is carried on the backs of the poor and the powerless. The English novelist Emily Brontë wrote, "The tyrant grinds down his slaves and they don't turn against him, they crush, instead, those beneath them." And because the poor and the powerless are, for reasons not yet fully understood, seen as immoral and unworthy, the system is given nearly carte blanche to exploit and demean them. Calhoun's argument that "slavery is a positive good," in slightly less poignant rhetoric, would have found sympathetic ears today.

After Mac leaves, Alabama gets up and goes down to the pool hall. He doesn't know where else to go. But a man's gotta go someplace. Man's gotta do something, he tells himself.

"Hey, Alabama, ain't you workin' today?" It's the rack boy.

Alabama doesn't answer. Pretends he didn't hear.

"You get laid off?"

"I'm retired," Alabama says. Then he sits down on a stool against the wall to watch the high flyer in the peg-leg pants make his run.

"Well, here's to your retirement," a guy sitting next to him says.

"Yeah, here's to your retirement," the rack boy says.

SIX

.•.

The Enslaving Myth of Prosperity

————————•.•.————————

*The primary function of myth is to validate an existing social order. Myth
enshrines conservative social values, raising tradition on a pedestal.*
— ANN OAKLEY, BRITISH SOCIOLOGIST AND AUTHOR,
WOMAN'S WORK, 1974

Then the owner of Sam's Billiards comes over where Alabama is sitting.
He has a potbelly and white skin that looks like it is about to peel off
of a blister. He is bald. But he wears cowboy boots that are shined up
nice. "Hear you retired, Alabama."

Alabama nods.

"I was lookin' for somebody to sweep up after closin'."

"What's the pay?"

"Payin' five an hour. Oughta be able to get 'er done in a couple hours
if you hustle. Shit. When I was a kid we got twenty-five cents an hour.
Had to fight for the job. Now I can't get nobody to work for five dollars.
Rather collect their unemployment. Country's goin' to hell."

"I was makin' sixteen at the plant. Plus I got sick leave and I was
supposed to get a retirement an' the likes o' that."

"Well, this ain't the plant. This is business. I ain't made o' money,
you know. Lotta expense here. Cost me two thousand a month to even
open the doors. Them cue sticks cost a hunnert apiece." Sam looks
Alabama up and down. "You look pretty healthy for workin' at the plant
all them years."

"Smoky in here," Alabama says.

"Well, you can't have no no-smoke tables in a pool hall. Pool players

smoke more cigarettes'n any other kind 'cept poker players." He gives
Alabama a long look. "An' I want the bar cleaned good. Got a reputation
for a clean place. Want the tables brushed and vacuumed. An' the
pisser—hate a stinkin' pisser. No matter what you do, these pool sharks
cannot hit the pisser. Never could figger it out—they can hit a pocket
backwards and with their eyes closed, but they miss the pisser ever'
time. I want the can clean enough you can eat off the floor."

"They used to say I kept the boiler room floor clean enough to eat
off of it."

"Well, I ain't payin' no boiler room wages. I pay five and no more,"
Sam says. "We stay open till one-thirty, you know. Clean up startin'
two in the mornin'. Then you lock 'er up."

"I reckon I'm worth more'n five dollars," Alabama says.

"Explain me why," Sam says back. He waits. And after a while Alabama gets up and walks out. "You're jus' like all the rest of 'em," Sam
hollers after him. "But I didn't mean to piss you off."

—THE NEW ROAD TO HELL—

At the beginning of the nineteenth century, America—both North
and South—remained a nation of land, and most Americans worked
the land and were reluctant to sell their lives for hire. In the North,
individual families in small villages were self-sustaining. But following
the Civil War, the machinery of the Industrial Revolution began to
accelerate. With the rapid appearance of a new class of manufacturers,
entrepreneurs, and large-scale merchants who utilized newly designed
machinery to turn out inexpensive goods—a class called capitalists—
the agrarian values of the nation began to disappear. Small farmers and
individual craftsmen found it increasingly difficult to survive, the gap
between those with little and those with much began to widen, and
the virus of slavery began to appear in a transmuted form.

The rich began buying up the farms of the poor. In 1800 only about
12 percent of Americans worked for wages. By 1840, over 40 percent
of Americans had become, as they were already being called, wage
slaves. Once independent families were forced to become tenants, or

were scattered into factories. Banks began to support the industrialist instead of the farmer. The metamorphosis occurred with great speed, emptying the Northern countryside into the cities. In 1790, less than one Northerner in ten lived in a town. By 1860, one-third of all Northerners lived in towns and cities, working for wages.

Immigrants swelled the ranks of workers. Children populated the sweatshops. Machinery increasingly made the skills of shoemakers, tailors, and other skilled tradesmen redundant. Pushed out or reduced to piecework, one craftsman complained, these manufacturers "seem to think it is a disgrace to labor; that the laborer is not as good as other people. These little stuck-up, self-conceited individuals who have a little second-hand credit . . . you must do as they wish . . . or you are off their books. They have no more employment for you." The forebears of the New American Slave had emerged.

—INDEPENDENCE, THE LOST TICKET TO LIBERTY—

James M. McPherson explained in *Battle Cry of Freedom* how the Industrial Revolution abruptly converted America from the original republic designed by the Founders to a developing slave state. At the time of the Constitution, Thomas Jefferson thought a prerequisite of liberty was independence. Such independence required that the free man own the means of his production. Farmers who owned their land were independent and, therefore, free. Skilled artisans who owned the tools of their production were independent and free. Women, who owned nothing, were, in most respects, slaves.

Before the industrialization of America, the independent artisan worked as much or as little as suited him. If he wanted to go fishing or join his friends in the pub during the working day, he did so. But in the factory all of the workers labored in lockstep, transformed, as they were, into appendages of the machines they now operated.

Wage laborers no longer qualified as the free men Jefferson had envisioned for his new republic. In the North, the once independent craftsman was unable to match either the price or the quality of the factory product. Soon he either joined the labor force of the factories or perished. Employed in the factory with its tireless machinery, the artisan became wholly dependent upon the new master for wages that, in turn, robbed him of his liberty.

Under nineteenth-century industrialism, the conflict between the new master and the new slaves became permanently rooted in the system. The employer—the corporation—*itself already a machine*—demanded its profit, which meant that efficiency, not worker or community, became paramount. Class distinctions soon became more pronounced, so that the very rich owned the means of production and the very poor owned only the value of their labor. In the marketplace, the value of their labor was meager at best and was bought and sold at a price established, for the most part, by the new master.

By the time of the Civil War, it had become apparent that capitalism and the republicanism of Jefferson were incompatible, for capitalism violated the underlying tenets of the new republic. According to McPherson, these included *virtue, commonweal, and equality*.

—THE BIRTH OF THE WAGE SLAVE—

Virtue required the employer (now the corporation) to put the best interests of the community ahead of profit. But under capitalism, the ultimate virtue *was* profit. The notion of *commonweal* required that the power of the republic be dedicated to the common benefit of all people, not a favored class. But favored charters were already being granted by Congress to banks and corporations, railroads and canal companies.

Equality, of course, as in any slave state, became a myth—one that persists to this day. With the loss of the craftsman's independence, equality was reduced to an indifferent shrug of the shoulders. Freedom was bartered away for survival, so that with the loss of his independence the craftsman also lost his equality as a person. As early as 1840, the wealthiest 5 percent of the population owned 70 percent of the taxable property, while the poorest half owned almost nothing.

In America, the idea of the wage slave is not a modern phenomenon. One orator at the turn of the twentieth century, in splendid rhetoric, cried out that wage labor was "drawing the chains of slavery, and riveting them closer and closer around the limbs of free labor." Ralph

Korngold, writing on the conditions of the worker at the time of the Civil War, described factory workers' hours in New England as extending from five in the morning until seven-thirty at night. The workers took off a half hour for breakfast and another half hour for midday dinner. Such off-time lent to their further exhaustion, since they were required to rush home, bolt their food, and return within the half hour or suffer a fine they could ill afford to pay.

In 1849, a report submitted to the American Medical Association by one of its members contained the statement that "there is not a State's prison, or house of correction in New England, where the hours of labor are so long, the hours for meals so short, or the ventilation as much neglected, as in all the cotton mills with which I am acquainted."

Korngold states that in Boston, Irish workmen were forced to labor fifteen hours a day, including Sunday. The death rate among the workers was grim, the average Irishman living only fourteen years after reaching Boston. In tune with the times, the Cochee Manufacturing Company required its workers to execute a contract to "conform in all respects to the regulations which are now, or may be hereafter be adopted . . . and to work for such wages as the company may see fit to pay."

The company store is not a modern device to enslave the company's workers. In those bleak days in the nineteenth century, most were in debt to their employers. If they tried to quit their jobs without paying what they owed, they were imprisoned. In 1831, in Boston alone, there were over fifteen hundred people in prison for debt, and more than half of them owed less than twenty dollars. At the time of the Civil War and afterward, such conditions of virtual slavery existed in practice in major areas of the industrial North.

—UNIONS: JOINING TO SURVIVE—

In defense of the workers, trade unions sprang up and were joined by yeoman farmers. Unions argued that all genuine wealth was derived from the labor that produced it and that those who produced it should own it. Their members lashed out at bankers, factory owners, stockbrokers, and the other capitalists, who were seen as "blood suckers" and "parasites" and who had "grown fat upon the earnings of the toil-worn laborer." Political parties developed out of such conflict, the anti-banking Democrats against the pro-banking Whigs, the Democrats arguing that the concentration of wealth in the nation's banks was the gravest threat to liberty since George III.

—SLAVES FROM NORTH TO SOUTH—

By the time of the Civil War, two classes dominated America. In the North, industry, with its wage slaves, owned the means of production and became the New Master. In the South, the planters also owned the means of production, namely, the land and the slaves. In the South, the slaves stood in place of machinery and labored on the land without wages and without rights so that many of the distinctions between the industrial slave and the plantation slave became distinctions only in degree.

—THE ENSLAVING MYTH OF PROSPERITY—

Bill Clinton was reelected in 1996 mouthing the myth of prosperity. The people, lumbering to the polls, were told that the government was in good hands—honest hands, caring hands, hands that were not in the pockets of the master—and that those hands had somehow created prosperity for America. Clinton boasted of the lowest unemployment rate in recent times. Downsizing of our corporations somehow miraculously did not render us a nation of unemployed.

We were told only half-truths: Supposedly 70 percent of the workers who lost their jobs from 1993 to 1995 found new jobs by February 1996. But the whole truth is that of the 70 percent who were reemployed, 204,000 found only part-time jobs and 926,000 found jobs paying below their previous wages. Added to this were 1.3 million who never found any job at all, part- or full-time. Thus, nearly two-thirds of those who lost their jobs remained unemployed, or the jobs they found were only part-time or for lower pay.

Today, Americans are beginning to ask why, in these years of rising profits, they are being laid off by the millions and wages remain flat or continue to decline. A *New York Times* poll showed that 19 million people, a number matching the adult population of New York and New Jersey, admitted that a lost job in their family had brought on a major crisis in their lives, "the most acute insecurity since the Depression." The crisis had produced "an unrelenting angst that is shattering people's notions of work and self and the very promise of tomorrow." In the meantime, the stock market rocketed to more than a hundred new highs in the same year.

Since 1979, 43 million jobs have been erased in the United States. *The New York Times* reports, "In the last fifteen years since Ronald Reagan was elected—in times of recovery as well as deep recession— millions of Americans have lost their jobs and begun to slide, some slowly, others rapidly, down the economic ladder." Although far more jobs have been created in an expanding economy, often the new jobs demand longer hours, offer less pay, accumulate no vacation time, and have no retirement plan. Through cynical teeth they are referred to as "McJobs," jobs without the security of any master. The country's largest employer is Manpower, Inc., the temporary-help agency that rents, like leased equipment, 767,000 substitute workers each year.

Many jobs have been taken up by immigrants who will labor for five or six dollars an hour. The boss says they are good people. Indeed, they are. They have families. They are eager to work at any price. The boss says, "Try and find a white or a black who will work like that for that money." Unskilled workers have lost the most. Adjusted for inflation, from 1980 to 1996 the median wage of workers with a high school diploma actually fell by 6 percent, and during the same period of time they continued to lose such benefits as health insurance, unemployment, and vacation pay.

—ROSEBUD AND HAMILTON—

I was having breakfast one morning with a man named Hamilton at Nora's Fish Creek Inn, a popular log cabin café in Wilson, Wyoming, population a couple hundred. Hamilton is a man of considerable wealth whose single goal in life is money-making. He moved from New York to Jackson Hole to get out of the smog and debris of the city. Liked to fish. I used to tell him that he habitually chased the dollar for the same reason that our dog, Rosebud, always retrieves a stick. Can't help herself. If you throw the stick out she'll chase it. No better reason. Rosebud couldn't eat the sticks and Hamilton didn't need another dollar.

Although Hamilton was compulsive about making money, there were parts of him he didn't like to show. I knew he quietly contributed to certain good causes and his children had grown up with sensitive social consciences. You can usually judge the best of a man by his children.

I had been reading the morning news. The article claimed there were more poor people today in America than in 1970.

"That's progress?" I said, shoving the paper over to Hamilton.

"Right," he said. Nora came by with the coffee. "If the rest of your food was as bad as your coffee you'd be serving garbage," he told her.

"We're famous for our bad coffee," Nora said. "What's the matter with you?"

I said, "Says there that over twenty percent of America's children live in homes falling below the poverty level. What about them, Hamilton?"

"Not my problem," he said. "There'll always be the poor."

"Does there always have to be hunger?"

"For Christ's sake," he said. "Nora, give me another shot of that coffee." He muttered, "Have to drink a quart of this crap to get a cup." He turned to me. "The poor are poor because they want to be poor."

"Right," I said. "The kid born in the projects wanted to be born in a three-story falling-apart walkup with a dozen other fatherless, scared, dirty kids. The kid chose a mother on welfare. And he chose to go to a school where he couldn't learn to read."

"You are a fucking knee-jerk liberal," he said. "You liberals all make me sick."

"What about the poor?" I said. I liked baiting Hamilton. "Don't you care about them?"

"I hate the fucking poor."

"Why?" I asked.

"They're a bunch of fucking leeches! They give the country a bad name." He was beginning to holler. I changed the subject.

"You and George going fishing? The river looks good." George was a river guide.

"I'll tell you one thing," he said. "The poor, if they will get off their asses, can make it just like I did."

"Right," I said. "All they have to do is be born again—to a rich father who gives them a free ride though Harvard Business School."

"That has nothing to do with it," he said. "They're lazy. You know it and I know it. I can't even find somebody to mow my lawn, for Christ's sakes."

"How would you solve the poverty problem?"

"Too many of 'em already. Shoot 'em," he said. Then he laughed and ran his fingers through his graying red hair.

—THE SLAVERY OF POVERTY—OURS—

Yes, there have always been the poor in America. Perhaps there always will be. I do not accede to the proposition, however, that people are poor by choice. People are poor because of poor genetic gifts. People are poor because of poor parental gifts. People are poor because of a poverty of vision, visions of hopelessness and despair. People are poor because of poor education, because of poor opportunity. People do not choose to be poor. Poor people have poor choices and sometimes have poor natural equipment with which to make such choices. Those who have been poor and who have somehow achieved wealth usually do no service to the poor they have left behind, for the few who succeed stand as apparent proof of the cruel argument that it is not the system that prevents success, but the sloth of the poor who would rather be poor than work.

Those who have inherited their wealth especially cherish that argument. Those who have superior genetic gifts or have been soaked in opportunity embrace the argument. In America, the few poor who have "made it" have always served as aberrant examples to prove one of the most debilitating myths of the system: that everyone, if he works hard enough and long enough, can enter the pearly gates of plenty.

Despite the alleged good times, tell this to the million men and women in America today who are in the prime working years of their lives and who have, in the past year, according to the U.S. Department of Labor, given up looking for a job. Tell this to 36.4 million people in this country who live in poverty, a number equivalent to every man, woman, and child who lives in the twenty-five largest cities in America, including New York, Los Angeles, Chicago, Cleveland, and New Orleans.

People are not poor because of inferior values or limited ambition. People are poor largely because they cannot help but be poor. The slave was born into slavery. And most of America's poor have been born into the slavery of poverty.

—THE POOR GET POORER—

From 1970 to 1993, the working poor in this country increased from 39 percent of our population to 45 percent. In the same years, the middle class shrank from 57 percent to 47 percent while *the affluent doubled*. See us now, this once proud nation of the soaring, hopeful middle class, which has instead become a nation whose population is nearly *half poor* with its middle class still shrinking.

John E. Schwarz writes in *The New York Times* of a family in which the husband is a house and sign painter and the wife a clerk at a discount store. The husband, a man with more than a high school education, has worked full-time for many years. Nevertheless, he is forced to "scrounge from food banks and hunt through dumpsters" to make ends meet for his wife and two children. "I see them every day, low-paid workers, offered the pittance of a minimum wage, the best they can find, and although all eligible members of the family are employed, they must, as one Denver couple reports, live for days on potatoes and eggs in order to pay their utility bills. 'You ever seen a hamster in a cage?' " the mother asked Schwarz. " 'It just runs and runs on its wheel and gets nowhere. That's what I feel like.' "

In 1970 the bottom 20 percent of U.S. families received 5.4 percent of the income, while the top 5 percent took in 15.6 percent. Such a spread permitted the top to engage in our celebrated "grab-most-of-it" ethics and the bottom to barely survive. But by 1994 the bottom 20 percent's share had fallen to 4.2 percent of the income, while the top 5 percent had increased its share to 20.1 percent. In short, *the poor are getting poorer*, and America's celebrated middle class is becoming another myth.

—PROSPERITY ON THE BACKS OF THE POOR—

Today, this nation rests its prosperity on the backs of the world's poor. Hunger and homelessness in the nation's cities increased in 1996 *for the twelfth straight year*, in this, the richest nation in the world. And the mayors of the twenty-nine major cities of the nation have predicted that cuts in welfare will exacerbate the problem.

Workers are being urged by Washington to reeducate themselves so they may be employed by yet another master, but this time, after extended reprogramming, at a lower wage. Those who were once earning ten to twenty dollars an hour will, after having completed a "retraining program," be able to earn between five and ten dollars an hour with reduced health care benefits. But the picture is still more dismal: Of ten workers laid off through downsizing, only five took the training made available to them. Of the five workers completing the training, only two found work in their new field, and only one found a job that paid a wage that was 80 percent or more of the wage he had previously received. The problem is worse for workers over the age of forty.

In their monumental exposé, first published in *The Philadelphia Inquirer*, Donald L. Barlett and James B. Steele asserted that "America is moving toward a two-class society: those who have more and those who have less." We have been bilked by the half-truths of the politicians. As far back as 1964, Lyndon Johnson was vowing that "for every billion dollars by which we increase exports, 100,000 new jobs will be created." George Bush made more conservative promises in 1991: "Each additional billion dollars in exports creates nearly 20,000 jobs in the United States." And in 1993 Clinton echoed the same figures. But only half of the story was being told. While the nation's exports were doubling between 1980 and 1995, imports *tripled*. And U.S. corporations were "de-hiring" American workers by the millions and employing cheap foreign labor by even greater numbers.

Barlett and Steele tell the story of a typical family working for an old-line American business, Colgate-Palmolive Company. More than $8 billion of its sales comes from outside the United States. Exports! But let's see what is left out of the formula. The sad saga of Lynne and Ed Tevis tells the rest.

When the company announced plans to close its Jersey City plant, the Tevises, faced with the loss of their jobs—and Ed Tevis but twelve years from retirement—were required to relocate to Kansas City, Kansas. They paid their own moving expenses—something in the neighborhood of $10,000—considering it an investment in job security. But despite the company's promises, in less than two years, and as a result of further thinning of the workforce, the Tevises were out of jobs.

But as the company was thinning its American workforce, it was hiring overseas by the thousands at shockingly lower wages. In the years between 1980 and 1996, Colgate cut its American workforce from 21,800 to 6,400. But during the same time, it added nearly 5,000 workers overseas, bringing employment in foreign countries to over 30,000. In 1980, U.S. workers accounted for 45 percent of Colgate's total workforce. By 1996 U.S. workers accounted for just 17 percent. Profit was it. Dividends went up 137 percent. The stock shot up 287 percent. Profits soared 374 percent. Colgate makes toothbrushes in Colombia and South Africa, Cashmere Bouquet soap in India and Guatemala, dental cream in Panama, dental floss in the United Kingdom, and powder puffs and pads in China. The company, but not its workers, is prosperous. You can hear the pain of Terry Darago, who, with her spouse, Stanley, a Colgate worker, was also relocated. "People got divorced. Some people had to sell their houses. Others had their cars repossessed. People struggled." And all the while corporate profit rocketed through the damaged ozone.

Unfortunately, the Colgate scenario is representative: The more the corporation sells abroad, the less it makes at home; the more it spends overseas, the less it invests in the United States. The more money that goes to the investors, the less it pays its workers.

All across America, the story is similar. Over the last decade, AT&T, by its own admission, has thrown more than 25,000 manufacturing workers out of jobs and transferred much of the work to Asia and Latin America. In the United States, about 2.6 million manufacturing jobs have been lost since 1979. These workers were the blue-collar workers at the core of America's vaunted middle class.

Today, many of them work in service industries for little more than minimum wage. Barlett and Steele do cite one exception to this bleak report: In 1994, when the jobs of thousands of phone workers who were manufacturing cordless telephones for AT&T were threatened by trade regulations, the U.S. government charged to their aid. But the jobs on the line were not American jobs. They were in Malaysia.

Where are our consumer goods manufactured? As we know, our cameras, televisions, and VCRs are made in Japan. The simple tools in the closet, the hammer and screwdriver, are made in China. Paper goods, like notebooks, are manufactured in Indonesia, a country where political and economic exploitation is endemic to the system. Many car parts, including windshield wipers, come from Mexico. Our cars and trucks are manufactured in Japan, Korea, Canada, Germany, Sweden, Mexico, and the United Kingdom. Nike hiking shoes are made in China and elsewhere, and Bugle Boy jeans come from Nicaragua. Ralph Lauren sweatshirts are made in Pakistan, and an official U.S. Olympic baseball cap inscribed BRINGING AMERICA TOGETHER was made in the Dominican Republic.

After the American worker, the largest loser in this war has been the small businessman. Unlike the giants in industry, the small businessman has little clout with the congressmen, for he has bought none. Barlett and Steele insist that "[w]hat is at stake is nothing less than the cohesiveness of American society, as the economy threatens to leave behind those without health insurance, without pensions, without good jobs."

—THE PROSPERITY OF THE MASTER, THE POVERTY OF THE PEOPLE—

The highly touted prosperity in America is not a prosperity for the masses of the people. The prosperity is for the masses of its corporate nonpeople and their cowbird managers who peck the choice worms off the back of the corporate beast.

America is prosperous in propaganda and myth. It is prosperous in the way the old South was prosperous when prices for cotton, tobacco, and rice soared. The Southern plantation owners were the only ones whose prosperity was measured, and the South was therefore said to be prosperous. The rest of the people, the poor whites included, were property. No one considers whether a machine is prosperous. The osmosis of prosperity rarely reaches the slave, not even for a new shirt for his back. The slave, like the machine, labors on the same, regardless of the prosperity of the master.

I think of the prosperity of the black slaves as they themselves related it in early interviews collected in the anthology *To Be a Slave*:

An hour before daylight the horn is blown. Then the slaves arouse, prepare their breakfast, fill a gourd with water, in another deposit their dinner of cold bacon and corn cake, and hurry to the field again. It is an offense invariably followed by a flogging to be found at the quarters after daybreak.

Then the fears and labors of another day begin and until its close there is no such thing as rest. . . . [W]ith the exception of ten or fifteen minutes, which is given them at noon to swallow their allowance of cold bacon, they are not permitted to be a moment idle until it is too dark to see, and when the moon is full, they often times labor 'til the middle of the night. They do not dare to stop even at dinner time, nor return to the quarters, however late it be, until the order to halt is given by the driver.

And quotas are not a modern invention that lay only upon the backs of modern workers. A slave reported the master's demand for quotas at his plantation:

When the order to halt was finally given, it was weighing-in time. Each slave was expected to pick at least two hundred pounds of cotton a day. That was the minimum for everybody. Generally the overseer learned how much more than that each slave could pick, and that was his daily task.

Millions of American workers are not enjoying their highly touted prosperity. That word slips only from the lips of politicians and the corporate overseers. Millions of workers are prosperous in fatigue and disillusionment. As for the individual who is unemployed or underemployed, he often believes himself to be inadequate, or he would be among those riding the fat cow.

The American worker is working harder and receiving less. Juliet B. Schor, Harvard economist, says that the total hours worked in the average household, both at home and at work, are increasing. She says Americans are suffering from a time poverty. "Nation-wide, people report their leisure time has declined by as much as one third since the early 1970's. Predictably, they are spending less time on the basics, like sleeping and eating. Parents are devoting less attention to their children. Stress is on the rise, partly owing to the 'balancing act' of reconciling the demands of work and family life."

Despite the prosperity enjoyed by the master, the people are working longer hours and earning less money. In 1995, the Bureau of Labor Statistics reported that 8 million workers sixteen years and over held more than one job. By 1994, 60 percent of our women with husbands were working.

—PROSPERITY—AT THE TOP—

In 1970, the CEO of a typical Fortune 500 corporation earned approximately *thirty-five times* as much as the average manufacturing employee. Then, according to Paul Krugman, a widely respected American economist, "it would have been unthinkable to pay him *150 times* the average, as is now common, and outright outrageous to do so while announcing mass layoffs."

There has always been a disparity between economic classes in America. But Krugman inveighs against the loss of the egalitarian ethic that limited these disparities. "That ethic," says Krugman, "is gone." He warns, "The notion of a middle-class nation has always been a stretch. Unless we are prepared to fight the trend toward inequality, it will become a grim joke."

Many of the corporations in this country are being run for the personal profit of the robbers who control them. The workers operate the machines, devote their lives to the company, buy the company product, and struggle under slave wages to survive, and the resulting profit, as much as can be legally stolen, is often grabbed by those who have captured the cow.

In 1994, Michael D. Eisner reaped a total harvest from Disney of $203 million, including company stock gains, and Sanford I. Weill of Travelers took a total remuneration of $53.1 million. *Industry Week* undertook a survey concerning the sky-rocketing salaries of America's CEOs. The respondents found it difficult to garner the adjectives to express their dismay. They referred to the salaries as "disgraceful," "embarrassing," "infuriating," and "sickening." Even Bill Clinton, in 1992, thought that paying CEOs 100 times more than their workers was a little out of line. By 1994 the ratio was 187 to 1. The sometimes social observer, Derek Bok, former president of Harvard University, wrote in cautious understatement: "Almost everyone seemed to agree that executive pay had reached unseemly heights."

I am not concerned with the theft at the top. I am concerned with the theft from the bottom, the stealing of the lives and happiness and security of millions of powerless people who, economically, are skinned alive in order to support the new slavery. In 1994, professor of economics David M. Gordon, in his book *Fat and Mean,* reported that supervisory employees in American corporations were paid $1.3 trillion. The trend is upward. As did Gordon, let us put that amount in stark, easy-to-understand context: While Americans in 1994 were receiving nearly 10 percent less than they were earning in 1979, *their supervisors' pay was four times the total federal bill for Social Security payments*—a bill that critics claim is bankrupting the nation. While people were often working two jobs, with a husband and wife sometimes working as many as four jobs just to keep a roof over their heads, the supervisory personnel running our corporations received *four times more than the total federal expenditures for national defense*. While over 20 percent of our children were living in poverty, corporate supervisors were paying themselves more than *fifty times the total payments provided to the Aid for Dependent Children program*.

If not already bankrupt, American workers are plunging headlong in that direction. Working longer hours than since the grim days of Reconstruction, a husband and wife working multiple jobs still cannot cover themselves with adequate insurance, educate their children, or even own a modest home. In comparison, in 1994 the entire federal government's tax bill was $1.34 trillion, which is almost the exact amount the captive corporations paid their supervisory personnel.

—EVERYBODY IS PROSPEROUS—EVERYBODY BUT ME—

So long as each of us believes that our individual slavery is a phenomenon peculiar to us, we shall all remain slaves. The way out of the slave quarters is to discover that we are all in the slave quarters together.

Here we sit before the television screen, soaking up the master's ballyhoo extolling the nation's prosperity. We are not out somewhere fighting the master's war. Inflation is allegedly down. We are told the nation suffers only marginal unemployment. Surely, then, our own poverty must be well deserved, or if not, we must be the chosen whipping boy of fate while the favored multitudes traipse light-footed through the garden of plenty. The television screen reveals middle-class families of all colors doing well, working, laughing, engaging in the good life. Everyone has a new Toyota and is jumping around with joy. Regular folks are loafing at the beaches, drinking Coors, and watching the pretties walk by.

We have not yet learned that television ads are designed to make us feel inadequate and excluded. Life, as we are shown it, is bounteous and grand *for all but us*. As we drive down the freeway, we see the new cars, but not the massive new-car loans that enslave their drivers to the banks. The only conclusion we can draw, then, is that we alone suffer, that we alone are going downhill, that we alone are getting poorer, more tired, more hopelessly choked in an ever-tightening noose.

Neither political party dares admit the truth—that America's workers are working longer, harder, and for less and less; that the crime we suffer has its tap roots in poverty; that the family breakdown we decry is mostly a disease of job-related stress, unhappiness, and hopelessness; that spousal and child abuse are the uncontained explosions of men and women striking out at those who are more helpless than they. I do not blithely sound the pessimist's horn or wail the crepehanger's tears. But neither ought one sprinkle the truth with sweet, euphoric dew.

—THE CHOSEN AND THE PITIED—

Still, those of power and position are not hanging on to the high rungs because they are massively superior. I have met many CEOs among the greatest corporations in America. I have broken bread with them, cross-examined them on the witness stand, delved into their souls, listened to them explain their philosophies of life, heard their excoriation of unions, their hatred of government, their disdain of workers, their fascination with celebrity, their obsession with money and power, and their love of golf.

I would not entrust some of the CEOs of some of America's largest corporations with the operation of a roadside pop stand. Many have achieved their positions because they are better intracompany politicians than their competitors. Most are power players who have trampled over those below them for the top job, for the benefit not of the company but of themselves. They sit at the top not out of managerial genius, but in the fulfillment of brazen personal ambition.

Those hanging on to the top rungs may be rich slaves, and although it may be preferable to be a rich slave than a poor one, nevertheless, those who have trampled to the top, dragging their atrophied souls along with them, may have paid a price in ethics and in life that many below them would refuse to pay.

—THE PAIN OF THE PEOPLE—

Today, the virus of slavery has mutated into an even more vigorous and subtle strain. We do not belong to a single master. Not in the eyes of the law. By law we are free. But the law deludes us. We are the "loose slaves" who, under the law, belong to no one. We have been freed not to grow and to bloom, not to pursue the dictates of our souls, but to bear the burden of the ultimate slavery—to acquire a master for ourselves. And, as was observed by the slave masters of old, slaves without masters may be the most pathetic slaves of all.

The pain of the people is the pain of the new slavery, an intolerable pain strange to the human organism. When we are injured by physical trauma or a malfunction of the body or hurt by the words of another, we can understand the cause. But the pain of a slavery that has been foisted upon us by an unseen force is nearly unbearable. How do we accept the pain when it is laid upon us without reference to worth or fault? Such pain demoralizes us. The pain is not one we must endure in order to live in a free society. Still, for many, the frightening scenario of Aldous Huxley's *Brave New World* has become the reality of today, one in which the enslaved citizen, with few other choices, embraces his slavery with all righteous passion.

Alabama drives his pickup over to Johnson Brothers' Happy Hills Trucking Company, a big warehouse on the edge of town. "I'm lookin' for a job," he tells the dispatcher. "Used to drive truck when I was a kid."

"How old are you?" the guy asks. He wears sunglasses like a movie star and is falling out of a muscle shirt with Michael Jordan's number on it.

"Fifty-five last June. I'm a good driver. Never had no moving citations."

"You look pretty good for fifty-five. I'd a guessed you younger."

"Took good care of myself. Only did break my right leg oncet when I fell down the tailin's shoot. Wasn't my fault. An' I was only out six weeks, an' it healed up fine. Don't bother me none."

"Well, the company don't hire past thirty-seven."

"That don't seem right," Alabama says.

"That ain't for me to figger out," the dispatcher says. "You can wait aroun' an' talk to the boss if you want. But I know what he's gonna tell you."

SEVEN

·◆·

The New Slave Master

——————·◆·——————

*Corporations are many lesser commonwealths in the bowels of a greater,
like worms in the entrails of a natural man.*
—THOMAS HOBBES, ENGLISH PHILOSOPHER,
LEVIATHAN, 1651

As a kid, Alabama used to work at Macy's Greenhouse, hauling in the humus, potting the plants, pulling the hoses around. In those days they didn't have those sprinklers that came on every few hours like automatic rain. He liked working at the greenhouse. Kind of sweet smell in there he liked. A feel in the air like Tahiti maybe—and then you go outside and freeze your ass off on the way home.

The porch steps of the Macy house are rotted. He steps to the side of the rot and knocks. The door sneaks open a crack, and when Mrs. Macy finally sees who it is she opens the door wide and says, "Why, Alabama, I haven't seen you since you were chasing butterflies in the greenhouse. You grew up."

"What did you expect?" Alabama says. She looks even older than his grandma, all covered with the skin of old people, like the bark of ancient oaks. When he was a kid he'd often think about her when he was going to sleep at night. She was a young woman then, and pretty in places that the girls at high school hadn't come into yet. "I come to see if you was hiring anybody."

"We shut the greenhouse down," Mrs. Macy says. They are still standing at the door. "George is dead, you know."

"Yeah, I heard," Alabama says. He doesn't know what else to say.

"Well, then, I'll be goin'," he begins, but as he turns to go, she reaches out and grabs his arm.

"I had to shut it down. They grow those mums and carnations in California, right out there in the open—whole fields of 'em. And they bring in those illegal workers from over the border. You can't compete with that. We had to shut it down."

"That's too bad," Alabama says. He sees the sorrow in her eyes.

"It didn't hurt me. I could handle it. I got my chickens still. But it put George in his grave." The way she says it. Then she says, "Do you want to come see my chickens, Alabama?"

—THE ESCAPE OF THE MONSTER—

If we are the New American Slaves, then who is our master? The New Master, like some monster escaped from the laboratories of a noble experiment called the American dream, is the sum total of an amoral coupling between government and business. It looms as a monolith hybrid that is neither government nor business and is composed of individual strands of power that include the president, Congress, the courts—mostly used to process corporate business—a multitude of governing bureaus and agencies, and an immense cluster of multinational corporations, some as wealthy as great nations.

Although this endless organism is melded together as the United States of America, it is neither a sovereign state nor a corporate conglomerate. Try to distinguish the Pentagon from General Electric, with its capacity to produce nuclear fuel, or the Federal Aviation Agency from Boeing, which dominates the commercial aircraft business of the world. Try as we may, we cannot sever Congress from the corporate crowd that manipulates and controls it, and the government agencies that approve the trillions of dollars of mergers that divide up corporate business into regions of the world like gangs that have their territories. I cannot remember the last time we, as citizens, had any say in it.

—THE INVISIBLE GOD-THING—

What if one day visiting neighbors from outer space came upon us and asked, "Where is your master? Let us see him."

And what if we should tell them the truth. What if we should reply, "Our master cannot be seen. Our master is invisible." Might they not look at us strangely, wondering: Are these Earthlings mad? We nor they can see their master?

How incomprehensible that that which cannot be seen or touched can control whole nations—indeed, the world; that it can bring on wars and so decimate the planet that every twelve minutes another of the earth's species becomes extinct. Yet the monster can no more be smitten for its wrongdoing, or imprisoned for its crimes, or rendered the death penalty for its killing than one can strike out at the air and change the weather.

If the corporation is, in a material sense, nonliving and nonexistent, then what is its nonlife's purpose? In this bizarre world, it has been created to perform but one function: to seek profit. In the fulfillment of that objective, it is as mindless as any machine and as soulless as any cement mixer. No ethical standards restrict it. Its only moral imperative is the accumulation of money. That a corporation may occasionally act charitably, especially in the advancement of its public image, does not change its single-minded profit-making compulsion. I think of the giant automobile company, which, at halftime, gives a mere thousand dollars to each of the competing universities and pays half a million dollars in advertising time to make a public display of it. In the same way, the state, which lies at the core of the entanglement, may, especially at election time, make noises that mimic humane sentiment, such as promises for better medical care or more jobs. But this does not alter the state's unabated support of the single goal of the corporate conglomeration—namely, profit.

What is this invisible thing that controls us? It is the mythical *they* we speak of: *they,* the government; *they,* the corporate employer; *they* who are watching us, depriving us, frightening us, controlling us. The New Master represents the most dreadful accumulation of power the species has yet encountered. It eats up the landscape, the deep jungles, the prairies, the pristine forests. It consumes anything growing, anything alive, to satiate its insatiable appetite for profit. It devours the people who labor for it. The thing is so enormous that it casts an endless shadow upon the earth that the people have grown to accept like the darkness that covers the sun in a never-ending eclipse.

Although this thing cannot be seen or touched, evidence of its existence can be witnessed everywhere. We hear the false promises of a president. Alabama, whose ears have become sensitized to the chicanery of political rhetoric, says, "If the sucker claims we are not going to war, well, we are about to bomb somebody. If he says yes, he means no. To understand the politician, you gotta learn English backwards."

The petty, deranged howlings of sold-out congressmen, the Newts, the yapping sillies on both sides of the aisle, are stark proof of the power of the mindless corporate glob over Congress. We see the sprawling industrial sites, much of the energy of which is devoted to the manufacture of useless products that suck the life from the people and the earth. We stare in horror at the great mountains of refuse, the oceans of plastic, the junked cars, and we know that although we cannot see the New Master, the New Master is ever present.

Every year we collectively discard 250 million tires. As one observer says, "You can't bury 'em. You can't put 'em in the water. No one will steal them. They're just there." We gaze at rivers so polluted they have caught fire, rivers poisoned and blocked like aging arteries so they can no longer reach the sea. We grieve over the great forests that have been laid bare and resemble more the mange on a dog's back than a wilderness. We understand the New Master as we understand our neighbor who claims to be a good neighbor but at night throws his garbage over the fence into our yard.

We stare at the desolate no-man's-land in our cities, schools that have become little more than juvenile jails, and penitentiaries teeming with wasted men. The United States imprisons 565 persons per 100,000 of its population, a per capita rate *six to ten times higher* than most other countries. France, typical of developed European nations, incarcerates only 95 persons per 100,000. China, a nation we attack for its trampling of human rights, imprisons only 107 per 100,000.

Today, America houses 1.6 million of its citizens in prisons, up from about 316,000 in 1980. In building penitentiaries and imprisoning our citizens, we have even outperformed the Russian penal state. In many

states, the spending for prisons and police rivals what we spend for
education.

—THE GOVERNMENT TENTACLE—

In the same way that we have never seen a corporation, we have also
never seen a government agency. We see the people laboring, the desks
in endless rows, the tons of rules and regulations filling whole libraries.
But all government agencies are equally invisible. One would be hard-
pressed to distinguish the bureaucracy of the large corporation from the
bureaucracy of any government agency. Like siblings at the dinner table, one perpetually complains about the other. But bureaucracies are
bureaucracies. They both enjoy certain features of immortality. Ford
Motor Company will likely be alive after the last diluted descendent of
Henry Ford has passed on. In the same way, government agencies, once
rooted in the political soil, do not give up life easily. Most outlive by
many generations those who gave birth to them. When people say they
work for a corporation and bow to the corporate employer, it is in some
ways like kneeling before God. Neither can be seen. To the faithful,
both are just there.

—THE WEDDING—

An eerie specter—these corporations, these less than nothings, these
mere concepts recorded in some obscure office in Delaware or elsewhere that dominate the world, that never sleep, that never die, that
never laugh or sing. Then one day we learn that the nation's corporate
cluster and the government gaggle of bureaucracies have been joined
in unholy matrimony. It was an arranged marriage, one of convenience,
one that was intended to serve both parties.

—THE CHARACTER OF THE THING—

And what, one asks, is the character of the New Master, this
government-corporate oligarchy, this thing that has no heart, no soul—

this thing that does not breathe? Does the thing possess ordinary human values and simple morals? Does it exhibit courage? Does it value beauty? Does the thing care? Does it know the difference between right and wrong? That is to ask, is the thing insane?

To discover its character, let us present simple questions: What are the goals of the New Master's system? If its overriding goal is the elevation of the human race, the alleviation of human suffering, the eradication of prejudice, the stamping out of hunger, the ennoblement of the human soul, the enthronement of human dignity—if the goal of the New Master is to support the individual in his quest for life, liberty, and the pursuit of happiness—then the New Master embraces a system dedicated to liberty.

On the other hand, if the goal of the corporate oligarchy is to grasp endless profit for nonliving entities, if it seeks the subjugation, the exploitation, and the bleeding of its subjects for more profit, if its goal is to ignore the disenfranchised while it builds large armies to dominate yet other peoples in the world, then such a system must be adjudged a system dedicated to slavery.

When any system has for its goal the advancement of the system over the betterment of its individual members, such a system is embedded in slavery. Let us consider the master's goal regarding the nation's workers. The workers, from the CEO to the ordinary laborer, constitute a fund—let us refer to it as the *worker fund*. The worker fund is composed of the lives of workers, which have been converted to hours, months, or years and the measured segments then made available for sale to the master. Such a worker fund constitutes the ultimate source of profit to the corporate mass. Although the fund belongs to the workers, it is readily available to the master, and as in the slave state of old, the master extracts from the fund nearly at will.

In most cases it remains the master's call as to how much of the worker fund it will appropriate. In making such a decision, the New Master will likely consider whether the efficiency of the worker will be enhanced by sparing him a modicum of free time. After all, even draft horses must rest. Indeed, draft horses are permitted to run in the pasture from time to time lest they become lifeless and inefficient. I remember how, when I was a young ranch hand, at haying time the embittered old rancher would work his men until they dropped, but he left the horses unharnessed on Sundays, since it was easier to replace a weary man than an exhausted horse.

I am put in mind of one slave owner who, in advising others on the management of their slaves, wrote how he approached his own. "Now I contend," said the slave owner, "that the surest and best method of managing Negroes is to love them. We know, from a thousand experiments, that if we love our horse we will treat him well, and if we treat him well he will become gentle, docile and obedient."

In the end, the New Master's decision on how he will work his employees will be based not on what is uplifting to the worker or on what will advance the worker's life goals, but on what will be most profitable for the corporation. Sadly, in this new, post–Civil War state, the decision has been to work the New American Slaves longer and longer hours for less and less money.

—THE MORE WE WORK, THE POORER WE GET—

Since 1948 the productivity of the American worker has doubled. To say it another way, the standard of living of the American worker (as measured in market goods and services), as enjoyed in 1948, can be achieved today in half the time. We could have gone to a four-hour day and lost nothing. We could work only six months a year, or every worker in the nation could be taking every other year off, with pay. But what slave benefits from his greater production?

Still, our corporate overlords claim we do not produce enough, that we must work harder and longer and produce more or lose our jobs. And if our economy lags behind that of the rest of the world, the master claims the fault lies at feet of the dawdling American worker.

I think of Alabama, his hands thick and callused, the nails split from years at the shovel. "The more you hunker your ass down, the lower they want you to get it," he says. "They want it busted. I was workin' ten years ago for more than I was gettin' when they give me the pink slip. It's like the harder you work, the less they pay you. An' then when they are through with you, it's good-bye—like you was never there all them years."

The corporate nagging over lagging worker productivity is the same whip that has been laid upon the slaves from the beginning. No manner of effort, no amount of sweat, has ever satiated the master, for sweat and work are the first source of its wealth.

Still, our chief global competitors, Japan and Germany, are far behind America in worker productivity. And most of the rest of the world ranks far behind them. According to a recent study by the McKinsey Global Institute, a Washington research firm, Japanese workers produce at a rate about 53 percent of that of American workers. German workers produce at about 90 percent. Today, Americans work 320 more hours each year than their counterparts in West Germany and France; in other words, Americans give up more than two months of their lives each year to their employers than do workers in those competing countries.

Contrary to what one might expect, however, these longer working hours are not producing greater wealth for the American family. David M. Gordon says it neatly in his book *Fat and Mean*: "The vast majority of U.S. households can barely make ends meet. . . . But given our wealth and productive potential, we can hardly boast about the struggle so many Americans endure in just getting by. The core problem, purely and simply, is that the average U.S. worker's wage doesn't put much on the table and the typical working household is working too many hours for too little return." In short, the New Master has made its decision—to dip deeper and deeper into the worker fund to realize yet larger and larger profits.

—THE LEGALIZED RIGHT TO ROB—

On a recent Saturday, I sat next to a young man who was flying from one coast to the other to be "up and ready on Monday morning" to do his company's business. He had a wife and a couple of young boys, and was lamenting the fact that he would miss the boys' baseball game.

"I am going to wake up one morning and they're going to be grown and gone," he said. He looked sad.

"Why are you traveling on Saturday?" I asked.

"Because that way the company can save fifteen hundred dollars."

"That makes you miss both Saturday and Sunday at home. What

about your time? It is *your* time they've taken to save *their* fifteen hundred dollars."

"I know," he said. He looked away. "They tell me they will pick up my tab for a night out on the town. Might cost them a couple of hundred. But they're still making a thousand or more off of me." Then he thought a minute. "What do I want a night out on the town for? I'd rather be at home."

"What would happen if you told them you don't travel on the weekends? That your weekends are owned by your family?"

"I'm not big enough at the company to do that yet."

"And so if you are small and have no power they can steal parts of your life from you?" I said. "Do you get overtime?"

"No." Then after a while he said, "They want all of us to show that we are on the team—that we are all gung-ho and rah-rah for the company. They tell us there are only two kinds of employees: those who are for the company and those who aren't."

"What do you think the company is going to say to you when you are fifty and they decide to downsize, and you try to remind somebody about all of the weekends you gave the company and about your boys' ball games you missed because you were rah-rah for the company? Do you suppose they will remember?" We know corporations have no memories.

"No," he said. "They won't remember. Hope I'm not there when I'm fifty." Then we didn't talk about it anymore.

I have never been against profit making. People should be free to make their profits in the same way that people should be free to worship or to speak or to assemble. I am simply against the imposition of raw power upon the powerless to extract yet more profit for the powerful.

—LAWS THAT PRESERVE POWER AND PERVERT JUSTICE—

What about our labor laws? Do they provide a clue as to the goals of the system? Ask the labor law attorneys. They will tell you that such laws provide pitifully little protection for the worker, that nearly every labor law purporting to provide worker protection instead protects the employer from the unprofitable nuisance of work stoppage and employee litigation.

The Employee Retirement Income Security Act, ERISA, passed in the seventies amid great fanfare that it would serve as the bastion of workers' rights, has become a nearly impenetrable shield for employers. ERISA, employers successfully argue today, was intended to eliminate the rights that workers had historically enjoyed under state law, the pretension being that ERISA, in its place, would provide this beneficent federal protection for workers.

But as the judges interpreted ERISA, the worker (who never voted on the issue) forfeited his right to pursue many of his traditional remedies. No matter how cruel the employer, the worker lost his right to recover damages for intentional infliction of emotional distress. No matter how criminal the employer in depriving the worker his pension, the worker gave up his right to seek punitive damages. Moreover, the worker must now exhaust all of his so-called administrative remedies before he is permitted to even knock on the courtroom door. This means he must first jump through all of the hoops required in the appeal provisions of the corporate pension plan before he can sue. And if he ever gets to court, the question is not whether the worker was treated fairly but merely whether the employer was arbitrary or capricious. And no jury will even decide that issue, for under ERISA the worker has also given up his right to a jury trial.

In one well-known case, the worker—let us call him Bill—had been denied his pension by the company. To complicate things, Bill was suffering serious medical problems, and while he was fighting the company for his benefits he died. His wife claimed his death was caused by the stress of fighting the company, and she sued. But the court ruled that her rights under state law had been replaced by ERISA, and since ERISA provided the worker with no wrongful death claim, she had no right of action for her husband's death even if it had been caused by the deleterious acts of the employer.

In race or sex discrimination cases, the worker must first present his or her case to the government's Equal Employment Opportunity Commission, or EEOC. Then the worker must await the outcome of the government's investigation before a suit can be brought. For any serious claim, the process is seen as a delay and waste of time, a procedure full of hurdles for the worker, who often is without funds to hire attorneys who can match the skill and expertise of the company's lawyers.

When the employee is injured at work, he is again restricted in his actions against the employer. If his boss runs over him in the street, he can sue for the full extent of his injuries and recover damages not only for his disability but for his pain and suffering, and, if his boss was reckless, he may even recover punitive damages. But if his boss runs over him on the job, his rights as a worker are greatly limited. Although he need not prove negligence, he will now be given only such compensation as the law provides, which is often not enough to pay his rent and put food on the table. His right to medical help is usually abbreviated, and his final settlement a pittance.

In short, the laws that purport to protect the worker and assist him in obtaining fair treatment against a gargantuan corporate employer most often cast the employee into an endless web of administrative procedures and court actions from which little but delay and demeaning frustration is gained.

—THE STORY OF GEORGINA CHENG-CANINDIN—

Even the employee's right to sue has been mutilated. In one well-publicized case, Georgina Cheng-Canindin had wanted to sue her employer, Parc Fifty Five Hotel in San Francisco, because she claimed she had been wrongly terminated for disclosing confidential salary information to other employees and, if that wasn't enough, being a "problem employee." The company said she couldn't sue because the rules spelled out in her employee handbook required that she agree to arbitration, and she had signed a receipt indicating her acceptance of the handbook's rules. In arbitration, Parc Fifty Five Hotel would even pick the arbitrators: two hotel managers and two hotel employees selected by the very executives who had discharged her. Moreover, the company's personnel department would determine who would testify on her behalf. If the committee deadlocked, one of the executives who had discharged her would break the deadlock. Even the employer-prone courts were unable to stomach that abortion of justice. The California court of appeals ruled that the hotel's arbitration process was so unfair that it was not legally binding, and the court permitted the suit.

The Cheng-Canindin case is an anomaly—not because overreaching employers are rare, but because it is only the rare employee who braves the system to seek the aid of the courts. But these days, a holding by a court that favors the employee is of some rarity as well.

Across the land, corporate schemes to deprive employees of their right to a jury trial are becoming the rule. Today, many employees must agree to waive their right to a jury trial before they are permitted to enter the workplace. So nothing much has changed. What old South slave had a right to sue his master, even when he was beaten, and what old South slave's wife had a right to sue the master for her husband's death, even when his life was beaten out of him?

—Minimum Wage, Maximum Slavery—

That a minimum-wage law is necessary in America is proof that if it were legal, the employer would exploit the worker by offering wages below the minimum set by Congress. That workers will line up to labor at slave wages—wages that cannot possibly provide them with supper— reveals something of the inequities existing between those who employ and those who seek employment, an inequity but one step removed from the pure slavery of old.

I know of an old Mexican man who worked for a mission for the minimum wage all of his life. He was the mission's chief custodian. Somehow, with the help of his wife, who stayed at home and tended their garden, they were able to raise a family of nine children on his meager wage. Year after year, he proudly labored for the mission. Over those years he had become irreplaceable because he alone knew every idiosyncrasy of the mission's ancient mechanical plant. He took but an occasional day off for emergencies, and no vacations. He was loyal and cheerful, and much loved by the people. But when he retired, he was still making only the minimum wage. He was rewarded for his more than thirty years of loyal service with Social Security, to which he had made his own contributions from his measly pay.

In the end, the minimum-wage law often proves to be irrelevant to the life of the average American worker. A worker will as surely starve on the minimum wage as on no wage at all. It only takes longer.

—THE IMMUTABLE NATURE OF THE BEAST—

When America's worker fund fails to provide workers who will labor with the highest efficiency at the lowest possible wage, the corporation acquires them in Third World countries such as Indonesia and China where it is said that young girls slave in sweatshops for fourteen cents an hour for employers such as Nike, while the same company pays the likes of Michael Jordan multimillions for a few hours' work on television to coax Americans to buy the shoes fabricated by the hands of such children.

General Motors and Ford recently announced auto-parts deals in China amounting to $450 million. GM will build its first car in China in the fourth quarter of 1998. GM also has a truck plant under construction in China. Ford will produce 150,000 engines a year in China. It is Ford's sixth venture in components in that country, its seventh auto-related deal. Slave labor wages are a principal attraction.

Today we, the New American Slaves, endure the state of our being in much the same way as did the slaves of old—as *the way of things*. Julius Lester wrote in his masterful account, *To Be a Slave,* "To the sound of the whip and the shrieks of black men and women, the slave owner and America grew wealthy. Yet it is all the more remarkable that even now these two hundred years of slavery are looked upon matter-of-factly and not as a time of unrelieved horror." I say it is all the more remarkable that even today we do not recognize the persisting enslavement of our people, but accept it as *the way of things*.

—THE MAGICAL VIRTUE OF MONEY—

Within this corporate oligarchy, money, itself an abstraction, stands for nearly every virtue. Even though one may not require as much intelligence as avarice to accumulate large sums of money, the more money one possesses the more intelligent one is presumed to be. I maintain there are as many intelligent people in the projects of Los Angeles with black skin as there are in the essentially white-skinned offices of AT&T, and as many intelligent people in the rural areas of Kansas as in the paneled walls of IBM. By any score, in the corporate oligarchy, those who are the most revered, who are seen as the most intelligent, the wisest, yes, the most beautiful people of all, may have nothing whatever to commend them to their vaunted heights except that they possess or control large sums of money.

I know a New York corporate raider who has become so rich he could actually provide a four-year college education for every child in the state of Wyoming. He is as personable as a post. He is as creative as a stump. He is as entertaining to be with as a side of moldy beef. I have never once heard him make an original statement, and when he speaks his voice sounds like mumblings escaping the grave. He has had three face-lifts. His skin is drawn over his skull like rawhide over a drum. He dyes his hair black. He walks stooped over, as if he is about to tie his shoelaces. To my knowledge he has never smiled. His eyes blink occasionally—like a snake's. His sport is big-game hunting. On safari he is driven in comfort, and when he gets out of the car to walk a step or two, black servants carry his rifle, hand it to him, and point out the poor unsuspecting beast, and he shoots it using a ten-power telescopic sight that permits him to hit the animal as surely as if he turned on the light with a wall switch.

People swarm around this man like adoring parents. They hang on to his every word, no matter how boring, no matter how mundane. They laugh uproariously at what they sometimes mistakenly believe are his intended jokes. They invite him to their parties, no matter how he deadens the affair. They drop his name wherever they go as if their friendship with him somehow reflects their own worth. Yet I know that were he to come up penniless one morning, his friends would pay no more attention to him than to any piteous bum on the street. In the end, we do not worship the people who possess money; we worship the money. When the money is withdrawn from the person who possesses it, there is nothing enduring left—if, indeed, there ever was to begin with.

—THE PERNICIOUS POWER OF MONEY—

We all need some money most of the time, and when we need it, it can become the succor of life. I do not renounce the possession of money. I reject instead the noxious bargain that is usually made for it. I pity the greed that poisons the person who seeks it as his life's principal goal. I abhor the sickness it brings on, causing the possessors of it to see themselves as having been kissed by God. I detest how we long for it, often coveting it over even the divine virtues. I loathe the changes it renders in ordinary people, often less than ordinary people—how it converts them in our eyes into celebrities or gurus or, when they publicly parade their gifts of a few piddling percentage points to charity, into saints. I detest the cruelty, the slavery imposed on the weak in order that the greedy might obtain more of it. Most of all, I despise the hypocrisy, the false arguments, the sickly rationalizations, the socially imposed dogma, that make the quest for money, at the sacrifice of human life, acceptable in a society that pretends to be humane. Money is like salt. A little of it lends flavor to the food of life. Too much of it destroys the pudding and a ton of it turns the kitchen into a salt mine.

—THE RELIGION OF THE SOULLESS—

This corporate oligarchy dedicated almost exclusively to the acquisition of money exhibits yet another strange but human foible: Although the thing is soulless, it is nevertheless deeply religious. It bows to a religion it has taken on faith, one to which it is unalterably and blindly committed. That religion is called Free Enterprise. To the New Master, the religion of Free Enterprise is the compendium of all good, and all else measured against it is evil, or at least suspected of evil.

From their earliest days, our children are taught this religion in the public schools. It is preached to us daily over radio and television. Under this religion, it is heresy to propose any reasonable restrictions whatever on the divine right of the New Master to practice its religion to its ultimate extreme. The religion is so sacrosanct, so inviolate, no one dare suggest its obvious and grievous faults, which account for incalculable human misery and, if left unchecked, will inevitably lead to the destruction of the earth itself. Should one dare criticize the religion, one will surely be burned at the stake of infamy, branded as un-American, as a Communist, or demonized by the scathing minions of the master as a cultist or a kook. In any event, one will surely be promptly visited by the Internal Revenue Service or investigated by the FBI.

—Slaves Pledging to the Master's Religion—

We have committed every resource on earth, and the life of every man, woman, and child who abides on the face of the earth, to the cause of Free Enterprise. Less than a decade ago, we were set to destroy the world through a nuclear holocaust in order to preserve that religion. And upon little provocation, we are ready and willing to do so today. Like other religious constructs, the principal goal of the national religion is to permit those in power to remain in power—to secure for those who are more able to take, the opportunity to take more.

Although the ideal of free enterprise could, indeed, lend itself to the uplifting of the human condition, when it is practiced for profit alone, it becomes but a license for the powerful to further enslave the weak. Ten million American children do not have health care, and the U.S. poverty rate for children is the highest among eighteen industrial nations. More than half the children in poverty live in families in which one or both parents work. But the religion of Free Enterprise, as practiced, is intended not to produce freedom from poverty for its human supplicants, but to make acceptable the victims of its excesses—the desperately poor and the obscenely rich alike. We have forgotten the admonition of Jefferson: "The care of human life and happiness, and not their destruction, is the first and only legitimate object of good government."

I do not argue against the virtues of a competitive system, for there are many. I agree with Mohandas Gandhi, who said, "Capital as such is not evil; it is its wrong use that is evil. Capital in some form or other will always be needed." But to accept capitalism and Free Enterprise as articles of faith without agreeing that we must be free to consider whether what is offered is free and freeing is itself enslavement. *Free-*

dom and *free enterprise* are not interchangeable terms. Indeed, they may not be wholly relevant to each other. Free enterprise is often far from free, although it may be more free for the large and powerful than for the small and the weak. As we shall see, many of the enslaving aspects of the system have been concealed behind the myth of free enterprise and are often held up as evidence of freedom rather than proof of our enslavement.

—FREEDOM IN THE BARNYARD—

By analogy, let us assume that a few huge beasts—bulls, perhaps—are loosed into the corral of competition along with a multitude of small calves that totter on their legs. The corn of plenty is provided in the feed troughs, and under the only rule of the corral, all who occupy the corral, big bulls and weak calves alike, are given an equal opportunity at the corn.

But before the day is over, the bulls have consumed all of the corn and have hitched the calves to the wagons to haul more corn to the bulls. By nightfall, the calves are left to nibble at the spillage. All the while the bulls bawl at the top of their lungs that the calves are too slow in hauling in the loads and, but for their indolence and disloyalty to the bulls, could have upped their haulage to what the bulls claim are their very reasonable goals.

The nearly infinite monster we call the New Master stands as the end product of the free enterprise system. Yet it cannot consume and expand eternally. The wealth of the earth is limited. The forests and seas have borders. The species of the earth are delicate and, save for the brown rat and the cockroach, are on the verge of extinction. Human tolerance of slavery, too, has its limits. The species cannot forever thrive in bondage or subsist on myth. The wealth derived from human toil is finite, as measurable as the acres of hay the rancher's old team of horses can mow. If the species is to survive, if the earth is to endure, the free enterprise system must be brought under intelligent control and transformed to serve man, and the New Master itself must, at last, be converted into the humble servant of the people. We shall see how in pages to follow.

Alabama is standing there looking at Mrs. Macy's Plymouth Rock pullets. "They lay brown eggs. Can't sell brown eggs," she says. "Used to have Leghorns. They laid white eggs and you could sell them. But Leghorns are tough eating."

"I remember you used to have them white chickens runnin' all over."

"Used to sell their eggs to the Peacock Grocery. But old Wilbur Peacock is out of business, too. Safeway came in. And Safeway doesn't buy any eggs from us local folks. So I got these Plymouth Rocks. Good eating, and their brown eggs are bigger." She smiles at herself. "Eggs are all the same on the inside." The chickens have black and white herringbone feathers. "You could run the greenhouse," she says.

"I don't know how to run no greenhouse," Alabama says.

"I could show you. We could raise tomatoes. I think we could sell fresh tomatoes in February when the people are snowed in."

EIGHT

..-

The Slaves Revolt

——————•·——————

You had better all die—die immediately, than live slaves and entail
your wretchedness upon your posterity.
—HENRY HIGHLAND GARNET, BLACK REVOLUTIONARY, 1843

The banker seems amused. "You want to borrow money to grow tomatoes in February?"

"Well, yes, sir," Alabama says. "I always done my bankin' here."

"I know," the banker says. He turns quickly to some papers. "Your
file shows you are three months in arrears on your pickup payments."

"Well, I been outta work. I figger on gettin' 'er paid up as soon as I
get me a job."

"I see. Well, we couldn't loan money to you when you are already in
serious arrears."

Alabama puts his battered straw cowboy hat back on his head and
gets up from the chair with the red leather back. "Well, I thank you,
sir. I was hopin' I could get the Macy Greenhouse a-goin' agin. Take a
little time, though, and a little workin' money."

"They ship tomatoes into this country from Mexico by the trainload.
Hundred cars at a time. You couldn't compete." The banker is still
smiling.

"Ours'd be fresher, an' better. Mrs. Macy don't use no bug spray at
all."

After Alabama leaves the bank, he goes back to see Sam at the pool
hall to ask him for the clean-up job.

—NAT TURNER—

You can see his kind old eyes, his easy shuffle. He touched the children with his hands and bowed very low to the master. He was a good slave, trusted, kind, the kind of slave a master values. In some ways, the story of Nat Turner stands as an allegory of our time.

He had learned to read and was a self-educated preacher who had come to know a world much wider than the Virginia plantation on which he labored. He bore the slave's calm face, the docile manner. But when he plowed the fields, he heard voices urging him to fulfill his purpose—to free his brothers and sisters of their slavery.

In August 1831, Nat Turner believed that time was upon him. He would gather a few of his trusted fellow slaves. He had only Henry and Hank, Nelson and Sam, Will and Jack, but their followers would grow, and their cause being just, God would provide the way. The slaughter of their white oppressors would begin that night, a slaughter so complete that no white person would remain behind to stop them.

The next twenty-four hours were transformed into a horror of bloody murder upon murder—the murder of every white member of every white family the gang came upon, man, woman, or child. There were no atrocities such as rape or mutilation, simply the relentless killing of all whites who came into their path, except for one family of whites who kept no slaves and who were likely saved to make the point.

At each plantation he encountered, Turner took on more recruits. They confiscated axes, mauls, guns, ammunition, whatever weapons they came upon. The murderous explosion that was ignited by lifetimes of torture and wretchedness was swift and terrible. By the second day, the mob had murdered some fifty-five white persons. But down the road, when they stopped to seek more recruits, they were surprised by a patrol of gathering whites with superior weapons. Turner's volunteers scattered. They lay in hiding that night, but forty reassembled the next day. Then once more an alarm broke them up, and by daylight the insurrection was over. But Nat Turner was not to be found.

For a number of weeks Turner lived in the woods of Southampton County, venturing out only at night for water and food. In the meantime, the whites retaliated against the revolting slaves with their own wave of terrorism. One North Carolina correspondent wrote, "The massacre of the whites was over, and the white people had commenced the destruction of the Negroes. Passengers by the Fayetteville stage say that by the latest accounts, one hundred and twenty Negroes have been killed in one day's work." Overseers pointed out any slave with a contrary disposition and the slave was immediately killed. Often owners watched helplessly as their slaves were slaughtered like vermin. Many were tortured, burned, maimed, their jaws broken, their hamstrings cut, their heads severed and stuck atop poles.

Fifty-five of Nat Turner's gang were given a trial, one as fair as local hysteria permitted. All were hanged. But still Nat Turner remained at large, and that fact alone kept the slave owners constantly on the edge of panic. Fayetteville and Raleigh, North Carolina, were put under military guard. Slaves were shot in Washington, D.C., and more heads hoisted on poles. In Tennessee and Kentucky, revolts—real or imagined—were discovered before they exploded. So, too, in Mississippi and Alabama.

In the growing panic of the slave owners, Turner was reportedly seen nearly everywhere. So great was the paranoia that a thousand men took arms in Southampton County consisting of two army regiments with units of artillery and cavalry and detachments from the navy. The dread then, as today, was that although the masters could look into the obsequious faces of their slaves, they might never know what furor, what violence, lay behind the bowing and the fawning. What docile, obedient slave might next be transformed into yet another Nat Turner?

Then, on October 30, a single patrolman came upon Nat Turner hiding in the woods. He was utterly spent from privation and hunger, and near death. The patrolman hauled him in. He was convicted on November 5 and hanged six days later.

What lessons did the slave owners take from the Nat Turner rebellion? Many actually moved out of Virginia. Of those remaining, they were, to the person, "dreadfully frightened about the niggers," and their response was predictable—further domination of their slaves, and harsher, crueler treatment. Realizing Nat Turner was educated, they concluded that no slave should ever again be permitted to read. Understanding that the rebellion arose from slaves congregating with one another, they decided that no slave thereafter would be allowed to meet with other slaves. Nowhere in the South, of course, was uttered the first suggestion that the solution to the slaves' rebellion lay in inviting their slaves into membership of the human race.

—THE GHOST OF NAT TURNER LIVES ON—

One thinks of Theodore Kaczynski, who in some ways stands as the Nat Turner of today. He killed out of a tormented, perhaps psychotic heart, but he killed purporting to forward the theme that modern man had become a slave to technology. Somehow he believed that killing would call the people's attention to his manifesto. His bombings, of course, turned the world against him, and where he might have once been heard by the few, he was feared and rejected by the many, none of whom would listen.

In our own times, we observe a nation of mostly white overseers laboring for the New Master. These corporate executives and their middle managers are often most fearful of the least powerful—the poor, the disenfranchised, those on welfare, those whom the industrial machinery has discarded.

On the margins of the city, the rich have grown even more strident in their hatred of the poor, and they turn to the power they wield in Congress to deprive the poor of welfare, to build more prisons, to impose longer and harsher punishments, and to further alienate those they oppress. The working man, too, fears those who have less power than he, the human leavings of the system who inhabit the urban wastelands, the sprawling, dangerous inner cities of the nation. In such desolate places, in the concrete swamps of filth and wreckage, lurk today's escaped slaves, mostly unclaimed, sometimes dangerous, and always feared by those who have oppressed them.

—THE UBIQUITOUS MEDICINE: BULLYISM—

I think of the tragedy in Oklahoma City in 1995. When the smoke cleared, the administration's reaction was not to discover the underlying cause of why citizens wished to strike out at their government. Instead, the response was to add a thousand men to the FBI, as if a thousand or even ten thousand more armed officers could prevent a similar tragedy.

Foolish devotion to brute force is always the mindset of those in power. It is called *bullyism*. Such simple-mindedness results in revolution, war, and the eventual demise of the bully. In 1962, John F. Kennedy said, "Those who make peaceful revolution impossible will make violent revolution inevitable." The United States, while it has the option of expending small portions of its military billions to relieve the pressure accumulating from the suffering of the poor, instead builds yet larger and more powerful forces to be exerted against them both at home and abroad. Today, the U.S. military budget exceeds the *total* of the next thirteen largest military spenders below it.

Dwight D. Eisenhower said, "Every gun that is made, every warship launched, every rocket fired signifies a theft from those who hunger and are not fed, those who are cold and are not clothed. This world in arms is not spending money alone. It is spending the sweat of its laborers, the genius of its scientists, the hopes of its children. . . . This is not a way of life at all. Under the cloud of threatening war, it is humanity hanging from a cross of iron."

When parts of Los Angeles were burned after the Rodney King verdict in 1992, the response was equally predictable. The dire misery of the projects was never addressed; the city simply enlisted a larger police force. When Nat Turner exploded into his insane rampage, the South in mindless response tortured and killed more slaves, raised an army, and in the end left innocent slaves more frightened, more helpless, and, as the slave owners were to learn in the years to come, more dangerous.

I have yet to hear a president, a congressman, or a mayor ask these simple questions: Why are the people so angry? Why are we abusing our children so? Why are we beating our wives? Why are we murdering our innocent? Why are our families so dysfunctional? Why is crime eating our civilization alive like a cancer at our throat? Why do we hate so? Fear so? And, at last, how can we deal with this massive discontent other than attack it with further repression? That makes no more sense than beating a child and, when he cries out in pain, beating him again to teach him not to cry.

Today the New Master responds to the cry of the slaves by punishing the fatherless child, by forcing the single mother into the streets, by emptying the mental hospitals under the ignorant and inhumane theory that it is too expensive for the system to care for the casualties of the system. The New Master builds more penitentiaries, not more housing. It passes yet harsher laws that further alienate the people from one another and from their government. Marshaling our best logic, we argue that the death penalty will teach the killer a lesson. Education for the poor has become a dream from which we have been rudely awakened. One remembers the old South's response to Nat Turner: Do not educate the slaves, for educating the slave can be dangerous.

Crime begets crime. Criminal growing fields can grow only criminals. In the inner city, white police take over black neighborhoods like occupying troops and, even in plain view of the camera (as in the Rodney King case), beat black men out of their senses. In the pristine halls of the judiciary, the courts are packed with judges who, with heavy but callous-free hands, lay down the law of the New Master.

In the ghettos, those who need the most are abandoned and become like cannibals, devouring each other with drugs and crime. In response to the slave's violence, the New Master, always paranoid, knows no other means by which to confront the violence it has engendered except by loosing a greater and more empty-headed violence of its own.

At Ruby Ridge, federal agents shot in the back and killed a child's dog, shot in the back and killed the fleeing child as well, and then blew off the head of that child's mother, who was standing at an open door holding her baby in her arms. And even after a cover-up was discovered, the federal government refused to prosecute the killers. At Waco, the government, employing a relentless program of unleashed violence, roasted twenty-two helpless children like wieners on a spit and cremated more than fifty adults in the same inferno. Yet no federal officers were prosecuted.

As in the days of Nat Turner, the New Master's response to slave revolt is further hatred, further banishment, further imprisonment, and further executions. No matter the inhumane act of the New Master, its own violence and cruelty are made lawful through the New Master's Congress and the New Master's courts, enforced, as always, by the New Master's judges and its ready police. Rehabilitation has become apostasy. Education, although cheaper than imprisonment, is never considered, since education is antithetical to punishment, and we have become a punitive people.

Job opportunities that will provide a decent living are not available to most of the unemployed. But the jobless are hated further for not securing jobs, for not laboring for wages that cannot provide enough food to feed the hungry children. In the painfully constricted mind of the New Master, the new swamp slaves should, indeed, be terminated.

—The Corporate Nanny, the Public Training Camps—

In a nation where money is power, the children are abandoned to the corporate nanny, also known as day care, a throwback to the days when enslaved mothers trudged to the fields, leaving their children under the eyes of old women whose fingers had become too arthritic to pick the cotton boll. As in the fearsome training camps of Germany, too often the objective is not to assist the children in their quest for growth and light but to cause the child to "buckle under." It is more important that the children walk in lockstep and deport themselves in such a fashion as to make the teacher, their first overseer, more comfortable in her work than it is for the children to express themselves, to create, to follow their curiosity. And today the New Master is proposing that it educate our young in privately owned and operated corporate schools for profit. One wonders, why not? Corporations run many of our prisons. Ought they not now be permitted to extend their grasp by taking control of our schoolchildren as well?

—The Domestication of the Species—

By the time we have achieved adulthood, we have become fully domesticated, docile and dull, the mirthless smile creased permanently into the muscles of our faces. Rather than rage, we more often feel an inescapable weariness, a heaviness so intense we cannot hold up our heads. Although many are healthy and comfortable, for many others, life drags on without meaning, and makes life often seem not worth the living.

The feelings most often expressed by the slave are exhaustion, impotence, and despair, a feeling that he is of little account when considered against society as a whole and that he can make no difference in the scheme of things. He feels as if he were screaming in an empty canyon; his voice is as loud as silence itself. He feels caught in a gigantic maelstrom that has sucked him up, that carries him along like some unattached object, the force of which he is utterly powerless against.

Alabama said it once: "I was out fishin' in the canyon one day. I looked around. Nobody but me was there, so I let a big one. Nobody heard it. My line got caught on a bush, and I come out with a string of cussin'. Nobody heard that either, then I hollered jus' to hear myself holler good. But nobody heard that. That's the way it was at work. Nobody heard you. Nobody give a shit. An' nobody gives a shit now."

Outside the sky may be blue, the birds singing, but the king of mammals is barely able to breathe. Because he cannot express his anger in any constructive or creative way, he turns his anger against himself. He hates himself with no just cause, and his anger, turned inward, ferments into that most deadly of all human conditions: depression, perhaps our nation's most pervasive illness.

—Depression, the New Plague—

The cause of our national depression is simple to diagnose. Slaves cannot bear to be slaves. A nation of slaves caught in their slave traps and helpless to free themselves are reduced to a collective depression. To appreciate the extent of this phenomenon, one need only consider the substances people employ to medicate their symptoms: cocaine, crack, alcohol, antidepressants, one or more of which have affected the lives of nearly every American. Denying our bondage, we drink ourselves to death, eat ourselves into the grave, smoke ourselves into oblivion, and seek to lose ourselves in the numbing network sitcoms where only the canned laughter is funny and where, at last, we are transported from our powerlessness into a world where nothing counts. And when we cannot escape this trap in life, we escape it in death, in premature heart attacks and cancers that eat out our bowels and our brains.

—THE DRUG OF CHOICE—

In still another institution of the New Slavery, the slave, beckoned to the equivalent of the old company store, is encouraged by every design and device to squander his few thin shekels at the master's shopping mall—for exercise, for the alleviation of pain, for the palliation of boredom. Under conventional wisdom, shopping has become the drug of choice for depression.

Do we not see ourselves there, today, this moment, we, the New Slaves, dragging no shackles, supporting no chains, wildly mobbing the shops, grabbing for trinkets, snatching wares for which we have no earthly use but to establish, beyond doubt, that we are free? For are not slaves powerless to spend their dollars as they please? Indeed, are not slaves dollarless?

We have adopted the slave's view of heaven. Erich Fromm describes it in *The Sane Society*: "Modern man, if he dared to be articulate about his concept of heaven, would describe a vision which would look like the biggest department store in the world, showing new things and gadgets, and himself having plenty of money with which to buy them. He would wander around open-mouthed in this heaven of gadgets and commodities, provided only that there were ever more and newer things to buy, and perhaps that his neighbors were just a little less privileged than he."

—THE ERUPTING REBELLIONS—

Today, as surely as in the days of the "slaveocracy," as William Lloyd Garrison labeled it, a sort of free-roaming rage inhabits the land. After the Civil War, Wendell Phillips, one of the nation's great leaders against "chattel slavery," threw himself into the labor movement. His words of 1871 might as aptly have been spoken today. "All we see at the present time is the substratum of society, heaving and tossing in angry and aimless and ignorant struggle, not knowing what it wants nor why it suffers, nor how it can be remedied, and daily becoming angrier and more soured, and more embittered. The question is, who shall speak to it, who shall educate these conflicting interests?"

When we could focus our eyes on a living monarch, King George III, rebellion was easy. But today we cannot strike at the master, for the master is present only in the soft clicking of long rows of computers, in the deafening sound of the machinery in the factories, and the deadly mumbling of the bureaucratic machinery behind the impenetrable walls of government. How do we attack a master that is as invisible as air, as ethereal as the firmament? The only object in sight for the rebelling slave to attack, the only living entity who can become the object of his fury, is his fellow slave.

—THE NEW MEANING OF *POSTAL*—

Like Nat Turner, most slaves are angry beneath the passive fixture of their faces. It is the way of slaves to present patently compliant gestures. But beneath the benign, a dangerous anger swells that will erupt at unexpected times and from the most unlikely ones. Thus, a new word has seeped into the vocabulary: *postal*, describing a person who suddenly and without apparent reason explodes into random violence, who, without provocation or warning, grabs his automatic rifle and blasts away at every living creature in sight. Everywhere we turn we see evidence of this underlying cauldron of discontent.

Those who are angry at government withdraw from it, call themselves Freemen, hole up in Montana, and, armed to the teeth, challenge hundreds of FBI operatives to bring them in.

Angry tax protesters, reeling out reams of constitutional rhetoric, refuse to become "tax slaves" and burden the courts with their unwinnable cases.

The maddened who can no longer identify their oppressors express their rage in random freeway shootings or burn the stores of small merchants in Los Angeles with whom they likely have had no dealings whatsoever.

The young, born in bondage and with desolate visions of a meaningless life, join gangs in which all human life is seen as being as cheap and as goalless as their own.

Across the land, vast segments of the nation, alienated and economically emasculated smolder in anger and, without thoughtful leadership, follow any who will but point to some race, some religion, any handy scapegoat at which to strike.

Because it is easy to identify the color of skin, we have a resurgence of racism, and the Ku Klux Klan takes on a new and venal life.

Because the angry can readily identify a religious or ethnic group, we are presented with such ilk as the Aryan Nations and their preachment of hatred against the Jews.

Like a geyser in Yellowstone, these troubled waters boil away under the surface and finally erupt in the Unabomber, whose genius became distorted by his reaction to the pressures of technology. And in Oklahoma City, some demented dissident, already at an early age wildly enraged, blows up a federal building, sending 168 innocent people to their deaths.

—THE SILENCE OF PAIN—

This violence is the bitter fruit of pain. Yet we do not speak much about our pain. The Republicans do not dare speak of it. And when the Republicans are silent, the Democrats, who are just as sold out, remain silent as well. No one speaks for the people. The labor unions, weakened by a history of incalculable corruption, speak out of both sides of their mouth—one side in conciliatory language to the master, the other scolding the workers for their docility.

But the master is not silent. The master points its non-finger at the people and claims they have failed again. Then, one evening at quitting time, the master makes its final, silent speech and ends the dreams of its loyal employees by dropping the ultimate personal bomb on the employees: the pink slip. The master uses cold, benign words. These human beings are "surplussed" or "nonrenewed." Despite its record profits, the master argues that it must "de-hire" its longtime workers in order to save the jobs of the survivors. But neither the survivors nor the "disemployed" believe it.

And when the people are pummeled in that pink paper storm, Wall Street cheers, and the corporate stock catches fire as if the discarded people have been thrown into the flames.

—REFLECTED CRUELTY—

Yet the anger persists, and anger consumes. But the anger is not always carried out in the post office or through the elaborate machinations of the Unabomber. More often it strikes at those closest to the worker: his spouse, his children. It is called spousal abuse, of course. It is called child abuse. Last year, disputes that started at home carried over into 60,000 cases of workplace violence; at least 1,215 children died from child abuse and neglect, and more than 1 million senior citizens suffered some form of abuse, according to the AMA. It cannot be excused. We can only attempt to understand its cause.

—VICARIOUS VIOLENCE—

The people are angry, and the people crave violence. Today we are caught up in the violence of the killers on the screen and the killing of the killers. We are enthralled by the state's killing of the killers in gas chambers and on gurneys. We spend endless nights staring at the talking heads as they dissect the murders of babies and young girls. We are crazed for the crazy killing because in our most dreaded, secret places it is *our* madness and *our* violence.

Although we protest the violence, we seek it and turn to it. The master, too, knows that the violence on the screen sublimates the violence within us. Eagerly, then, we await the evening news, which will provide us our daily dose of mayhem and murder, confirming that we are not alone in our murderous urges. And we are grateful—grateful that the violence has once more proven to be *theirs,* not ours. And because of *their* crimes, by *their* having revealed in us our own most fearsome passions, we hate them all the more.

According to one authority, local TV news spends nearly 50 percent of its time covering crime and disasters. Rarely do the producers of the evening news show us the generous gifts of human kindness that every day are offered out of the underlying goodness of the species. The words *mercy* and *redemption* have disappeared from the national vocabulary. In our isolation, we are led to the conclusion that America abounds in child molesters, kidnappers, urban terrorists, mad bombers, drug pushers, robbers, and murderers. We are able to associate with each other only by watching the same violence, the same dull blather on television, each of us alone, each behind our own bolted doors, prisoners of ourselves.

The violence that we observe—that, indeed, we demand—of course brings on fear. We pass by each other on the streets without a smile, without a word, and, within inches of each other, we stand silently staring at the elevator walls, never once peering with our lonely eyes into the lonely eyes of our fellow passengers.

We are alone. And afraid. We are afraid of our neighbors, of those who, like us, are afraid. We cry for more police. We protest when the criminal exercises his legal rights for fear he will be set free. We call his rights legal loopholes. And, in blithe ignorance, to save ourselves from the criminal, we are willing to sacrifice those same constitutional rights that also belong to us.

Some of us demand that the people disarm. But we do not demand the disarmament of the master of the most violent weapon of all: the undeserved, randomly fired pink slip that kills more Americans than all of the nation's nefarious killers put together.

—THE ATTACK AGAINST OURSELVES—

Since the institution embodying the last hope of justice in America—the jury—is composed of our neighbors, and since we no longer trust our neighbors, many join in the mounting campaign to maim the jury system. In England, where the jury was born, the maiming is nearly complete. Jury trials have been taken from the people in all but a few specific cases. Distrusting our neighbors, we join those who would put caps on jury awards, never realizing that we are disenfranchising ourselves of our own justice. Told by the master that punitive damages raise the cost of goods, we join those who would disallow such damages against corporations, robbing ourselves of the only weapon remaining to punish the corporate criminal. Still fearing our own neighbors, we agree that those charged with crimes may be convicted with less than a unanimous vote, thereby endangering ourselves should we be wrongfully charged. We argue that the legal system no longer works by pointing to freakish trials such as the O. J. Simpson case, or the woman who was awarded millions for her burns from a cup of too-hot coffee at McDonald's.

Never are we permitted to intelligently discover the truth of those cases, to understand that the juries, according to the evidence presented, have been right in most of them. Instead, we judge the juries' work *solely on what the voice of the new master tells us:* that juries should be abandoned in favor of other, more efficient and reliable systems peopled solely by judges, who, of course, are nearly always the appointed minions of the corporate state.

—"GIVE ME LIBERTY"—

What if Patrick Henry had been black? Would his words have been lost to history? Here is the cry of Henry Highland Garnet, the black revolutionary. Are not these words, uttered in 1843 and now nearly lost to memory, as poetic, as stirring?

*If you must bleed, let it all come at once. . . . In the name of the merciful
God, and by all that life is worth, let it no longer be a debatable question
whether it is better to choose liberty or death!*

Still the lesson of Nat Turner lives on. Slaves dare not revolt lest the
miles of marching troops be called in and the flame-throwing tanks be
thrown against the people and the innocent children burned. But so
long as the slaves hate each other, white hating black, gentile hating
Jew, rich hating poor, the New Master shall always prevail.

—OUR FATHERS, OUR MOTHERS—THE SLAVES—

Looking back, we see the twisted vine and bitter fruit that have
grown from the roots of slavery. Today's "common man," his overseer,
the nation's men of wealth and power, all labor for the New Master.
All are, in fact, economically genetic kin to the slave. In the old South
and in the North, black and white alike, we have found our ancestors,
the black slaves, the industrial wage slaves, humans utterly without
value to their masters except for the profit they could produce by their
sweat and their blood.

Still, as we have seen, the forces of freedom are relentless. In those
dark days of slavery, abolitionists took great risks, at times even sacri-
ficing their lives to eradicate that evil, and in the great Civil War, over
600,000 Americans gave up their lives. But can opposition today still
matter? Are the forces of freedom still relevant? Do any still care? Or
have we, indeed, entered the world of George Orwell's *1984*, in which
all emotion is transformed into hate, all thought dulled, all pain anesthetized, all revolt dissolved, a time when the lie passes into history and
becomes the truth?

From this brief revisitation of our American genesis, we have begun
to understand the underlying psychic composition of the nation. In the
chapters that follow we shall consider whether we can alter the machine
that has become our New Master—for we struggle at the brink. Are
we too late, the consuming plague of slavery already irreversible? Can

the operative parts of the machine that has become our New Master be reformed to free us? Can the machine's code be reprogrammed to foster liberty rather than to inflict a yet more subtle bondage upon us and our children?

I think of the man, Martin Luther King, Jr., ensconced in infamy in the Birmingham jail, his crime: leading blacks and whites in their historic quest for racial freedom. It is 1963. Black people are still wending their way to the back of busses, their heads bowed, their place in the nation a mockery to the promise of equality. He writes from the jail that if the cruelties of slavery could not stop them, the opposition they faced would surely fail. He insists that the goal of America is freedom. King believed that the destiny of the enslaved was tied up with the destiny of America itself. His words are equally prophetic today. So, too, the destiny of we, the New American Slaves, is permanently, irrevocably affixed to the destiny of the nation.

And still the sound of Patrick Henry's crusty old voice reverberates across the land and into the firmament, and moves us onward: "*Give me liberty or give me death.*"

So I have asked: Are we slaves?

I have told you nothing you have not already known. My voice is your voice. It is only that we hear the voices of others better than our own, even when the voices, theirs and ours, are burdened with the same message.

We are slaves.

Our nation was founded on slavery. It grew and prospered on the backs of black slaves for over two hundred years. It ate up the lungs of miners and chewed up the bodies of helpless factory workers. It floated to wealth on the sweat of children in sweatshops and prospered beyond all dreams on the ungodly toil of the poor. We are slaves because we were born into this state. Born in the cage. Born in the zoo. Yet, to be sure, it is a better zoo.

They say we are free. The teachers say it. The politicians say it. The parents tell their children. The people tell each other. The voice of the master, the media, tell us.

We are free.

We enjoy the most obvious accoutrements of freedom: the right to speak, the right to protest, the right to be charged and tried under due process, tried before a jury of our own. They even say we choose our representatives who make our laws, although we are never told why the laws are against us.

We are taught freedom, speak freedom, exercise freedom, and yet it is all a puff in the wind if, at last, no matter how we strain at the invisible chains, we cannot set the course of our own lives. And if our nation has become only an instrument of power for those in power, if no matter how we, the people, try we cannot change its course, we are only the ants crawling on the deck of a vessel at sea destined for Lord knows what port.

Although we are slaves, we are the envy of the world. The wretched pound at our borders to get in, for ours is a more gentle slavery, a more civilized slavery, and, to be sure, a more deluding slavery. I cherish the freedom we enjoy, and, like you—indeed, like most—I would fight and die for it. Yet the idea of freedom in America has become much more our liturgy than our experience. We cannot be free, either as individuals or as a nation, if our perception of slavery is clouded by a fog of fancy. I have endeavored, therefore, to clear our vision so that we may see what we have known from the beginning. We are not free. Not yet. For *partial freedom is not freedom*. Freedom to wiggle the toes is not freedom to walk. And freedom to walk is not freedom to escape the cage.

This has been a cry exhaled out of love for the walking dead. This has been a cry for a nation benumbed and buried under more than two centuries of false promises and deluded dreams. This has been a call to Americans to awaken, to rise up from under the moldy shrouds of myth so that one day we may inhale the clean, crisp air of liberty, so that one day we shall fulfill for ourselves the original, the sublime promise—the promise of liberty and justice for all.

"Well, I didn't think you wanted the job," Sam says. "I jus' hired me a clean-up man—Romero over there. Acts like he wants the work."

"I was lookin' for somethin' better," Alabama says.

"A guy shouldn't be too choosy," Sam says. Then, to make things all right again, Sam orders up a Bud for Alabama. But before the bartender pops it, Alabama has already gone.

PART II

Freeing the Self

PART II

Freeing the Self

Overture

The zoo, the walls, the wire mesh above. Slam up against the concrete wall. Beat in the skull. The wall is, at last, the mind. The
wall is, at last, the prejudices foisted upon us by those who wish to
own our minds. Hate our brothers. Love God. Hate the color of skin
and love green money. Pay the priest. Pay our taxes, and the television cable company. Shun knowledge, shun the dearness of questioning and the joy of shivering naked in the early morning sun,
alone. Shun freedom.

We are slaves to ourselves. Preserve a closed mind and what you
have is the walking dead. All slaves are a form of the walking dead.

Is it not time to throw off the shroud? Is it not time to speak out,
to cry out, to fly, to test wings, to fall, and to laugh with joy over
the divine bruises?

NINE

·+·

Empowering the Self

————— *·+·* —————

*Our deepest fear is not that we are inadequate. Our deepest fear is that we
are powerful beyond measure. It is our light, not our darkness, that most
frightens us.*

—NELSON MANDELA, SOUTH AFRICAN PRESIDENT

AND ANTI-APARTHEID ACTIVIST

—THE ELEVENTH COMMANDMENT—

One night as a boy I was down under the kiln, down in that hellhole
shoveling the spill with an old guy named Bill. We were talking. I said
I was going to become the greatest lawyer in the history of the world.
It was just noise, just the sound of my voice against the deafening roar
of the kiln, but there was some small entity playing in me, that dancing
little fellow called "Hope."

"Well, now, that there sounds like a lotta bullshit to me," Old Bill
said. "I will tell yo one thing, boy. You be lucky to keep this job, and
we'll both get our asses canned if we don't quit fuckin' the dog." He
started shoveling harder and faster, and I joined him. "Better get this
motherfucker cleaned up afore the boss comes by."

We kept on shoveling. When the wheelbarrow was full he got between the handles, lifted them up with the hoist of his old legs, and
toted the load up over a two-by-twelve plank into the plant proper, and
after pushing it outside the kiln shed for what amounted to a couple
of city blocks, he dumped the load where one day a backhoe would lift
it into a dump truck to be hauled off. Next load was mine.

When Old Bill got back with the empty wheelbarrow he jumped right in with his thoughts. "Boy, you best pin yer ass to the grass. You best not go bullshittin' yer self about bein' some big-time lawyer. Them big-time lawyers go to them big schools and wear clean underwear ever day." He laughed. "They ain't our kind. I'll tell ya that much."

I didn't say anything.

"Nothin' wrong with bein' poor. Don't ya ferget that."

Never did. Never have.

"But there is somethin' wrong with bullshittin' yerse'f," he said. "Ya know what the eleventh command is, boy?"

"No," I said.

"The eleventh commandant is, 'Thou shalt not bullshit thyself.'" Then it was my turn to lug out the load.

—POWERLESSNESS, THE CONTAGIOUS DISEASE—

Something there is about feeling powerless that makes us wish the world around us to be as powerless as we—something about feeling weak and worthless that causes the human animal to inflict weakness and worthlessness on his fellows. Our sense of worthlessness, spoiling as it does our chance at life, brings up feelings of hostility. We give policemen badges and guns, train them to subdue us with brute force, and wonder why such people, naturally attracted to the work because of a deep sense of their own powerlessness, beat our powerless citizens senseless. We give the IRS authority to audit us, to sniff into every corner of our existence, to attack us with a cold, smileless, authoritarian arrogance. And Old Bill, working with a boy under the kiln saw life as cruel and brutal, and people as worthless and weak. You can tell about folks, for as they see others they also reveal themselves.

—THE PERFECT POWER OF THE SELF—

All power is in the self. We were born with all the power we require to live, and all the power we require to die. We do not need to seek power from others. We do not need to marry a powerful person or submit ourselves to the power of others to acquire our power. We have it already. To obtain power, we do not need to join a church or embrace a religion and adopt its enslaving myths and mumble its dogma. We already have the power. No God with whom I care to carry on an interchange would demand that we submit to him. No loving God could want our servitude.

Each of us has been endowed with the perfect power to be free. *Slavery is a state of mind that fails to acknowledge the slave's own power.* Lavinia Bell, the black slave who was born free, knew such power and, once having felt it, could not rest until she had recaptured it. The nation abounds with Lavinia Bells, men and women who have tasted freedom and who, in ways often inappropriate, even unlawful, strike out to regain it.

On the other hand, the ghoul of slavery knocks at the door of every soul who sees himself as weak and worthless. The ghoul demands that the slave give up his power. The ghoul of slavery demands that we see ourselves as lowly and worthless. The ghoul at the door demands to be worshipped by his slave, for without such worship the ghoul is powerless.

—THE INCOMPARABLE SELF—

I will tell you a laughably simple truth. It is nothing new. It is a truth that has not been invented by any man, nor taught by any guru. It is a truth born in the genes of every person. It is as much of the person at birth as is his first cry of life. It is as much a part of human history as the thumb is part of a functioning hand. The simple truth is that each of us is *unique*. And because we are unique we cannot be compared with any other person. And because we cannot be compared with any other person we are perfect. And because we are perfect we are not required to surrender to any power that is not our own in order to realize our power, our fulfillment, our destiny, our lives.

See it this way: Do you see your fingers? Each finger has a print that is different from the print of any other finger. Every person has ten uniquely different fingerprints. And every person in the world who has ever occupied space on this earth, and every person who will ever be born until the end of time, has ten prints that are different and unique from all others in the history of the world, or the world to come.

So it is with the imprint of the person. We are uniquely different from all other persons living or dead. We are uniquely different from any other person who will ever again grace the face of this earth. Such uniqueness renders us incomparable, elevates us as the standard, not for anyone else, but the standard for ourselves—the *only* standard. We are, therefore, in the sense of our absolute uniqueness, perfect. It is only when the perfect self is relentlessly attacked by the forces of slavery that we become wounded, that we begin to grow into ourselves, that the scars of the soul begin to bind and confine and strangle until at last we become enslaved.

—Attacking the Innocent Child—

I see the perfect child enslaved by the misery of prejudice. And the child takes the judgment of others onto himself. I see the perfect children of the world injured by poverty and the stultifying forces of ignorance and hatred. And the child with no other vision than the crime and destitution that surrounds him takes onto himself the judgment of the system: that he is worthless.

I see the creative genius in our children—that budding flower that stands for the incomparable power of the human species—debased and corrupted by parents who feel worthless and powerless themselves and who in turn visit their dysfunction upon their children. I see with horror the perfect people of the world, powerful from birth, coerced through fear and endless device to adopt as their own the neuroses of other slaves.

I see, with the deepest grief, the perfect people become absorbed in the blinding fervor of a political party, in the religion of an economic philosophy, in the hatred of children of other innocent and perfect people, in the insane teachings of the insane, in such ideas and beliefs and myths that destroy the perfect child, that denounce the perfect adult and manipulate us into slavery.

—Taking the Gift of the Self—

The gift of the self cannot be given to us. It is an incomparable gift that has already been given. We have possessed it from the beginning. Ours is the gift of our perfect uniqueness that cannot be purchased by buying a new car, by wearing certain designer clothing, by appearing in the "right" crowds, by joining the "right" clubs, or by speaking or thinking in the "right" way. The gift cannot be given to us through money or through things. The gift cannot come to us through our domination of others, through their enslavement and their submission. The gift cannot come to us through riches. The gift was already given, and thereafter stolen from us by the forces of slavery.

Having understood this perfect and simple truth, we must also understand that the stolen gift can be taken back, simply—like *that!*— like turning on the light, the blessed light.

TEN

·•·

The Slave Within

————— ·•· —————

Man's main task in life is to give birth to himself, to become what he potentially is. The most important product of his effort is his own personality.

—ERICH FROMM, 1947

—THE FALL—

In the same way that nations are the product of their history, so, too, does each of us own a personal history. To whatever extent each nation possesses a past in slavery, so, too, has each of us, to a varying degree, experienced an individual slavery. The deeper we have fallen into slavery, the more difficult it is for us to recognize it, especially if we have been ravaged by its power at an early age. The colt broken to the lead before it has run free is the easier to harness. Still, are we free enough to yet ask, "How did we become slaves? And how may we free ourselves?"

—THE FIGHT AGAINST FREEDOM—

Once enslaved, few want to burst out from under the leaking roof of the slave hut to be free and to stumble in the cold night alone. In the back part of our hearts we equate freedom with terror. To be free leaves us isolated from the other slaves. Better that we rage until we are palsied, point and squall and wail at fate, shake our fists at God, blame the system, blame anybody, everything, because to be free demands that we take responsibility for our bondage. No, we do not want freedom. We were born in the zoo and it is too frightening outside. We want, instead, *a more comfortable slavery,* one gilded with bountiful excuses for our bondage.

On the underside of freedom lurks the sense that we are as puny as a dust particle at sea. We stay imprisoned in bad marriages because we are afraid to be alone. We endure every manner of indignity and outrage, every agony and tedium, because we are afraid—afraid to throw off the traces and experience the naked terror that so permeates the idea of freedom. We kiss our shackles. We stay at home with the old folks, or never leave the farm or the neighborhood. We linger on in daddy's business or hang on to the same old job until we have worn a track around the thing like the knee-deep trail of the old gristmill horse, because we are too frightened to march out into the wilderness alone.

Already we know that no one is ever really free. Not the president, not the chairman of the board, not the husband or the wife, not the haughty businessman, the playboy, or the idle rich. Freedom, we believe, is for the birds. And even birds are securely bound by their instincts. No, no one is free, and no one wants freedom. We want to talk about it over a beer. How can one be free and be so frightened? To many, freedom is death. And if we awakened one day to confront pure freedom, would we not scurry back into our little holes as fast as terrified mice?

—THE PESTIFEROUS LONGING—

Still we long for freedom. And in the end, we must have it. When the infant's cord is severed, the infant experiences the first power of freedom. It can cry at will. And it does cry, exercising its freedom to protest the external forces already laid against it. The babe can be heard, and it *is* heard. It can respond to its bodily demands. Already it is an entity to be reckoned with. It has a will of its own. It can exercise its will, and although its dependence is clear to see, its dependence, as in all dependent relationships, enslaves the parent as well. Yet freedom is the biological goal of every creature, babe or brute. The hawk is free. The squirrel. The worm in the wood. We are born to become free. Only man devours the soul of his brother. Only man enslaves himself.

—Born in the Zoo—

Zoos are zoos, whether constructed of steel and concrete or of the fabric of the mind. Like all experiences, freedom is registered in the mind, without which there can be neither freedom nor slavery. The mind sets the limits of bondage and provides the gate to liberty. That which each of us takes as our freedom is our experience within the zoo. The infant monkey in the monkey house is as free as its counterpart born in the jungle—until, at last, the imposing boundaries of the cage are discovered. Even then, having been born in a cage, the captive monkey is more likely to accept the walls of its cage.

Today we have constructed new cages in old zoos. I remember when one simply bought one's ticket and hopped on an airplane. Today we are terrorized by terrorists. Yet there are probably no more than a few score of people in the entire nation whose madness would cause them to plot the willful destruction of hundreds of innocent passengers. As a consequence those few, whoever they might be, control 260 million people. Today we take it as an unquestioned part of travel, as *the way of things,* that we must identify ourselves with an official picture identification—the precursor of tattoos on our wrists. Today we accept as *the way of things* that our bodies must be searched mechanically, that our luggage must be inspected, that once aboard we must behave in numerous purposeless ways that have little or nothing to do with our safety but control us perfectly, like cattle run through the chutes. We know that if someone wants to manufacture a bomb and blow up the plane and its passengers, all of the endless procedures we have endured are only the known landscape over which any terrorist can travel with ease.

We do not provide ourselves safety. We have only given up our constitutional right against unlawful searches and seizures for the *illusion* of safety. Yet no one complains, or if a complaint is heard, it is in the form of an impotent mumble to which a security guard, who may not even be able to read the regulations he has been hired to enforce, responds by warning us to comply at once. Otherwise we can take the bus to Chicago.

Today one's every move, every decision, every act, is governed by rules and regulations devised, ostensibly, to permit masses of people to function together in harmony. We dress according to rules, eat according to rules, excrete according to rules, sleep according to rules, and die according to rules. We mate according to rules and rear and educate our young according to rules. To build the simplest house requires compliance with a mountain of rules that would confound all but modern man, who has been born into this bureaucratic cage. The rules that govern our daily lives would fill tons of fine print on tissue-thin paper. Still, the human species, more than any other creature, is perfectly able to adapt to nearly any environment. We can swelter and prosper in the jungles. We can tramp over the ice and multiply in igloos. The rules and laws and the multitude of man's endless impositions on man that consume our freedom have become a part of the daily environment to which we have also adapted with little more than an occasional whimper.

—FREEDOM INSIDE THE ZOO—

Yet we cannot be free outside the cage unless we are able to experience freedom within it. Consider the wild monkey who, lately transported to the zoo, hurls itself against the walls until it is battered and exhausted. Consider how it refuses to eat within the cage and may eventually die. On the other hand, his cage brother, born in the cage, sits peacefully munching on whatever morsel the zookeeper has tossed him and bounces off the concrete walls as if he were but swinging from tree limb to tree limb.

Slavery and captivity are not synonymous for either man or monkey. The wild monkey can be captive in the jungle itself. Relegation to an inferior rung on the monkey ladder, it is subject to a monkey-imposed hierarchy. In the jungle itself, it is pinioned to a territory with limits, to the safety of certain trees the leopard cannot climb. In or out of the zoo, the monkey may fail to recognize its cage and accept the limits imposed upon him as freedom.

—PERFECT FREEDOM—

Perfect freedom does not exist except when we are finally freed of life. Then the mind is unprisoned, and the soul is free to fly. Death frees life, releasing it like a bird that soars without fear of its enemies, like the sparrow with no fear of the hawk. Absent death, perfect freedom does not exist, which is not to argue that we should accept slavery in any of its multifarious forms. What I argue, instead, is that freedom for monkey or man, without regard to the exterior forces that enslave us, cannot exist if we have not first freed the self. *And the self is ours to free.*

—THE ETERNAL "NO!"—

From the moment we are freed from the imprisoning womb and the cord is cut, not only do we begin to assert our freedom, to search for it and grasp for it, but at the same moment powerful forces are loosed against us to enslave us. Whereas we were born to become free, the mother, the community, the law, and the system begin to fling the *eternal "No!"* at the child. As the child reaches for a glass on the table, he hears the eternal "No!" He hears "No!" as he toddles toward the door. He hears "No!" as he reaches for the nose of his father's face. He hears the eternal "No!" echoing in his ears from cradle to grave. The Ten Commandments with their "Thou shalt nots" ring in his ears. His teachers, more dedicated to their own comfort than to the child's free expression, smother the child with the eternal "No!"

His life is cut into segments of time. The fence of time captures him. There is a time to sleep, to arise, to go to school, to eat, to play, and a time once more to go to bed. Never has the child been permitted to revolt against any of the enslaving forces that domesticate the human animal and convert him from the wild aborigine of his genes to the human machine that will eventually perform as predictably as a wind-up toy.

—THE REBEL WITHIN—

By puberty, the war between the forces of freedom and slavery explodes to the surface. The child, now brimming with hormones, begins to assert his individuality. He strikes out in unpredictable ways against all authority—against his parents, the school, the law. He experiments with alcohol, tobacco, and drugs. He tests his sexuality. No matter the love of a parent, the supplications of a parent, the pleading of a parent, the threats of a parent—nothing will divert the child from his rush toward individuality. One cannot experience individuality in the womb, attached to the placenta, suckled at the breast, held by the maternal hand, or contained within the parental fold. Like the slave who breaks his chains, one can achieve individuality only through the rebellious forces of freedom.

But no sooner does the child begin to assert his independence during puberty—although usually with the wisdom and aplomb of a wild hare—than the forces of the eternal "No!" are reapplied with even greater vigor. In high school he is no longer coddled. School has become a higher-stakes penitentiary. The rules are impersonal and rigid. The juvenile's own social system, too, has rules. One can belong only if he complies and accepts the way of the gang. His genetic longing for the tribe shouts in his ear. His need to become a functional, recognized member of the tribe dominates his decisions. To *belong* is the paramount goal. Parental approval and acceptance in the larger social order bear little weight for the adolescent. His is not the adult world, nor does he wish to enter it. He does not respect it. The adult power structure is the enemy. Yet it is that power structure from which the eternal "No!" pounds perpetually in his ears, that threatens, that punishes, that enslaves.

—THE EVIL BITCH—

By the time the child blunders into adulthood, other forces have come to assert their power against him. Mother Nature has stricken him with the ultimate disease: falling in love. Her weapon, the evil bitch, is chemical warfare. The hormone, a magic potion still not fully understood by science, strikes at the human brain, causing its victim to fall prey to the disease, to mate and to thereby plunge into a new slavery from which he will likely never recover. The forces of the malady cause him to woo, to fight, to copulate, and to produce children. Now he must provide his offspring a nest and nourishment, and in the utterly predictable progression, he must make certain bargains, which usually require him to sell himself as a commodity at the slave market. Thereafter he makes bargains from year to year, from job to job, that ensnare him until he is rolled into his grave.

We are creatures enslaved by our genes. We are, indeed, like salmon predictably fulfilling their genetic course. Mindlessly we swim with the school into the great seas and back up the river of our birth to spawn, to die, and to be eaten by the waiting grizzly on the bank. Such freedom as we experience is only that which we encounter within the genetic cage of our birth, within the confines of the mammalian creature that we are and from which we can never escape.

The first halting step toward freedom of the self is the acknowledgment of one's enslavement to the forces that define the species. We were not born to become free. We were born to fall in love with Mary Jane or Mike, to marry, to father or mother those three little drippy-nosed rascals who will bedevil us until the day we gasp our last exhausted breath, and then, as true to the equation as dandelions going to seed and thereafter withering in the first frost, we too will complete this seemingly purposeless cycle established by the ultimate force that some call God.

—TESTING, THE WAY TO FREEDOM—

Like the child realizing he is locked in the basement, we can now begin to explore and search for a way out. Having acknowledged our servitude, we are freed to test ideas, to test religion, to test that which is said to be right and that which is said to be otherwise, to test the rules, the rhetoric, the declarations of freedom—in the end, to test authority. Ah, to test authority, every strand and thread of it that entwines us! To test the authority of government, of the law, of the enveloping system, yes, even to test our perception of the universe! I say, test it all.

I say, test all inner authority as well. Test the loud-mouthed tyrant called conscience, that inner voice that shouts and nags and wails, that orders us to perform that which it defines as duty. I say, grab the inner despot by the throat. Call it up to answer. By what authority does it command us to accept a religion, to bow to an icon, to salute a piece of cloth, to perform services we detest or disrespect, to fulfill the expectations of parents and children and those who prevail upon us and suck from us under the guise of friendship? By what authority does it command us not to deviate from the norm, not to try new behavior, not to stray one step from the rutted path? We must make demands of our own and hurl the question back. For the shackles are slipped over us in our silence, while we, the compliant, make no sound whatever. Silence gags us in the dark as if we are chained to a stake like the village goat, like the slave to the whipping post.

Freedom is always at war with the opposing forces of slavery. Always. Freedom to think, to explore, *to wonder,* is at war with snarling religions that command that we think nothing, explore nothing, and accept on faith whatever is flopped before us on the plate of life. Freedom to experiment, to try the new, to reach out, to look over the abyss, is at war with the system's demands that we slink up to the master and, like good slaves, fulfill the master's expectations. The penalty for being who we are—and, therefore, for being different—is to face the deep and intense fear of being banished from the tribe. Freedom itself is at war with the myths of freedom. The myths of freedom blind us like fog settling in over the front porch. And only by exposing the myths that surround us and by revealing their enslaving nature can we hope to regain our liberty.

—BELIEF, THE INVISIBLE SHACKLE—

One needs to begin by taking an inventory of the *self.* What is this conglomeration of beliefs, likes, prejudices, habits, customs, and thought processes that make up the self? Take each into the fingers of the mind like one examining an egg for cracks. Turn each over and over again. Does such a belief or prejudice close the doors to experience? A belief is dangerous to embrace. We are slaves to beliefs—to a point of view that leaves us with locked-tight, jammed-shut minds and imprisons us to petty habits. We are slaves to our hatreds, our prejudices, our miserly view of our own worth and the worth of our neighbors. We are slaves to values, which are usually set not by ourselves but by others.

The most formidable chains are forged from beliefs. Ah, beliefs! Beliefs tear out the eyes, and leave us blind and groping in the dark. If I believe in one proposition, I have become locked behind the door of that belief, and all the other doors to learning and freedom, although standing open and waiting for me to enter, are now closed to me. If I believe in one God, one religion, if I believe in a God at all, or if I embrace none, if I have closed my mind to magic, to spirit, to salvation, to the unknown dimensions that exist in the firmament, I have plunged my mind into slavery.

We are animals who travel the same trails in the forest every day. If that were not so there would be no trails in the forest. We get up every morning and proceed through the same routine. We turn on the coffeepot, let out the dog, stagger to the shower, brush our teeth, blow our hair dry, let the dog in, and pour a cup of coffee. Anything that intrudes on the routine brings on immediate irritation. Every day we drive to work over the same route, have lunch at the same place, usually with the same people, and, in sum, perform the same daily routine that has finally left us benumbed. At last we fall into bed to watch the same inane sitcoms on television, which will paralyze the few remaining brain waves that dare slither across the mind's blurry screen.

When we proceed through one day in one way, certainly we have experienced that day. If we repeat the same routine on the second day, we have lived only one day—the first. Some people have spent a lifetime engaged in the monotonous repetition of the first day, day after day, and at last die having lived little more than that one first day of their lives. Routine, habit, and fear of something new have become the venal thieves of freedom.

Most of us are enslaved by the economic or social class in which we exist. Rarely does the wealthy man have lunch with the plumber. I know black men and white men who have worked together in harmony every day until their retirement but who have never enriched themselves by having had dinner with each other's families. Often the self-professed intellectual has never tried to discover the intelligence of the truck driver who holds insights not discoverable in the books. The psychologist who counsels people every day in accordance with the procedures he learned in school has never talked to an Indian shaman about man's relatedness to Mother Earth, nor talked to the street-corner guru concerning the state of the species. The physician whose deistic view of himself sometimes leaves him pathetically ignorant has never talked to a Chinese herbalist and knows little of any medication that has not been first explained to him by the marketers from the drug companies.

Most of us are trapped—trapped by our education and the minutiae of our experience. Although the freed self is the source of all knowledge, most of us are imprisoned in a false sense of self, the authority for which is often little more than transplanted prejudice and half-truth. Nothing serves us so handily, so frequently, and so well as blithe ignorance. Our system of likes and dislikes, which renders us as predictable as the clock that strikes on the hour, reduces us to machinery—machinery waiting to be manipulated, turned on, turned off, used up, or wasted according to the need of the master.

—THE QUESTION, THE CURIOUS WEAPON—

Still, I say, *question!* That is the great weapon against slavery. By what right do parents, teachers, professors, the media, the government, and the church enslave us? Question every word, every phrase of propaganda fed to you. Strip naked every myth to its rattling bones. Propaganda and myth are evil potions administered to us by the witch doctors of the system that anesthetize the mind and leave us limp and lifeless on the system's operating table. Skepticism, not cleanliness, is next to godliness. Skepticism is the father of freedom. It is like the pry that holds open the door for truth to slip in.

I say, question, and question again. Authority cannot bear the glare of the question. Question every "truth," for that which is true for the master is rarely true for the slave. And the self? Can the self be the receptacle of truth? I say, question the self. Are not the ideas that cling to the walls of the self like barnacles on the ship's hull—the ideas of parent, of church, of religion, of politics? Question every prejudice. Ask, whom do my prejudices serve? If we are prejudiced for an economic theory, the prejudice may serve the structure in power. If we are prejudiced against a race, our prejudice likely serves the rich against the poor. But in the end, such prejudices rarely serve us.

When, because of prejudice, we separate ourselves from other members of the species, our sense of brotherhood is diminished. Such alienation always serves the few who, by dividing and separating us from one another, conquer and devour us. Think of the fate of the wolf if a thousand sheep in the herd, in unison and in deep caring for themselves and one another, descended upon the beast with four thousand stamping hoofs.

—The Brothers: Fear and Freedom—

We are fearful of leaving the pack. We are terrified to stand alone, vulnerable, tender, and free. But listen to the words of Nietzsche, the nineteenth-century philosopher: "Do you have courage, Oh, my brothers? Are you brave? Not courage before witnesses but the courage of hermits and eagles, which is no longer watched even by a God. Cold souls, mules, the blind, and the drunken I do not call brave. Brave is he who knows fear but conquers fear, who sees the abyss, but with pride. Who sees the abyss but with the eyes of the eagle; who grasps the abyss with the talons of the eagle—that man has courage." And that man is free. Fear and freedom are brothers.

—The Yoke of Political Correctness—

Today, most of us are starched up stiff in the high white collar of "political correctness." That which is deemed politically correct is as likely to enslave as are our prejudices. Many are prohibited by political correctness from discussing that which distinguishes man from woman, black from white, Jew from gentile. We are not all alike. Nor are we any longer permitted to celebrate our differences. Political correctness silences us. It eliminates our right to ponder the issues important to our lives and to think for ourselves. In an allegedly free society, it has become society's censor. It separates us from one another, for if I cannot express myself to you lest it be politically incorrect, you cannot respond to me in such a way that I may learn from you. Political correctness is the hollow voice of power urging the slaves to let the master think for them.

—Revealing the Truth: an Act of Love—

We are told that in this free system, our destiny rests solely in our hands. But when we strain against the chains of our slavery, we conclude that there must be something inherently wrong with us. Since the rest of the nation is said to be free and enjoys freedom's rich rewards, it must be that we who suffer this powerful sense of insignificance, of aloneness and enslavement, are somehow defective. We must be weak. We must be at fault. We must be worthless.

On the other hand, for those who have been lulled into the sweet security of bondage and exist contentedly within the walls of the zoo, for those who embrace myth and splash like happy babies in the bath of blissful conformity, the question naturally arises: Why should they who are content in their servitude be disturbed? Why make happy slaves miserable freemen?

But the destiny of the human race can never be fulfilled under the yoke. The potted plant in the window can never produce its most prodigious blooms. I say God delivered to Adam and Eve the ultimate act of love by ejecting them from the Garden, for confined within the garden they existed without the knowledge of freedom, and without suffering its pain the slave can never seek the splendor of the self.

ELEVEN

·-·

Freeing the Spirit, Releasing the Soul

---·-·---

Question with boldness even the existence of God; because if there be one, He must approve the homage of Reason rather than that of blindfolded Fear.

—THOMAS JEFFERSON

—THE SLAVEMASTER'S STAKE—

"Religion," said Carl Jung, "is for people who want to avoid the experience of God." Religion is not "the opiate of the people," as Marx claimed. Religion is the often dutiful overseer that chains the people to the slave master's stake. Often it serves the master rather than the slave. It teaches that to think for ourselves is treacherous, that independent thought puts the soul in danger of eternal damnation. It teaches that to permit one's thoughts to stray from the Scriptures is heresy punishable in hell, that to marvel at the mysteries of life and death outside the liturgy of the church is the evil scheme of the devil.

Religion can introduce us not to God, but to slavery. It can deprive us of our freedom to explore the mind as well as the wondrous and endless possibilities presented to us by an infinite universe. The birds, provided with wings, are permitted to fly. The fish, provided with fins, are permitted to swim. Should the antelope fold up its racing legs and the bee cease making honey? The door to enlightenment is the mind. The door to freedom is also the mind. Having provided the door, are we to understand that God commands that the door remain locked?

Nothing is more enslaving than a mind choked by the tentacles of intolerant dogma. Yet, as we shall see, religion itself has always been indentured to the power structure, and during the Civil War, in both the North and the South, religion was fully committed to the institution of slavery in America.

—RELIGION AND THE SLAVE—

In 1859, the Agriculture Society of Union District, South Carolina, made a study to determine the bearing of religion on the productivity of their slaves. The published report concluded that it was "the best policy and the highest interest of the master to afford good religious instruction to his servants." *Religion paid.* It "aids greatly in the government and discipline of the slave population." The report recommended the employment, even at considerable cost, of religious instructors. "The investment is not as great as the actual dividend in [the] way of improvement." The report cited such benefits to the master as "a stronger sense of duty upon the part of the Negroes to obey" and "a feeling of fear to offend against the obligations of religion."

Yet one planter, a year later, wrote to his fellow slaveholders, "I do not think—with sorrow I pen it—that [the Negro slave] is capable of moral elevation to any very appreciable extent. . . . That an inscrutable Providence will eventually work out his moral elevation, through the agency of the white man I have not a doubt; but it must be done by 'moral suasion,' coupled with a smart sprinkling of that great civilizer— the cow hide."

From the earliest times, man has used God as his authority to enslave his fellow man. One planter wrote his advice to fellow planters: "Let us remember that it [slavery] is an institution ordained of Heaven, and that we are the chosen instruments for the melioration and civilization of the downtrodden and oppressed African race. Placed in this position by Providence, we should feel and appreciate the responsibility and importance of our station, and so discharge our duties as to fulfill Heaven's designs toward us."

From the standpoint of the slave, the master's religiosity became the final evil. Wrote Frederick Douglass, the great runaway slave leader, to his former master, "When I saw the slave-driver whip a slave woman, cut the blood out of her neck, and heard her piteous cries, I went away into the corner of the fence, wept and pondered over the mystery. I had . . . got some idea of God, the Creator of all mankind, the black and the white, and that he had made the blacks to serve the whites as slaves. How could he do this and be *good*, I could not tell. I was not satisfied with this theory, which made God responsible for slavery, for it pained me greatly, and I have wept over it long and often."

Susan Boggs, a black runaway interviewed in Canada in 1863, said of the religious slave masters: "Why the man that baptized me had a colored woman tied up in his yard to whip when he got home that very Sunday and her mother . . . was in church hearing him preach. He preached, 'You must obey your masters and be good servants.' That is the greater part of the sermon, when they preach to colored folks . . ."

—SLAVERY AND THE CHURCH—

Indeed, the church itself has often condoned slavery. In 1610, Father Sandoval of Spain wanted to know the position of the church on slavery and inquired of the matter to a brother. Here was the reply:

> I think your Reverence should have no scruples on this point. . . . We have been here ourselves for forty years and there have been among us very learned Fathers. . . . [N]ever did they consider the trade as illicit. Therefore we and the Fathers of Brazil buy these slaves for our service without any scruple.

The church owned many slaves. Even before the Jesuits began to import Africans to the New World, the church was active in its promotion of slavery. In the fourteenth century, Pope Gregory XI thought slavery was justice for those who had struggled against the papacy, and ordered the enslavement of excommunicated Florentines whenever they were captured. And in 1488 Pope Innocent VIII accepted a gift of one hundred Moorish slaves from King Ferdinand of Spain and divided them up among the various cardinals and nobles.

Saint Augustine himself pronounced that "the chief cause of slavery, then, is sin . . . and this happens only by the judgment of God, in whose eyes it is no crime." Pope Pius XII, although aware of the Nazi concentration camps, turned a blind eye, and in fact the Vatican is said to have facilitated the escape of more Nazis after World War II than any other government or institution.

—GOD, THE NORTH, AND THE SLAVE—

The view of the religious zealot so prevalent in the old South was equally widespread in the industrial North, where slavery took on only a slightly different form. In 1902 George Baer, the president of the Philadelphia & Reading Railroad, who spoke on behalf of the coal operators, answered striking coal miners who begged for Christian treatment. "The rights and interests of the laboring man," he announced from the pit of his sanctimoniousness, "will be protected and cared for—not by the labor agitators, but by the Christian men to whom God, in His infinite wisdom, has given the control of the property interests of this country."

In 1914, at Ludlow, Colorado, the striking workers' tent settlements at John D. Rockefeller's Colorado Fuel and Iron Co. were burned to the ground and the tenants, including women and children, burned and shot—not by raiding Indians but by Rockefeller's private army, backed up by the U.S. Cavalry. Rockefeller, a deeply religious man, was said to have monitored the struggle at Ludlow with great pleasure.

One miner, William Snyder, was called as a witness at the coroner's inquest over the death of his eleven-year-old son, who had been shot through the head:

"They set fire to the tent?" Snyder was asked.

"Yes, sir. My wife then said, 'For God sakes save my children.' "

"What did they say to you?" the coroner asked.

"They said, 'What the hell are you doing here?' I told them I was trying to save my children and they said, 'You son of a bitch, get out of here and get out quick at that.'

"My wife was out by that time. . . . I told them to hold on. I had a boy killed in there and they told me to get out damn quick. I picked the boy up and laid him down outside so I could get a better hold of him.

"I asked some of these fellows to help me carry him to the depot and one said, 'God damn you, aren't you big enough?' I said, 'I can't do it.' I took him on my shoulder and [lifted his] sister on the other arm and then one of these militia men stopped me and said, 'God damn you, you redneck son of a bitch, I have a notion to kill you right now.'" Then Rockefeller saw the unfettered work of the entrepreneur as God's work. The master cannot exist without slaves. The idea that God has, in his munificence, graced the planter, the businessman, the industrialist, and the born rich with the divine right to enslave others has always been the central argument for slavery.

In the South during the Civil War, the church was, as is its wont, aligned with power. Archbishop John Hughes declared that "we Catholics, and a vast majority of our brave troops in the field, have not the slightest idea of carrying on a war that costs so much blood and treasure just to gratify a clique of Abolitionists." The abolitionists themselves seemed blind to the nearly complete enslavement of hundreds of thousands of white children by the industrial North in its own sweatshops.

After the Civil War, Free Enterprise became the dominant religion of the industrial North. As always, religion served the master, and as always, the master required an endless supply of workers who would sell their labor cheap, workers who could be manipulated into all but giving their lives away. Henry Ford proclaimed that "work is the salvation of the nation." Indeed, workers were the salvation of Henry Ford, who saw them as little more than fungible parts and who believed that "a great business is really too big to be human." He preached to his workers, "If you are a high-priced man you will do exactly as this man [the foreman] tells you, from morning 'til night. When he tells you to pick up a pig and walk, you pick it up and walk, and when he tells you to sit down and rest, you sit it down. You do that right straight through the day. And what's more, no back talk."

Ford, who was considered by his workers to be an absolute tyrant, told a journalist, "I have a thousand men who, if I say, 'Be at the northeast corner of the building at four A.M.,' will be there at four A.M. That's what we want, *obedience*." It made no difference that the new slaves were wage slaves. Slaves were slaves and, by the Bible, had always been slaves. Religion over the centuries has served the master well, admonishing the worker that he can row himself to heaven only up a river of honest sweat.

Today, the church, in its eternal attraction to power, lends its blessing to a system that encourages the unfettered exploitation of the New American Slaves by the corporate power structure, and American industry, without a flinch of conscience and following the gospel of Free Enterprise, uses up the impoverished workers and their children in the Third World like so much coal to fire the money boilers.

—THE MAGICAL DIMENSION OF SPIRITUALITY—

I do not reject the magical dimension of spirituality. I leave open the possibilities of a wondrous, boundless universe. I cherish the fantasy, even the hope, of other adventures in other realms to come. But how can we ruin that most precious of all gifts—life—with the rope of religion around our necks? It chokes freedom with its dogma. It pinions us to the stake of superstition. It binds us with fear to a system in which the masters themselves have become the obedient slaves of Mammon.

—THE RELIGION OF FREE ENTERPRISE—

The religion of Free Enterprise preaches that it is acceptable, even laudable, to destroy the earth and to starve the people in pursuit of profit. It is a religion that worships things more than it cares for the soul, a religion in which a wealth in gold is more cherished than a wealth in freedom.

The religion of Free Enterprise promises deliverance in exchange for submission. It returns us to the Garden, but the Garden is molded of concrete and perfumed with the smoke of industry. There one is blinded to the beauty of the earth and must join in its systematic destruction. In the Garden one cannot hear the angels sing. In the Garden one hears only the endless moaning of the workers laboring for things.

Bob Dylan sang in "It's Alright Ma, I'm Only Bleeding":

Everything from toy guns that spark
To flesh-colored Christs that glow in the dark
It's easy to see without looking too far
That not much is really sacred.

—THE RELIGION OF PATRIOTISM—

I am not against loyalty to a system that is loyal to its members. But blind patriotism is another form of religion that often enslaves the people for the benefit of the master. Do we not understand by now that blind patriotism—the stirring rhetoric, the flags unfurling, the bands marching, the people charging off to war—is not always good for the health of the people? Do we not understand by now that the message of patriotism is often an invitation for the people to serve the system rather than for the system to serve the people?

All forms of nationalism become religions. The Nazi party, the Communist party, the notion of the sacredness of capitalism, indeed, any party or economic theory, any government that demands the submission of the individual to the interests of the state, is an invitation to slavery.

—RELIGION OVER MAN—

To the religious, whether it is a religion of God or money or patriotism, it is the religion itself that counts. Religion, the product of man, is not responsible to man. It is responsible only to itself. It has no duty to free the soul of man. It has only the duty to capture his soul. It has no duty to elevate him. It has only the duty to frighten him, to cut off inquiry, to block his discovery of the self, and to at last own him. Religion has too often become the debasing negative energy that demands that we praise religion and ignore man.

In a broader sense, as religion serves the aristocracy of money, as it bows to the god of business, as it recites the dogma of Free Enterprise, we trudge into a strange and frightening world, a world where religion, not the people, is paramount. In that unearthly world, the Holy Ghost is not a loving God but an enslaving force, not a freeing spirit but a master that enslaves us through myth and fear and, at last, through madness.

TWELVE

·—·

The Religion of Work

————·—·————

*A tremendous number of people in America work very hard at
something that bores them. Even a rich man thinks he has to go down
to the office every day. Not because he likes it but because he can't
think of anything else to do.*
—W. H. Auden, poet

—The Work Psychosis—

What of the religion of work, the deep, neurotic worship of work that
proclaims that work in itself is the ultimate virtue? What of this religion
of work, America's traditional Calvinist notion, that preaches that work,
whether it be for beneficial purposes or not, is deeply laudable, that
work is the way to salvation, that work is not a means to an end, but
the end itself? Oh, the glory of work without ceasing, work that has
become the neurotic, compulsive objective of the species. We have
become like slack-mouthed beasts madly scurrying in an eternal circle,
working, working, forevermore working.

In an earlier, perhaps healthier time, work for its own sake was a
foreign idea. As Max Weber, the philosopher and economist, demonstrated, in those societies that predate the Industrial Revolution, beginning as early as the tribe itself, man suffered no passion for work beyond
the need to maintain his standard of living. The so-called workaholic is
a casualty of the Industrial Age and is the piteous progeny of religion—
the religion of work. The most cruel punishment of all, one that would
cause the most heartless sadist to flinch, is to lay upon the life of a
man meaningless, empty work that uses him up like axle grease.

You can see him there today, the mad worker, scraping, scheming, toiling endlessly in a wild fury to build his money-making machine—the farm, the business, the great corporation—to which he has now become enslaved. And the machine he has built, no matter how large and powerful, is but a cog in yet a larger money machine, finally an economy of machines that grind away, mostly under their own power. Before the Industrial Revolution, the machine was the tool of man. But today, man has become the fuel of the machine.

—THE NEW SLAVE CHILDREN—

The great industrial society could never have been set into motion but for the availability of an abundance of workers willing to be used up under the prevailing dogma of the religion of work—that work is good, that to slave all of one's life provides the road to salvation. And when the machinery runs out of cheap enough labor in America to provide the fuel for the machine, the machine reaches out, as we have already demonstrated, to the overt slavery of the Third World, employing the labor of small girls who sew up our clothing.

The labels inside do not say, "Made in Indonesia by children with blistered fingers and blinded eyes." And when I protest, the answer I get is, "Well, they'd be starving if they didn't get their fourteen cents an hour," or "They'd be sold into prostitution if they didn't have that job." We hear the slave ghoul arguing once more. We remember, of course, John Calhoun, who made a similar argument a century and a half ago. "Slavery provides a positive good . . . the African race never existed so comfortably, so respectably, or in such a civilized condition." Today we strike the same bargain: We enjoy cheap clothes, and the little girls do not starve as quickly and are not sold into prostitution as soon.

—THE IGNOMINY OF WORK—

Work as an abstract activity, undertaken for itself, has no merit. Native man did not work. He hunted, which was his pleasure. He gathered, which was his joy. Anthropologists insist that in his nascent state man was engaged in providing himself food but an hour or two a day. And that was not work. It was his play, his adventure, the fulfillment of his genetic purpose. Work was unknown to native man.

Smohalla, who belonged to the Nez Percé Indians, saw work as evil.

My young men shall never work. Men who work cannot dream, and wisdom comes to us in dreams.

You ask me to plow the ground. Shall I take a knife and tear my mother's breast? Then when I die she will not take me to her bosom to rest.

You ask me to dig for stone. Shall I dig under the skin for her bones? Then when I die I cannot enter her body to be born again.

You ask me to cut grass and make hay and sell it and be rich like white men. But how dare I cut off my mother's hair?

Only a harsh master could force us to the relentless drudgery of endless meaningless, numbing toil. It is the religion of work, like all religions, that creates our anxiety. It is against the religion of work to embrace the moment, to feel, to experience one's relatedness to the earth and its occupants. It is insane to stop and hug a tree. In light of the endless work that lies waiting, its foot tapping in impatience, it is irresponsible to stop and to wonder at the simple beauty of a forest fern.

The notion of work, and its puritanical elevation as among the greatest of virtues, is a religion that converts the diamonds of human creativity into the coal of the industrial machine. The religion of work has transformed human life and all of its potential, its great capacity for joy and fulfillment, into the inert fuel that is dumped into the furnaces of the New Master. Out of this religion is produced the gadgets and trinkets we purchase from the puddled sweat of our work, and out of this religion is produced the great war machinery that is destined to one day destroy the human race as the final vengeance of the insane machine against its insane inventors.

Yet I do not wish to confuse the idea of work on the one hand with slavery on the other. Work and slavery are not reciprocal concepts, although slaves work. On the other hand, the mere fact that people work does suggest that they are slaves. Free men work when their work is their joy. Free men work when they are also free not to work, when they work but remain the masters of themselves.

—Work, the Virtue That Enslaves—

Elevating the drudgery of work to a virtue is our dubious gift from the Puritans. Martin Luther and John Calvin laid the way in the late Middle Ages. Erich Fromm, the renowned American psychoanalyst, thought that the Reformation's doctrine of predestination—that is, that God, at the time of our birth, has already made his choice as to who will and who will not be saved—created in man such an anxiety over not knowing his eternal fate that it was necessary for him to treat the pain of his anxiety with compulsive, meaningless activity.

Fromm likened the phenomenon of ceaseless work to a man awaiting the pronouncement of the doctor as to whether he is afflicted with a terminal disease. The man, waiting, waiting, paces the floor to assuage the terrible pain of his anxiety. But the American worker does not engage in a fury of meaningless activity to ease the anxiety described by Fromm. He works because he is enslaved. He works mostly to eat.

In the new industrial state, the rich and the powerful, too, are compulsively at work, impelled by insatiable greed, greed born of man's terror of death, for no matter how hard and long he works, no matter how much money he accumulates, no matter the power he wields, he still can never conquer death. Here he stands, this puny man bearing the burden of a free will that, at last, proves useless as a weapon against the grave.

The work ethic in America, flowering from the original doctrines of Luther and Calvin, fulfilled the requirements of the industrial state. Indeed, man might achieve salvation if he were honest, diligent, and responsible and worked hard in accordance with the model set by Henry Ford—which is to say that man could enter the Pearly Gates if he in all ways qualified as a good, reliable, and efficient worker-slave. And he might feed his family as well. If one worked at lawful work, even at worthless work, even at work that might bring misery or death to many, still, because of such work alone, one could be adjudged worthy.

One thinks of the workers at Los Alamos in the early 1940s, laboring away on a nuclear bomb that could destroy the world. One thinks of the workers in the tobacco fields and the cigarette factories. One thinks of the clever gurus on Madison Avenue whose creative advertising will hook three thousand kids on cigarettes every day. Such work is respected not because it produces good, but because it is work. Such workers are respected not because they produce a useful product, but because they work.

Under the Puritan doctrines, even the sinner, if he worked hard enough, could finally earn the respect of his neighbors. Hard work was the only means by which the poor could, in the eyes of the community, rise above the degradation of poverty. "He was a hardworking man" were the words spoken over many a corpse.

Today, we still embrace the empty ethic that if one works long enough and hard enough, one will, if nothing else, receive the blessed kiss in heaven. Yet, on the last day, the difference between the worker and those who have snatched the fruits of his labor is that the former dies in a hard bed, the latter in a soft one.

I do not argue that people ought not work. But let us for once be practical about it. Likely one must work if one has not chosen his parents carefully for their stock portfolio and has not thrown off the troublesome eating habit. Moreover, a man must likely resort to work to find a mate and feed and educate the squalling aftermath. But aside from the plain necessity of work and its status as the most laudable evidence of a person's worth, what, I ask, is there about work that makes it intrinsically right?

—"Here Lies Elsie"—

I say, work is good mostly because our fathers and mothers have said it is good. It is good because our parents, dominated and enslaved, had to work, and the sins of the father are visited upon the child. It is good because our mothers worked and were enslaved by their work—slave to the house, to the stove, to the bawling kids and the dirty diapers. How would we like to read on our tombstone, "Here lies Elsie. She was a slave to an eternity of diapers"? Well, she was. And she worked all of her life, and she was said to have had a good and fulfilling time of it because she was indentured to her kids and her kitchen and the pails—ten thousand five-hundred and forty-three pails of dirty diapers, by actual count.

—A Gold Watch for Homer—

The old man slaved all of his life working as a bookkeeper at the railroad shops ten, sometimes twelve hours a day. He was management. No overtime. And when he retired, they didn't even give him a gold watch. Gold watches are so much corporate propaganda, we all know that. Yet we wouldn't mind working all our lives for the company if, when we retired after thirty-some years, they'd give us a gold watch. But no—like the old man, we get nothing but a swift boot in the hind end. "Get out of here, you stinking old fogey. You are finished—used up. You can't even stand up straight. Been crouched over those books for so long, your face looks like a set of books—white with a lot of foolish lines."

One day after he retired, the old man got cleaned up to go to Mose's funeral, the master mechanic who worked with the old man those thirty-some years at the railroad. The old man looked in the mirror. He could see the clean gray hairs in his nose, and the little hair that had stayed the course on his head was washed and all frizzy. What the old man saw in the mirror everybody else had been seeing for a long time. It frightened him. He couldn't put words to it. Never was good at words.

He walked out the front door, and he stopped in the middle of the sidewalk and looked up at the sky as if he were waiting for the clouds to part and for a voice to say, "Homer, you done good. You were honest, and you never stole a fucking nickel from the railroad, and you put the kid through junior college. You are an all right man, Homer. Plum all right."

But nobody and nothing said anything to the old man. Then he got into his Chevy Malibu and drove off to Mose's funeral. When he came home, he kicked the kid out of the house. "Been hangin' around too damn long," he said. The kid was almost twenty and had taken art in junior college. Could have gotten into advertising if he'd tried—good money there. But the kid just wanted to paint a lot of those silly pictures. Went through junior college, and he couldn't even paint a picture that looked like anything.

"You oughta go to work," the old man said. "Nothin' wrong with work, you know. Make something of yourself. I was already workin' at the railroad when I was your age."

—WORK AS VIRTUE—

Work in itself is not godly. Work in the abstract is not virtue. I do not disparage work as an honest means of survival. But work to feed the hungry mouth is not the first level of slavery. *The first level of slavery is the worship of work.*

Work to experience the deep pleasure of creativity is virtue. The potter throws his pot and experiences the ecstasy of his creativity. The farmer tills his fields and feels the earth between his fingers and feels the joy of his work. The carpenter steps back from the studs that will support the roof and feels the pleasure of his gift. The doctor ministers with compassion to the dying, heals the sick, and feels the touch of God at his breast.

Work to free the self is virtue. Work to gain endless power or endless wealth is not. Such work is but currying the deep misery of a frightened soul. Such work is but medicating a profound addiction for wealth that has grown out of bottomless insecurity. I say one must free one's self of the religion of work.

Thoreau insisted that man should not work for six days and rest on the seventh. Instead, he argued, man should work one day and leave six free for the "sublime revelations of nature." In the end, if the worker has served the work rather than the work having served him, the worker is enslaved.

—THE BETTER-FITTED ZOO—

In America, freedom and work are often incompatible bed partners. We are free to work, all right, or, as somebody said, we are also free to starve under the bridge. But as we have seen, many want neither freedom nor work. They want to frolic around in a better-fitted zoo. They want to lounge in an easy chair and sell themselves for a higher price so they can buy more beads and more trinkets. They want those long warm winter vacations and bigger TVs and fancy basketball shoes like the tall, bald-headed guy wears. They want to *feel* free by driving a certain sports car. They want to swagger and *look* free by wearing certain "out there" clothing, and to come off as free by smoking a certain brand of cigarette. They are willing to indenture themselves in order to buy the *symbols* of freedom sold by the ad makers on Madison Avenue, but they do not wish to experience freedom.

They want to bellow on the talk shows with all great asperity about their First Amendment rights and their civil rights, their right to remain silent and their right to die and their right to life. They want the right to harass without being harassed, and they want the right to marry somebody whose whiskers are as itchy as their own, but they do not want to experience freedom. All this talk about freedom is just self-serving palaver exhaled in six-second sound bites to entertain us.

—THE BREAD SNATCHERS—

I know many a rich man who says he accumulates wealth to "keep score," whatever that means. But how can the hoarding of money to keep score be acceptable human conduct? Consider how we might envision a dollar as a loaf of bread. Ten dollars equals ten loaves of bread. What do a million, a hundred million loaves of bread look like?

Do you see the hungry children? What of the billionaire whose excuse for his billions is his need to keep score? What is this insane game? Having acquired the first billion loaves, he must seek another billion? And of course, he must protect the bread he has already acquired from being stolen. He must protect it even from the hungry children.

Can you see the bread piled up high, the billion loaves towering to the sky, covering whole blocks of a city, a high fence around the expanse of bread to protect it? Can you see the children, their faces pushed up against the fence, wanting but a part of a loaf? Where is the virtue in this game? Is this not an evil game, a mad game played by madmen? If one of these bread snatchers gives away a few loaves of bread, we call him a philanthropist, and we admire him. If he speaks, we listen with great respect. I am not arguing for a Marxist solution. I am simply freeing our minds of the myth that there is virtue in the mindless, endless accumulation of wealth.

—Playing Our Lives Away—

When young people ask me what they should do, I say, "Play. Play all of your life away." I have played most of mine doing that which many would consider work. No one ever asks me, "What are you playing at?" They assume I must be working, sitting here writing these words, standing there in the courtroom speaking those words. I could not be without my play. It does not burden; it frees. It does not exhaust me with deadly drudgery; it sends me into the depths for an archeological dig of the self where all our unknown treasures abound.

If one's play results in money, such is an acceptable side effect— that is, it is not necessary to the activity in the first place, like strengthening the heart comes as a reward from the joy of a good walk up the mountain. *I say, play your life away.* Play until you are worn out, for play is the fulfillment of your life, like bees play flitting from flower to flower gathering the nectar, like bears play climbing the tree for the bees' honey. Play exalts the gifts of God to man, his talent, his creative energy, his uniqueness, fulfilled by that which brings him joy, which is his play.

God played in the universe. You can see the pleasure He must have had fiddling around in the firmament, creating order and disorder, amusing himself in his infinite creations, lolling about in eternity. If man, then, is created in the image of God, ought he not play as well? I have never been a slave to work. I am only enslaved in my play, which is a slavery I can endure, and one I commend to you.

THIRTEEN

·•·

The Power of Aloneness

———·•·———

I went to the woods because I wished to live deliberately, to front only the
essential facts of life, and see if I could not learn what it had to teach, and
not, when I came to die, discover that I had not lived.

—HENRY DAVID THOREAU, *WALDEN*, 1854

—THE FEAR, THE POWER OF ALONENESS—

Let me take you to a forest in the high mountain country of Wyoming.
The spruce and lodgepole pines rise like tall grasses to the ant. No
sound except the wind through the needles. No sound except the chip-
ping of an irreverent squirrel. And then no sound at all. I have stood
there as a frightened child for many an endless day, the snow falling,
each horizon looking the same, the same towering trees in every direction blotting the way, the forest brimming with ghosts, with the staring
dead, and perhaps, I think, with grizzlies too.

I have stood there too frightened to breathe. I would not dare cry
out in fear. I would dare not break the hush, the sound of my voice,
tiny and high as a peeping chick, smashing into the silence, for the
universe would surely come hurling down in an avalanche of fury and
scoop me up into the horrible void.

I have stood there alone in the forest waiting for my father to return
from the hunt to fetch me, like a doe returning for her waiting fawn. I
have strained my eyes to see his dark form appear from the shadows,
the legs long and sure, the toes turned slightly in, like the Indians'.
Where is he? I peer into the dark trees ahead, but the way is dark, and

the snow falls on the lids, leaving large drops on the lashes. What has happened to my father? He is the only God I know, for he is the only God I can see. What if God, who is up in the sky, who is everywhere watching, is angry at me? The terror of it. To be alone in the forest where one's breath must be eased from the nostrils, for even the sound of one's breath can awaken the devil.

To be alone on the earth is the abysmal terror. The fish swim in schools. The birds fly in flocks. The buffalo wander in herds. And man has his tribe. Alone in the forest, I am free, but the aloneness is unbearable and the freedom it provides is fear.

Now I see the movement through the shadows. I stare, my eyes bulging like the eyes of the fawn in panic. The movement is in my direction. I cannot make out its form in the shadows. Then I see my father moving easily through the trees. He walks as silently as any forest creature. Now he sees me, and he smiles, his face the face of God, the snow gathering on his shoulders, the steam coming from his lungs. He has come for me, and all is right in the world once more, and I will never, no never, be alone again.

As he walks up to where I stand, it is as if he had never left, as if I had never been alone. His presence is the infinite magic of God. He has changed my world in an instant. The hunting was good. You can see it on his hands, bloody, the brown elk hair stuck to them, and the small pack on his back bulges with the elk's heart and liver.

What is it in the human soul that so fears aloneness? We are born in the presence of mother, but only we alone experience our birth. We may be in the presence of others at death, but only we alone will experience our death. It is the fear of death that terrorizes, the fear of the unknown. To be alone is equated to death. Banishment from the tribe is death. Alone, one is vulnerable to the attack of one's enemies. Alone, one may be killed and eaten as the deer separated from the herd is run down by the wolves. Aloneness warns of impending death.

Yet the fear of death is irrational. Socrates thought death quite fine. Death would deliver him to his friends or drop him gently into a dreamless sleep, and to him, either was acceptable. As the poet John Dryden wrote:

Death is nothing; but we fear
To be we know not what,
We know not where.

The irrational fear of death has, of course, a biological purpose. If the species is not blessed with the fear of death, it cannot escape danger. It cannot survive. We hurl the young and foolish into battle because youth has never seen the face of death. Old men never fight.

Alone.

Without aloneness, without taking the fear of it into the self, without knowing it, what is the use? Birth and death happen there. And life as well happens there. The power of the self happens there. The rest is distraction. The rest is escape for those who are afraid of themselves. Alone.

I have never known a daffodil that bloomed with the aid of a sister. I have never known a chickadee who flew with the aid of a brother. I have never known a man who grew except alone. I tell you, there is nothing to fear in aloneness. Thoreau wrote in *Walden*, "I have a great deal of company in my house; especially in the morning, when nobody calls."

Alone.

Then is when it happens. The conversations with the self are tentative and hesitant. The radio off. Oh, no—how could the radio in the car be off? I have seen people panic at such silence, grabbing for the knob like a drowning person for the life buoy. When the voice on the radio is off, they are like ducklings who, when the mallard mother has ceased her soft quacking, swim in tight little circles in a great pool of terror.

—OUT OF ALONENESS, THE POWER OF THE SELF—

People who do not experience aloneness have breathed only the stale air of others. But in aloneness I say it happens. I write alone—my gift to myself and to you. I dream alone. I feel, and the feelings are mine, out of my aloneness, out of my belly, out of the place beneath my heart, out of the deepness. It is *my* deepness. I learn, but the learning is *mine*. I listen, but the words fill *my* ears. I touch, but they are *my* fingers, mine alone.

We wish to be swallowed up. "Swallow me up," we say to the system. "Swallow me up," we say to belief. Swallow me up, take me. It is better to be taken than to be alone. It is better to be a slave in the presence of slaves than to be free in the presence of only the self, the frightened, lonely self. Henry David Thoreau was alone when he wrote, "I have never found the companion that was so companionable as solitude."

Out of aloneness rises the power of the self. It will face the man within, affirm him, and learn to respect, yes, even to love him. Out of aloneness is built the shelter of the self. It is the most secure of all places on earth. No citadel offers such protection, no fortress such safety. Once one has found the shelter of the self, the need for the authority of another—of the guru, of government, of the church, of religion, of God—is gone.

—THE AUTHORITY OF THE SELF—

Already God has given away all authority. It is called "free will." God does not want it back. It does Him no good on earth or in heaven. Why should God covet authority? What can God, the ultimate authority, do with any more authority? And what loving God wishes to be worshipped? He who requires worshipping is insecure in himself, and God is not insecure. It is we who need to worship, not God who requires the worshipping. It is we, the frightened, the alone, who seek the object of worship, and we call him God, and we fall on our knees and pray out of our dismal fear of aloneness.

If, indeed, we are to achieve the kingdom of God, we must achieve the kingdom of the self. Truth does not set us free. The self sets us free. And should we come face to face with the self, we shall come face to face with the final authority—the final authority not for another, not for the neighbor, not for the child, not for the state, but the final authority for the self. And that is enough. And that is godly.

That alone man should become his own authority is the goal of any loving God, for no loving parent wishes that his child be dependent.

No loving parent wishes that his child stay attached, unable to grow and to bloom. No true God wishes to be worshipped any more than any true guru, any true prophet, any true parent, any true friend, wishes for it.

—THE WAY TO FREEDOM—

The way to freedom is alone. I do not mean that one must live alone. I do not mean that one must not have a mate or friends, that one must not communicate with others, that one cannot learn from others, that one cannot become a member of a tribe, of a community, of a nation. I say only that freedom does not come from others, from the tribe, from the community or the nation. Freedom does not come from a social club. It does not come from the mumbo jumbo of a secret order. Freedom does not come from the liturgy of the church. Freedom cannot be given to us by man or by God. *Freedom is the gift of the self and only the self,* and this gift of all gifts is not given in the presence of the car radio or the television or the jabber of friends. It is not given in the madness of the freeway or the insanity of the workplace. It is not given in the conjugal bed. It is not the gift of the pope or the political party. Freedom is the gift of the self, to the self, alone.

·—·—·

FOURTEEN

The Magical Weapon: Withholding Permission to Be Defeated

·—·—·

However sugarcoated and ambiguous, every form of authoritarianism must start with a belief in some group's greater right to power, whether that right is justified by sex, race, class, religion or all four.
—Gloria Steinem, American feminist and writer

—The Enemy—

How often I have seen the enemy. The enemy comes in many forms. The enemy is our false sense of duty to those to whom we owe no duty. The enemy is a prissy conscience that lets loose its clanging alarm when in justice it should be silent. The enemy is our fear, causing us to quake like a rabbit before the drooling lion when instead we should embrace our fear as the source of our strength. The enemy is the bastard voice from within that has been implanted by society, by religion, by ideas that bespeak of our helplessness and powerlessness. The enemy says we are impotent and weak and not worth a whit in a windstorm. The enemy is everywhere, encountered daily, especially at work, in a system that shows us no respect, that reduces us to lifeless plodding automatons. The enemy is the fish in the school of millions that does not realize that his smallness is as mighty as the greatness of the great white whale, that no one harpoons a minnow and sells its blubber.

The enemy most often encountered today is *our vision of ourselves* as only another digit on a balance sheet. The enemy is our vision of ourselves as an insignificant and anonymous occupant of the streets, where we merge like blades of grass with thousands of others to make up the lawn upon which the master frolics. The enemy says we have already been subdued, we are already owned by the system, we are already hopelessly enslaved. The enemy says we were born into the ghetto of servitude, when instead we were born in a palace of freedom.

The enemy says that to be loved, to be rich and powerful, we must first submit. The enemy lies to us. And the lies are deep and enslaving. The lies destroy our children, squash their free hearts, box in the pain of traps, and box out the joy of growth. The lies tell our children they are not perfect. The lies tell our children they are not beautiful and worthy, that they must submit to fear—fear of their lesser selves, fear of the power of others, fear of a God who watches them like the eternal voyeur in the sky, fear of free thought, fear of the new, fear of their own blessed individuality. Such lies to our children are the gifts of slavery.

I was talking to a cabdriver the other day on my way to the courthouse. "Me, I ain't nothin'," he said. "Me, I'm just a cabby. Nobody gives a shit about me. The only difference between me and everybody else is that me, well, nobody sees me. But if I'd been the limo driver for O. J. Simpson, I woulda been seen. I woulda been somebody then." He laughed an unlaughing laugh.

To be seen! To be somebody! The cabby had, of course, given the power to *them,* whoever they are. If they chose to look at him, he could thereby become somebody, or they could condemn him to eternal nothingness by refusing to see him. To the cabby, one cannot be special without *them* saying so. I think of the flower in the deepest forest. Is it not as beautiful, seen by me or not?

Unless we are recognized by *them,* we are nothing. Unless we are approved by the boss, by our spouse, by somebody, anybody, we are worthless. Unless the priest or the clergyman blesses us, we cannot achieve salvation. Unless we submit to the religion of our parents, we will be condemned to eternal damnation. Unless we bow to the religion of Free Enterprise, we will be viewed as un-American. Unless we respect those who are disrespectful of us, we will be banished.

—WINNING BY WITHHOLDING PERMISSION TO BE DEFEATED—

The power the enemy has extracted from us is *permission*—permission to be defeated, subdued, manipulated, used, and used up. There was a time in my life when, young and inexperienced but full of fight and brimming with ignorance, I was losing cases for deserving clients—for the waitress whose small boy was injured and who, because I lost her case, could not provide medical help for her son; for the farmer who had been cheated out of his crop by a scam artist and who could lose his farm because I couldn't get justice for him. The losses were painful, painful beyond reason. I felt as if a sword had been thrust through me and I was bleeding to death. I could not bear the pain. I saw deserving clients walk out of the courtroom with their heads down, their faces empty of hope. I had no excuse. I had prepared. I had done my best. But I had lost.

"Why do I need this pain?" I asked.

"You need the pain because you have lost cases that you should not have lost," the voice within replied. "Do you see that crippled boy who will now go through life without proper medical attention and who was entitled to justice? You suffer the pain because you should suffer the pain. You deserve it," the voice said.

"Why did I lose?" I asked.

There was no response from the talkative self. Silence.

"Why did I lose?" I demanded again. Still there was silence for many days. I thought I had lost because I was unskilled, because I was inexperienced. I was weak and worthless. I lost because I had no talent. I lost because I was ignorant, stupid. How could the likes of me ever win?

I had not graduated from a big university. I knew no powerful people. There were, perhaps, more people in a square city block of New York or Chicago on a given day than in the whole state of Wyoming. Besides that, I didn't understand all the cartoons in *The New Yorker*. (I still don't.) How could a country lawyer win against the fancy city lawyers with the pretty suits and the pretty language and the slick minds and the heavy intelligence that came slamming against me like merciless, indomitable waves?

I thought I was nothing. I needed power. I prayed.

But the prayer gave away the power I had already been given. The prayer needed to be directed to the self, where all of the power I sought was already vested. As an old woman once said to me, "You already have what you seek."

Finally, in the darkness of the early morning, in that state when the conscious and the unconscious wrestle for power, the voice came to me. Without providing answers, it asked questions.

"Why," the voice asked, "do you give your adversaries *permission* to beat you? Do you need to be defeated? Is the pain of defeat necessary in your life? You try. But trying is not winning. Trying is only what you do *after* you have given *permission to be defeated.*"

Suddenly I saw it, the simplicity of it—as truth is always simple. They could not defeat me without *my permission.* We give permission for them to defeat us when we adopt as our own appraisal of ourselves that view imposed upon us by *them.* We give permission to be stepped upon when we see ourselves as ants—as, indeed, we are seen by *them,* by those to whom we have given our power.

I am not speaking of an obnoxious conceit. I am speaking of our failure to make an accurate appraisal of ourselves that acknowledges ourselves as unique, as incomparable. I do not demand that they change their view of me. *I only demand that I change my view of myself.* How can they defeat me if I do not give them the power? They can own my property, they can imprison me in their walls, they can deprive me of justice, they can speak better and more eloquently than I. They can wield their power over me from high places, from the bench, from the pulpit, from city hall, from wherever power is wielded over those who have given permission to be enslaved, but without my permission they cannot defeat me. They can withhold their favorable judgment, they can withhold what I seek, but they cannot defeat me.

—THE STATURE OF POWER—

It is a stature, a position, an image of oneself that, without consciousness, is communicated to our adversaries. My brother, Tom, speaks of it. He has lived major portions of his adult life in the dangerous parts of the city and has never been mugged. Never attacked. It is an aura—not one that's put on, but a genuine sense of self that is communicated in the walk, the language of the face, in the way of the person. It is not a fierce mask. It is a powerful soul, empowered by the self that refuses to give permission to be defeated.

You see it in animals. A certain dog's dominance is established, though it's not always the larger and physically more powerful dog. Rarely do two dogs fight to establish the hierarchy. More often they sidle up to one another, take each other in, their hackles up, their stiff, hostile tails wagging, their fighting teeth exposed. Then one walks away, and at that moment both know which holds the power, which has refused to give permission to be defeated. In the wolf pack, the alpha wolf prevails. In the boxing ring, the stronger man does not always win. The victor more often is he who has refused to give permission to be defeated.

—PERMISSION TO BE ENSLAVED—

The essential elements of slavery can be identified in the makeup of nearly every culture from the beginning of civilization. When civilization was invented, the slave and the master were also defined and became the opposing forces that propped up the culture. Nothing has changed except the culture. Slavery, as we have seen, takes whatever form, dons whatever disguise, as may be necessary for one class to wield its power over another. And as long as there are people who give their permission to be defeated, to be denigrated and oppressed, to be used and used up, there will be those who will oblige them.

We give permission for *them* to enslave us when we take their judgments of us as our own. When the teacher tells the child her drawing does not look like a tree, when the professor tells the student he has no talent, when the psychologist tells the person he is abnormal, when the doctor tells the patient she is neurotic, when the lawyer tells the client his case is worthless, when human beings are judged by their skin, the place they live, the language they employ, the dress they wear, the car they drive, when the banker tells a young person she cannot prevail in business, when the entrepreneur discourages a new idea, when we are told that our most passionate goals are impossible, or our most heartfelt longings stupid, when we are adjudged to be slow, or dull, or unimaginative, when we are compared to others as not measuring up—to a brother, a friend, to some other who is pushed up in our faces—these are judgments foisted upon us daily that, when taken as judgments of ourselves in turn grant them permission to enslave us.

—Granting Permission to Be Judged—

By what right do *they* judge us? By what authority? They judge us by the authority we have given them to judge us. We cannot prevent their judgments, but their judgments are as useless as ciphers unless we accept their judgments as legitimate for us. Eleanor Roosevelt once said, "No one can make you feel inferior without your consent."

We even permit others whom we do not know, and whom we do not care to know, to judge us. I am often amused at our concern for our appearance. We dress to the teeth to go to dinner, lending extreme care to our appearance for the benefit of a public that does not know us and, unless we have dressed in some greatly inappropriate way, will not give any more thought to us than we give to them as we stroll to our tables. At the same time, we may wear the sloppiest clothes and maintain the most uncomely appearance among the people closest to us, who will surely see us and take note. I am not against spiffying up a bit from time to time. I comment only on how we deliver to strangers the power to judge us, even though the power is in our minds, and by the wheelbarrow of our minds we deliver the power to them.

—Respecting the Respectable—

The noble crown of respect should be affixed to the head of every person who has achieved the *status of personhood*. I mean those who not only have empowered themselves, and thereby respect themselves as their final authority, but who also hold a deep and enduring respect for every person, no matter how humble.

But should the slave, therefore, respect the master? Should we respect the employer who cares more about profit than about the welfare of his workers? Should we respect the corporate overseers who are incapable of respecting their most menial workers, who see them as mere mechanisms to accomplish the assigned tasks of production? Should we respect the moneymonger whose primary passion is his insatiable greed for money?

How do we respect a judge who is committed not to justice but to the power interests that have enthroned him? How do we respect the law when it is more committed to the protection of property than to the protection of the rights of people?

As a young lawyer, I was instructed by old heads of the bar that we should "respect the robe" no matter what judge wore it. When these old heads demanded that I respect the robe, I was essentially being ordered to respect their cronies, the men they had put on the bench with their money and their influence. By endowing the robe with respect, without regard to the rogue who wore the robe, I was asked to respect *their* power over my client's right to justice. When I give respect to only the robe, I have lost the right to rise up against the injustice imposed by a judge who wears it.

Similarly, we are admonished to respect our elders. How do we respect elders who have no respect for us? I have seen many a parent, too many—and as a young man I found myself among them—who did not fully understand the respect the child deserves from the parent. "Children are to be seen, not heard" was the old cruel, enslaving saw. Teach the child to respect that which is not respectable and you teach the child the first requirement of slavery: submission to unjust authority. Children are persons. They are small persons whose perfect souls have not yet been ground through the meat grinder of slavery.

—RESPECTING THOSE CLOSEST TO THE ANGELS—

Children, as persons, are entitled to the greatest respect. Children are given to us as free-flying souls, but then we clip their wings like we domesticate the wild mallard. Children should become the role models for us, their parents, for they are coated with the spirit from which they came—out of the ether, clean, innocent, brimming with the delight of life, aware of the beauty of the simplest thing: a snail, a bud, a shadow in the garden. Children are closest to the angels.

I say that we must respect children as we respect sages, as we respect the venerable of history. Give me the wisdom of a child over the erudite colloquy of Samuel Johnson. I say we should look upon the child as our teacher, that we should learn to free our souls as the child's soul is free. Like the child, should we not learn to cry out at the joy of small discoveries, learn to express our anger and our fear, our love and loneliness? How delightful to be delighted as the child is delighted. Like the child, should we not learn to be with the self as the happy child is happy with the self, to ask as the child asks, to know that not to know is all right, to learn that ignorance is the beginning of all knowledge?

No child takes anything on faith except the love of his parent and the goodness of the species. I say, of all the occupants on the face of the earth, of all of the great persons of science—the artists, the caring healers, the true statesmen, the saints—of all who have achieved the *status of personhood,* the child is entitled to the greatest respect of all, for the child has lately been closest to God.

—Respect, Yes; Submission, Never!—

Respect offered out of fear is not respect but submission. Submission to God or to man or to the religious madhouses constructed by man transports one into the endless tunnel of slavery. Respect for the bully who takes on many forms is our entry into the tunnel.

I remember my father telling me when I was a child that I should not be afraid of the bully. But I *was* afraid of the bully, and therefore I thought myself a coward. My father said, "When the bigger kid knocks you down, get up. And when he knocks you down again, get up again. And get up every time he knocks you down. After a while it will be he, not you, who is afraid. He will learn you cannot be beaten. You can be knocked down, but you cannot be beaten." But I was still afraid.

My father was speaking to me about *permission.* One cannot respect the bully whom we encounter daily in numerous forms, nor give the bully permission to defeat us. Permission is given when we respect overt power. Overt power ought not be respected simply because it appears powerful. We may protect ourselves from it; we may, being sensible, not confront it. But we do not respect it. Do we respect the brutal police because of their power? Do we respect the goose-steppers because of their power? Fear and respect are not the same.

I feared the bully, but I did not respect him. And if I had been brave, which I was not, he could not have beaten me. Only by killing me with an ax could he beat me—and even then he would not have truly beaten me, he would have only killed me. Such is the indomitable spirit that lies at the bedrock of every person. Yet layer upon layer of the stultifying judgments of others prevents us from accessing the spirit—the spirit of the child, the spirit of the invincible. It is such spirit that permits the meek to prevail over the tyrant whose puny weapon is rank power.

Recently I received a letter from a seventy-five-year-old woman who told me that she had been wrongfully dealt with by a multinational corporation over an increase in her rent. No one in the company would talk to her—not the CEO, not the manager, not the company lawyer. After months of being stonewalled, she decided to take the matter into her own hands. She went to the county, bought a peddler's permit to sell pencils, and with a sign protesting the rent increase, began selling her pencils in front of the company office. She said you could not imagine the flurry of activity this caused.

Old friends became distant and critical. How could she do such a thing? She was a nuisance. Some called her a smart-ass. The company lawyer tried to intimidate her, but instead of being intimidated, she threatened to walk out of the meeting that the company had finally arranged in order to settle this embarrassing matter. Finally the company gave in. The $200 a month she won wasn't much, she said. But in the end, it was everything.

—"It Takes Two to Tango"—

"It takes two to tango," they say. It also takes two to "accomplish enslavement": a master and a slave. Each is utterly dependent on the other. In the same way, one cannot be dominated or manipulated without one's permission.

We can be fired by the boss, but we have not been fired from the self.

We can be thrown out of the club, but we have not been thrown out of the self.

We can be disdained, mocked, hated, rejected, banished, but we have not been defeated. Defeat takes two. It takes a conqueror and a vanquished who agrees to surrender.

I do not suggest intractable rebelliousness as a way of life. Self-destruction is not liberty. What I denounce is our delivering to anyone or anything permission to conquer our soul, to extract from us our free will. Defeat comes only when we have given permission to be defeated, to feel it in the deepest lining of the belly, to acknowledge it and submit to it in the tenderest marrow of the bones.

—BLESSED FEAR—

Sometimes I have looked into the face of a client and seen fear. Sometimes I have looked into my own face and seen it. Fear is the protector of life. It is the genetic implant of survival. The great buck with the majestic stance and the widely spread horns is the first to bolt at the snap of a twig, for he knows danger, fears it, and has survived to become the lord of the forest. Despite his fear, he is the king. The small buck who knows no fear, who encounters danger but does not recognize it, stands before the hunter, his eyes blinking, and soon his liver is sizzling in the hunter's frying pan.

Fear is the friend of the old buck. In the same way, fear is the friend of man. Although the big buck in the forest responds to fear, he does not give it permission to defeat him. He avoids the hunter's bullet, but he does not give up the majesty of the self. He is majestic in retreat, his great antlers shining in the sun, his neck expanded, his head thrown back. He is free to run, to hide, and to survive.

I say, embrace fear as a friend. It is nature's gift to us. It is the best weapon for liberty. We do not give our permission to be enslaved by acknowledging its presence. Instead, it permits us to escape into the forest if we must. But it does not prevent the boy from rising off the ground one more time to defeat the bully. Fear is presented to us as a signal of danger. It permits us to escape or to fight with power beyond our ability.

Once I had learned that simple lesson, I could no longer be defeated in the courtroom. I have faced opposing counsel who were armed with endless expense accounts and whole armies of backup lawyers who finally gave up. I have had lawyers from mammoth firms fold with heart attacks and prosecutors who refused to come out for the final argument. It is not because I am brighter, more powerful, better schooled, or even better prepared. It is not because I am braver than they. It is because they had waited, waited, finally in panic waited, for me to grant permission to be defeated. When permission did not come, they were left alone with weapons that proved useless.

That a person is indomitable in his advocacy instills its message to the enemy. Once more the small boy rises up from the dirt. Once more the weak and the powerless withhold their permission to be defeated and become the ultimate power in the courtroom, the boardroom, the workplace, every place. And those who judge feel the power. It is not a power spoken in a loud voice. It is not a power coated in anger. It is a power so deeply rooted in the person it becomes the person. The judge feels it. The jury feels it. The power of the indomitable, when aligned with justice, cannot be defeated, for defeat, at last, requires permission.

—BOB ROSE: THE ETERNAL HEART—

I think of my dear friend Robert R. Rose, Jr., to whom this book is dedicated. He was past eighty years of age when he died. He was blind. He could not breathe without the oxygen tubes in his nostrils. His heart was too weak to endure the bypass surgery he needed. He could not walk across the room without panting. He called me shortly before he died, wanting to talk about the opening statement he was about to make to a jury. He was excited. His voice sounded like the voice of a young warrior. His case was just. His excitement was about his learning, about his ever-expanding self. He was so consumed with life, he had no time for dying.

The man could not be defeated. Not then. Not ever. For although he had given his life to the cause of justice, having served many years as the chief justice of the Wyoming supreme court and before and since as a trial lawyer, and always as a teacher and mentor, there was but one part of the self he would not give—and that was permission to be defeated.

I was with him when he died. He was surrounded by his wife, his secretary of many years, his faithful assistant, his son and daughter, another close friend, and me. He could not see us, but he could hear that we were with him. The breathing tube was down his throat, so he could not speak, but that did not prevent his lips from forming words as he stared into the space I occupied.

"I love you," his lips said, and he reached up to feel where I was, and he found my face, and he felt it, and stroked my hair. And after that we were with him when he made his decision. The lungs were filling from a failed heart. The heart was too weak for an operation, the lungs gone, but not the spirit. Not the power of permission, even at death.

I remember how we held on to him, as if that would enable him to stay one more hour. His wife and children were at his head, his wife holding a hand, his daughter with her head at the side of his old racked ribs, his son holding his other hand. We held on to his bare feet, one each, his secretary and I. And then, still retaining his power over life, he gave the sign—the cutting motion of the hands across the space in front of him. It was time. His time. His decision. Not ours. Not the doctors'.

Then the nurse came, and she pulled from his throat the tube that had provided the caked old lungs life's oxygen, and he motioned for his dentures to be put back in. (No one wants to go on such a trip without one's dentures.) And he was very calm, as if he were waiting for a waiter to bring him his soup. Perhaps he did not see it as bravery. Perhaps it was but his resignation to his impending birth.

We were all with him. His wife spoke softly to him, as did his children, but by now he was alone. We were the rocks and the music in his garden, and he walked through the place quietly. We watched the monitor that told us of his oxygen intake and his blood pressure and the beat of his heart. They began to fail, of course. It took an hour, perhaps a little more. Then he left us, walking on into the firmament, us still holding on but not wishing to go with him, glad for him, and in deep awe of the miracle of death.

Finally the machine told us it was over. And I knew he had gone. The face was relaxed, and the muscles of the mouth that had fought so many word wars, that had argued for so long for justice, that had delivered so many sounds of love, were soft and easy. The monitor said the blood was clinically void of oxygen, the blood pressure level.

"He's gone," the nurse confirmed, even though his old heart kept registering on the monitor in small sputters. Still, having watched him go, I was surprised at his having left, like one awakens to find one's wife has risen silently from the bed while he slumbered. Then a great cloud of peace descended into the room and the peace soaked up the sadness.

We stood together beside him, still holding on, staring at the monitor, taking one last look at the old shell that was no longer relevant to the man. In nearly forty years, although we were often apart, I had never felt his absence. Suddenly I felt lessened, as if something important had been stripped from me. Once more I was the child alone in the forest. But even as we left the room, his old heart did not give permission. As we left I saw it beating faintly on. I doubt it will ever stop.

FIFTEEN

·-·-·

Black and White Together

——— ·-· ———

Humanity will not be cast down.
—Winston Churchill,
at Dundee, 1908

—Chains Are Chains—

Not long ago I talked with an outspoken advocate for the rights of African-Americans. "The black community is in disarray and in trouble," he said. "And any who do not adhere to the mainstream black position are immediately attacked and ostracized from the movement."

"Yes," I said. "Nothing changes." Black or white, we are taught never to speak out against power. The irony is that such is the lesson taught by all masters to all slaves, black or white. The slave father, long since freed of his master, imposes a slavery of the mind on his son. According to this young man, the mainstream black leaders of the nation seek by coercion and the whip of banishment to force their power upon the minority. It is one thing to present a unified front in the war for liberty; it is another to present a unified front of new slaves, all perfectly contained, all perfectly in line, all marching to the new goose step of their leaders.

Yet we misperceive. There is no "mainstream" black movement in America as distinguished from any other yearning of the people, black or white, to be free. There is a *single* movement. It is the struggle that has engaged mankind from the moment Adam stumbled from the Garden. It is the quest of every man and woman, black, white, of every hue, of every color, for liberty. When the myopia of our black leadership becomes too extreme, it becomes functionally blind. What has the black community accomplished as it struggles to elevate black slaves to the level of white slaves? Within the walls of slavery, no hierarchy can exist. Slaves are slaves. Some may enjoy more privileges. There has always been the privileged slave, "the house Negro." Some may have positioned themselves to scrape more than their share of the crumbs from the master's table. Some may display the ornaments of a different class—the overseer who has whipped his own but who whipped them for his master. In the end, there are only two classes of people in the world: those who are free and those who are not. There are only two races (and they are not distinguished by color): those who are free and those who are not.

And what has the struggle for liberty gained the black man if he awakens to find that the chains, although prettier chains, are still upon him? Chains are chains. Are we content to say we have climbed the ladder to a higher rung of slavery? The goal of the slave is to be free, not to look down from the upper bunk in the slave hut on his fellow slaves. I do not argue that at the slave table our fare should be so unfairly distributed, as it is. But white or black, despite our share at the table, steak or crumbs, we are still all slaves.

—New War, Old Issues—

The issues of the great Civil War remain like a garish tattoo on the body of the nation. Today, as in that war, the matter in contention is not white or black. Slavery remains the issue. But from the beginning, black and white have fought together.

In the great Civil War they fought at Milliken's Bend on the Mississippi above Vicksburg. That post, defended mainly by two regiments of blacks, mostly untrained and armed with antique muskets, turned back a Rebel brigade that intended to disrupt Grant's supply line. "The bravery of the blacks," reported Assistant Secretary of War Charles A. Dana, surprised at what should not have surprised him, "completely revolutionized the sentiment of the army with regard to the employment of negro troops." Despite the general wisdom—wrongly formed and ignorantly embraced—that slaves were too cowed to ever fight, in the attack at Vicksburg two Union regiments of Louisiana blacks died as valiantly as their white counterparts alongside them.

Black and white, we have fought together for freedom. In 1863, in the campaign against Charleston, two Union brigades assaulted Fort Wagner, which defended the entrance to Charleston harbor. Leading the attack was the 54th Massachusetts Infantry, the North's showcase black regiment. In the attack, the 54th took the greatest casualties, losing half its members. The 54th's gain in the battle and its losses of men wrought a massive change in the North's perception of its black soldiers. "Through the cannon smoke of that dark night," cried the *Atlantic Monthly*, "the manhood of the colored race shines before many eyes that would not see." *The New York Tribune* declared that this battle "made Fort Wagner such a name to the colored race as Bunker Hill had been for ninety years to the white Yankees."

After Fort Wagner, Lincoln, writing to the Democrats in defense of the Emancipation Proclamation, said, "You are dissatisfied with me about the negro. But some of the commanders of our armies in the field who have given us our most important successes, believe the emancipation policy, and the use of colored troops, constitute the heaviest blow yet dealt to the rebellion. . . . You say you will not fight to free negroes. Some of them seem willing to fight for you; but, no matter. Fight you, then, exclusively to save the Union. I issued the proclamation on purpose to aid you in saving the Union." And, the president concluded, that when the war ended, "there will be some black men who can remember that, with silent tongue, clenched teeth, and steady eye, and well-poised bayonet, they have helped mankind on to this great consummation; while, I fear, there will be some white ones, unable to forget that, with malignant heart, and deceitful speech, they have strove to hinder it."

—THE MASTER'S POWER—TO DIVIDE—

How can there be a war among the races when men and woman of all races are enslaved? And enslaved we shall remain so long as we deliver to the master the power to divide us. So long as we, the people, are at battle with each other for the crumbs, so long as slaves of every color struggle in the slave quarters for a better bed by the window, for a larger portion of salt pork and greens, for the trinkets and the toys, we shall be enslaved.

The war among the races has proven to be not a war fought for equality, but one that, in the fighting, absorbs the power of the people to free themselves from the master. No army ever won a war while the troops within the barracks murdered one another.

In our fight for liberty, the racial struggle reveals itself as a disabling strife imposed upon us by the master, a fissure among the people fought within the master's system that strips the people of their power. When whites shun blacks, when Mexicans are seen as subhumans who hoe our lettuce crops, when our young fight mindless gang wars against one another that often have a racial basis, when we pass referendums that destroy the right of minorities to achieve a foothold of opportunity, when we have imprisoned in concrete or by probation or parole over 40 percent of the nation's young black men, when we fight among ourselves for occupation of the lowest rungs on the class ladder, white against black, Korean against Mexican-American, gentile against Jew, we enslave ourselves. Racial and ethnic strife serves no other master than the corporate oligarchy itself.

Bowing, as we do, to the master's religion of Free Enterprise, the liturgy of which sets slave against slave, race against race, the powerful against the weak, the rich against the poor, and the poor against themselves, the plaintive song of the slave, "We Shall Overcome," will only be hummed in hollow notes. So long as we strike out at each other, the vital energies of freedom will be sucked from us as leeches suck on the hide of liberty.

And all the while the master watches, and the master gloats, and the master laughs his empty laugh. Out of its insatiable greed for profit, the master continues to lay the whip to the backs of its subjects, to the backs of us, the New American Slaves.

The fight for freedom is not the exclusive cause of the black man. Nor has it ever been. The French philosopher Alexis de Tocqueville had it only partially right when he wrote, after his 1831–32 visit to America, "If there ever are great revolutions [in America], they will be caused by the presence of the blacks upon American soil. That is to say, it will not be the equality of social conditions but rather their inequality which may give rise to it." But the cause of the coming social revolution is not the cause of black men alone. The cause is the cause of every man black or white, of every hue.

—THE NEW REVOLUTION—

The new revolution will not descend to fighting in the streets with clubs and rocks and guns. The victor in such a revolution becomes merely the oppressor against which the next revolution is waged. The true revolution begins with the self, and experiencing the revolution of the self extends to an understanding of the condition of one's neighbor. If we wish to know something of an old-fashioned chocolate malt, we had better taste one, ingest it, and change its form from drink to energy. Only then will we know the true taste of a chocolate malt. If we wish to know something of a revolution, we must take part in one by becoming the revolutionary, the masks removed, the blinders off, the knowledge of revolution having become the product of our having tasted the self, of having ingested the self, of having felt its power.

And having experienced one's self, one comes to the awareness that the hue of one's hide is irrelevant. The cage is relevant. Our neighbor in the cage is relevant. Slavery, as the putrefying plague of the nation, is relevant. Our struggle against it is relevant. So long as class is pitted against class, rich against poor, religion against religion, the master shall always prevail. So long as racial strife exists, so long as women and men struggle, one sex against the other, so long as dissension rages in the slave quarters, the master shall always wield his whip.

The French novelist George Sand once commented, "No one makes a revolution by himself; and there are some revolutions . . . which humanity accomplishes without quite knowing how, because it is everybody who takes them in hand." Such is the way of the true revolution— when the man on the street, the worker, the housewife, the children in the schools, and at last, even the rich themselves become aware of the enslaving myths and the stultifying chains that dominate us, then the revolution will be upon us. Individual awareness is the first weapon of the true revolution. Awareness seeds change. And revolutions are the product of change, not the other way around. One cannot walk any distance without opening one's eyes in order to see the way. Change occurs in opening the eyes of the self. Change occurs in a nation of selves marching together, our eyes opened.

I do not agree with Mao, who said, "A revolution is an insurrection, an act of violence by which *one class overthrows another* [emphasis added]." In America, the classes are classes of slaves. The racial strife is strife among the classes of slaves. The New Master is not a member of any class, since class implies membership in the human race.

The revolution comes like the blooming of a field of wildflowers in the meadow, an individual bud at a time, individual blossom at a time, until the whole field is afire with their blooming. The revolution comes through the blooming of awareness, one person at a time. And so the people ask, "How does awareness come about?" But I say, having asked the question, are we not aware of the way?

SIXTEEN

Security, the One-Way Ticket to Slavery

The people never give up their liberties but under some delusion.
—EDMUND BURKE

—THE INSECURITY OF SLAVERY—

Slavery offers no security to the slave. It never has. Slavery offers only slavery. Slavery provides security from making one's own decisions, security from thinking for one's self, security from being responsible for one's acts, and security from experiencing one's life. A strange security persists—the security *against being free*.

Only the dead are secure.

The struggle between freedom and security is eternal. The American colonists, by wresting their liberty from the king, gave up the security of his protection, of his armies and his powerful navy. They gave up the security of his laws and his exchequer. Yet there is no security under the yoke. The chicken in the chicken house is not secure. Saved from the coyote, the chicken will be eaten by the farmer.

The security traded for by workers at the workplace is an empty bargain. We have always known it. If the worker is not first thrown out as excess, he is excessively used up and excessively enslaved.

The master, then or now, can offer no security. How can we be secure and become property? How can we be secure when we are used up, when we can be discarded like the potato skin after the potato has been eaten? What security abounds when the master's intelligence is substituted for our own, when our creativity is stunted and ignored? What security is there when we grow old in the traces?

—THE DEVIL'S BARGAIN—

To bargain freedom for security is the devil's bargain. Having made the bargain, one enjoys neither freedom nor security. Every slave is a machine. The master cares for his machinery until it is worn out or obsolete or, on a passing whim, the master obtains different machinery. The owner of a large South Carolina plantation spoke of his machinery in 1833: "A plantation might be considered as a piece of machinery. To operate successfully, all of its parts [the slaves] should be uniform and exact, and the impelling force regular and steady; and the master, if he pretended at all to attend to his business, should be their impelling force." Today the corporate manager seeks uniformity with the same great passion: an army of workers, all humming along like well-greased machine parts, one worker as easily replacing a worn-out or damaged part as the next.

Despite tales to the contrary, slaves were not secure in the old South. The master could rape the slave, beat the slave, or cripple him. And when the master died, the heirs, fighting over the slaves like vultures, could split up the slaves' children to suit the needs of the settlement. Security in today's workplace is an equally deluding fiction. *Security is the sweet sister of death*. It wraps its arms around us, cuddles us, and lulls us into sleepy narcotic waves of apathy. Its price is the waste of the person, his perfect uniqueness imprisoned in some dank cellar called "the secure job" and there left to rot.

Listen to the old slave master: "What I mean by a perfect understanding between a master and a slave is that the slave should know that his master is to govern absolutely, and he is to obey implicitly. That he is never for a moment to exercise his will."

Ask most workers if they are entitled to think, to create, to grow on the job. We know, of course, the Japanese style copied today by some American companies: the fiction of the friendly family, the encouragement of workers to drop their ideas in the suggestion box, small groups working, thinking, creating together. But is there ever a better form of slavery? The corporate master is as incapable of appreciation as it is incapable of any other human virtue. Ask any worker if he owns a tiny fraction of his invention. His patent enriches only the master. Ask the worker if he ever got one percent of the savings he brought to the company from his discovery of a better way. The bonus went to the CEO, who also got rich on stock options bestowed upon him for his genius in producing a better profit picture for the company.

Security? How could we want security? Here is how the best of the slave masters saw the security of his slave:

> The man [the slave] feels confident that the master will only require what is right of him and will abundantly provide for all his wants and that of his family. When he or his children are sick, he knows that he will have his master's physician to minister to him. When he is naked, he knows he will be clothed; and when he is old, he knows that his wants will all be supplied to him in his small cottage; during winter he will be warmed by his master's fire and clothed from his master's flock; and at all times he knows that he will be fed from his master's crib and meat house. The man looks even beyond death and knows that when he shall have died he will be decently buried and his children after him provided for.

Surely we begin to understand that security masks the reality of slavery: life without life, death while still breathing.

—THE LAW OF THE MIRROR—

Yet, curiously, the bargain is equally destructive of the master. Slavery reduces the master to a brute. The child born as a slave lives a life of dejection and pain. But the child born as the master lives a false life, one of empty loftiness and cruelty. Which is more to be pitied— the child born to be whipped, or the once innocent child who will grow up with the whip in his hand? Which is more the lost soul—the slave with frightened eyes, or the blind bigot who believes he performs God's will when he enslaves another person?

The law of slavery calls up *the law of the mirror*. When the slave is chained to the master, the master is chained as well. When the slave is beaten, the master is also reduced, and his arrogance leaves him dull and stupid. And when the master discards his workers, he unintentionally frees both master and slave.

Today, the downsizing corporation, itself enslaved by the bottom line, frees its workers with its pink slips. At the same time, it also unwittingly teaches workers the truth—that the only security is the *security of the self*. I say there is more security in the swamps than in the slave quarters. And should we, too, become bottom-line gazers, we shall discover that whenever the worker is worth a dollar to the corporation in profit, he can be worth two dollars in profit to himself.

As another corporation downsized, John Farrell, the head of Chase Manhattan Bank's human resources department, was quoted as saying, "I can't imagine any corporate entity owing anyone a career." He is right. But the other side of that equation he leaves unsaid: One cannot imagine an honest corporation promising anyone a career and, at will, breaking the promise. But many corporate managers acknowledge that promises are but useful tools in the service of profit, and they may be broken in the service of profit.

Despite John Farrell's shrug of the shoulders at the idea of career promises, corporations do promise careers. The corporate structure itself is founded on the workers' critical need for security, workers who will devote their lives to the corporate journey. The corporation entices the young and the eager, and holds up those at the top as role models. It extols success as "upward mobility" in the corporate hierarchy. It establishes goals, both for the worker and the corporation. The golden carrot it dangles is career advancement, even over economic betterment.

Although John Farrell's statement is an arrogant spit in the faces of any lifelong loyal employees provided such promises, it again activates the law of the mirror: I, too, can no more imagine a corporate entity owing anyone a career than I can imagine anyone devoting his life to a soulless fiction. The law of the mirror always prevails. When the master provides security, both master and slave are enslaved. When the master discards the slaves, both are liberated. The road to freedom as well as to slavery always runs both ways.

—THE UNION OF MANY—

The idea of a union of workers has always existed. It existed even in slavery. In the antebellum South, there persisted a sort of unionized slavery—that is to say, standards for the slaves' work were established, not out of love for the slaves, but to prevent them from running to the swamps, which proved a great nuisance to the master—a striking of the slaves, as it were, that led to work stoppage and discontent. Under this "Organization of Labour," slaves were said to work better. The amount of work expected was set by custom at some plantations, and the planters who adhered to those standards claimed that the amount of work should not be increased very much since "there is danger of a general stampede to the 'swamp'—a danger the slave can always hold before his master's cupidity."

But today's unions have largely become but another hole into which the frightened worker can scurry and hide. Today, the best union is often but another bad corporation. Most unions are no longer a brotherhood or a sisterhood. Today's unions, for the most part, have become but another depository for our liberty.

Too often, at the union's head, the gross, the crooked, the sold-out, and the ignorant speak for us in one gravelly voice. How can they who make their under-the-table bargains, load up their own silky pockets, and betray the workers, provide us security?

The unions in the days of the robber barons were the working man's only hope. But already we have forgotten how the rank and file fought shoulder to shoulder. They fought against brazen serfdom, the children laboring in the factories, the mothers bone weary, the fathers beaten down, hungry, and hopeless after the twelve-hour day. They fought against the master's police, who beat them and murdered them, and against the master's courts, which hanged them. They fought for their lives, and they stood and bled and died together.

Today, we have forgotten their blood. Instead, we have abdicated our power to the white-collar men of organized labor, those with the pin-striped suits that are indistinguishable from the suits worn by their counterparts in management who sit as comfortably on the other side of the table. Today's union is often but one corporation engaged in a fight for power against yet another corporation, the managers of both reaping the principal spoils of the battle.

—THE UNION OF ONE—

The new and most powerful union of all will be a *union of one*— one man, one woman, one worker with special skills, an inquiring mind, and an independent attitude, his creativity intact, his love of life blooming. The union of one will be peopled by one man or one woman who is *alive*. Such a person is always sought by the intelligent manager. In the new-age workplace, the master will no longer be the master. The worker will be his own master. He will enter a place of work voluntarily to do a job for a price, *his* price. He will leave as he chooses. He will cherish his freedom, which is his security. He cannot be lured into the trap. The master cannot own him. This one man belongs to the union of one, is owned by no one, and represents only himself.

The new-age worker belonging to the union of one has made himself an expert in whatever job he or she undertakes. Perhaps today he is employed as a baggage handler for the airlines. But he does his work with an expertise that brings order and efficiency to the task. He works to satisfy himself, not the master. But he is also a fry cook because he takes great pleasure in cooking. He can go to work on any day at any restaurant.

She may have acquired one great and ever-growing skill, as in the case of those enamored with electronics. But she can work for herself as easily as for her corporate employer. She is not one glued to the corporate teat. She may have followed her renaissance nature and become both writer and editor, both draftsman and artist. He may be a mountain guide as well as a designer of mountain clothes and skateboards. He may be a ski bum and a forester. She has followed her dreams. Explored the self. Found the bounteous treasures within. Loved them. Cherished them. Kept them and sold them dear. He has time to become a father. She has reserved for herself the most important time of all—the time to mother.

The time is upon us when America will return to the mind of the artisan, the attitude of the individual craftsman. Workers will again become independent, workers who own their own tools. I see it already. The cameraman for the network television, an independent contractor, brings his own camera to the news scene, does his work, takes his camera home, and goes scuba diving the rest of the day.

Because the new-age workers have been freed to engage in that which brings them joy, and because they are of an independent lot, they are respected. Coveted as workers, they are self-starting, intelligent, involved, *and they create*. They can find new ways! More profitable ways. They are not plodding drudges in old ruts. They have pride— pride in themselves that engenders pride in their work. But they will be gone in the morning if they are not treated fairly, if they are not happy, if they cannot create, and the new-age employer respects them for it.

The new-age member of the union of one and Henry David Thoreau would have understood each other: "Simplicity, simplicity, simplicity! I say, let our affairs be as two or three, and not a hundred or a thousand . . . simplicity of life and elevation of purpose." And what higher purpose in life could there be than to do a good day's work when one pleases and, when one pleases, to toss a fly out on a ripple?

In the new-age workplace, the engineer, the draftsman, the computer wizard, the designer, every professional and every skilled artisan—yes, a skilled ditchdigger as well—can belong to the new union of one. The union dues are free. And the union of one will represent them honestly. The union head cannot be bought off. If management doesn't meet the union of one's demands, its member can go on strike in the same way that today's corporations, exercising their power, threaten to replace all striking workers with docile, fully obedient workers. If the employer does not meet the demands of the union of one, the new-age worker can replace the employer—like *that*!—with a more intelligent, more responsive one, one that better suits the taste and needs of the new-age worker.

Although most employers do not yet understand the truth of it, the free man or woman with an alert, creative mind is the most valuable of all workers and ultimately costs the employer less even though such a worker is paid more. The most valuable worker for the corporation is the worker who no longer demands all of the spangles and sparkles of security (which soon dim), the pensions, the paid thisses and thats, the advantages and benefits that somehow end up enslaving rather than freeing.

The old way has become a dismal game in which both master and slave, chained together, hate each other, and fight each other with their respective weapons—the master with its bullying power, the slave with his aggressive passivity. The worker, seeking security, as did the slave of old, does not seek to *do* work but to *avoid* work. The employer, on the other hand, has an opposite goal: to extract as much labor from the worker as possible. The worker's goal is not to live at work but to become embalmed during the working day and to lie in the company's casket until the quitting bell resurrects him. Then, exhausted and despondent, he is ready for his just deserts—not the sense of a good day spent, but a beer at the tavern partaken with the other part-time corpses who are his fellow workers and friends.

The worker who seeks security cannot exhibit the free mind necessary to spring ahead on his own. He requires an overseer, a time clock, rules about work, rules about vacations, rules about sick leave, rules about having babies, rules about rules. He requires laws to protect him and commissions to hear his complaints and representatives to represent him. All of this consumes endless paper and energy, and the ugly wrestling deadens the spirit of both master and slave and leaves them both weary and both hating.

Wars ought never be fought in the workplace. But today, both sides, labor and management alike, become entrenched in war. When wars are fought in the workplace, there is no respect on either side, no caring on either side, no pride or creativity on either side, and no joy or sense of having done a job well on either side.

—THE INTOLERABLE RISK OF SECURITY—

The best employment with the best corporation offering the best lifelong security is at best a poor bargain. *Get out,* I say. We must get out if we can. Walk out. Run out. Break down the doors, but get out. The risk is always greater in the slave quarters. The promise of security is but a promise to be broken, and *the risk of security itself is too great.*

The risk is that one will live one's entire life with an anesthetized soul, that one will live out one's entire life as a dead machine in the workplace. To die before one has lived is an unacceptable risk for the living.

When we are free, our minds run free. Perhaps we will see that we must begin our own small business. We cannot know what it is like outside of the zoo in which we have been captive until we break out. Perhaps we will see that we must go back to school. Trust the freed mind. Tested, the freed mind will rise up and show itself and find the way. Answers will spring up. They will come flashing before us, bursting like great fireworks in the liberated brain.

We will, of course, be afraid. But fear is the guardian of our success, the energy of our liberation. And the fear we feel is a fresh, raw fear unclouded and untainted by the fraud and lies of the master. In the end, what price do we place on our new liberty? Are we not rich with it?

—FREEING THE MASTER—

The worker who is ready to be fired at any moment on any day is the worker who is the most valuable to his employer. By being ready to walk off, he has kept possession of himself. By possessing the self, he is alert and alive, willing to take risks, to express himself, and to be creative. By shunning security in favor of freedom, he becomes more valuable to his employer and, ironically, enjoys more security. The docile, horsewhipped sycophant whose best skills are fawning and sniveling will be the first to go when downsizing time comes around.

Slavery dulls the master in the same way that it stupefies most slaves. If the new workplace requires a new liberated worker who belongs to the union of one, it also requires a new and enlightened employer. How can the master compete in a dynamic world when its managers, its CEOs, swagger and blow in that rare and heady atmosphere, believing themselves to have been enthroned by the gods? These are the great and blustery dupes of business who scurry about in jets, inhabit golf courses, languish in plushy French restaurants, and take home multi-million-dollar bonuses, but, at day's end, don't have the first idea concerning the value or the meaning of their own lives.

—The New-Age Worker—

The new-age business will recognize the worker as the source of its wealth, respect the worker, provide the worker a place of self-discovery and self-expression. The new-age master that survives in this brutal holocaust of business will share its power with the worker in exchange for the worker's uncommon wisdom. The new-age manager, knowing that the success of the employer must always rest in the hands of the worker, will provide the worker a fair incentive in profit sharing, and will move the worker toward his independence by assisting him in his growth and education, since the enlightened worker enlightens the workplace.

Former secretary of labor Robert Reich said, "As corporations have focused more and more intensely on increasing shareholders' returns and less and less on improving the standard of living of their workers, it should be no surprise that the stock market has soared while pink slips have proliferated and the paychecks of most employees have gone nowhere. Do not blame corporations and their top executives. . . . If we want them to put greater emphasis on the interests of their workers and communities, society must reorganize them to do so."

Despite the power of the new-age worker, the corporate conglomerate, unless "reorganized" as Reich suggested, will still be able to afflict whole communities, hurl nations into war, pollute the entire earth, and destroy the species itself. I shall give attention to the matter in a later chapter. Suffice here to say that in relation to the employer, the new-age worker will become more aware of his uniqueness and his value. And he will embrace his freedom as his personal wealth. At the same time, the new-age corporation will have abandoned its blind and stupid role as the manipulator and exploiter, and will have come to realize that its future depends on a fund of independent, creative workers who will, at last, free the master.

But I do not endorse the suggested remedy of the former labor secretary, who wanted the tax code rewritten "to reward companies that promise to avoid layoffs in profitable times and give their employees a stake in the company, good medical coverage and broad retraining opportunities." Must we bribe corporations with *our* tax money to do that which is right, that which will, in the long run, enhance corporate profit?

No one pays the worker a bribe to slave for the master. No tax incentives are given the people to struggle in those windowless office cubicles. No one provides a tax incentive to the three thousand women who are pinioned to their computer monitors in South Dakota or Texas fighting deadly boredom until their tendons fail and their wrists give out and their backs grow brittle. Why must we deliver such bribes to the nonpeople to do that which is moral, to do that which is just and profitable? The American economist John Kenneth Galbraith said, "Clearly the most unfortunate people are those who must do the same thing over and over again, every minute, or perhaps twenty to the minute. They deserve the shortest hours and the highest pay." I say, if any are entitled to a tax incentive, it should be delivered to such workers for their bravery and their endurance.

The new-age employer and the new-age worker, supported by the new-age union of one, will redefine the relationship of worker and employer. The new-age employer will become more a partner, a supplier of opportunity, an educator, a sharer in dreams, a sharer in profit. The new-age worker will become his own master. He will decide his fate and make and follow his own dreams. He will explore not the master's poisonous caverns of slavery but his own unexplored reaches, in which he will discover his unique self, cherish its value, and encumber it to no one.

SEVENTEEN

Success Redefined

The moral flabbiness born of the exclusive worship of the bitch-goddess SUCCESS. That—with the squalid cash interpretation put on the word success—is our national disease.

—WILLIAM JAMES, FATHER OF
AMERICAN PSYCHOLOGY, 1906

As often as not it isn't the money itself that means anything; it is the use of money as the currency of the soul.

—LEWIS H. LAPHAM,
AMERICAN ESSAYIST AND EDITOR

—THE GUILT OF WEALTH, THE PARADOX OF POVERTY—

I bear no affection for socialism. Socialism is merely another face of the same slave master. But let me say it with words as stiff as splinters: The worst enslaving trait of all is greed. I rail against the substitution of money for worth, the idea that dead money can furnish life to sold-out souls. I have made much noise about it.

Then one day Imaging, the woman I call my wife but who is the trunk of my tree, said to me, "If you feel so guilty about what money we have, give it to the poor and we will live poorly with them. I'll go with you." And she would. That put the issue in perspective. And of my work I thought: What a devilish irony that we who speak loudest for the poor often profit most from the argument.

I do not wish to be poor, not in *any* way poor. Not money poor, and not poor in the riches of the self. But what rots most deeply is greed, the endless appetite for wealth. I do not disparage those with money. I am only opposed to those who use the power of money to extract yet more from the poor.

—Greed, the Ultimate Virtue?—

Said John Kenneth Galbraith, "The man who is admired for the ingenuity of his larceny is almost always rediscovering some earlier form of fraud. The basic forms are all known, and have all been practiced. The manners of capitalism improve. The morals may not."

Based on calculations made by the Washington Institute for Policy Studies, the 358 billionaires on this shuddering earth in 1995 possessed a collective wealth of $762 billion, which equaled the income of the poorest 45 percent of all people on the planet. By 1996 that number blossomed to 447 billionaires who were worth $1.1 trillion—equal to the income of the earth's poorest 52 percent. *We are speaking of but 447 billionaires with wealth equal to that of approximately 2.5 billion human beings!* At that rate, the holdings of the exclusive billionaire's club will soon equal the annual income of the entire population of the world. Considering the starving of the world, these calculations profoundly create the most accurate definition of obscenity.

In one year, Microsoft's founder, the billionaire Bill Gates, more than doubled his net worth, from $18.5 billion in 1996 to $39.8 billion in 1997. It would take a U.S. household earning the median $35,000 some 600,000 years to make as much as Gates did *last year*. In 1997, the average worker barely kept up with inflation, while the combined wealth of the *Forbes 400* increased 31 percent, from $477 billion in 1996 to upwards of $624 billion in 1997.

—The Disadvantaged Rich: Worms to a Corpse—

Yet we should be compassionate, for greed consumes the greedy as well as its victims. Consider the rich man who has inherited his wealth. More than likely he grew up as a disadvantaged child. If he were demented we would call him "challenged." I say the child born rich is also challenged. He has likely never worked or worried, and was likely never given an opportunity to grow from the struggle. He is as likely to turn out as "poorly" as any child in the projects of Chicago. His visions are as limited and distorted as theirs.

I think of the Menendez brothers, whose values were as shallow as rain on pavement. They became members of an effete class who are more concerned with how they *look* than how they *are,* a class held up by the corporate image makers as superior, the deadpan models in *GQ*, who stand for the notion that clothes, not conduct, make the statement, or the ambulatory fence posts in *Vogue,* who stand for the proposition that beauty and anorexia are somehow related.

I think of the lost du Pont heir whose money so deprived him of his chance to become a person that his greatest contribution to mankind was the murder of an innocent athlete. His life was spared only because he was found insane. Must we not pity those whose only claim to personhood is dead money? Which is not to say that wealthy persons cannot become persons, but that persons who are *only* wealthy are, at last, nothing at all.

Said de Tocqueville as early as 1840, "Nothing is quite so wretchedly corrupt as an aristocracy which has lost its power but kept its wealth and which still has endless leisure to devote to nothing but banal enjoyments. All its great thoughts and passionate energy are things of the past, and nothing but a host of petty, gnawing vices now cling to it like worms to a corpse."

—A New Paradigm for Success—

The new paradigm for success in America must be *person-based*, not money-based. A successful person is one who has acquired not great wealth, but great personhood. The wealthy man who has not become a person is only an empty machine powered by churning greed. The individual who has achieved personhood is a lily in perpetual bloom. The paradigm of wealth as virtue, of money as success, of profit as the ultimate human goal, is the most enslaving value of all.

According to the current standard of success, the successful man can squeeze still more interest from the poor and ignore the hungry children, and if he has become rich enough, even at the pain of millions, he will be admired. We know him, the man who, having been crowned by money, exhorts the world to bow down in its worship and his. He can buy whatever engages his fancy: the fifty-thousand-square-foot palace often done in garish poor taste, the long phallic automobiles that may stand in service of his impotence, the women who find the power of money obscenely seductive. I have never known an ugly rich person, man or woman, who could not secure one of the opposite sex who, on the surface, appears beautiful.

Recently I was talking with a young female producer about this subject. A well-known personality with mountains of money had just married a pretty young woman. He walked with a toddle and was old enough to be his bride's grandfather. He was reputed to have the personality of a guppy.

"How can this happen?" I asked the producer. "What could she possibly see in the man?"

"She sees his money."

"I know," I said, "that's obvious. But how can the money attract her?"

The young woman looked at me as if I were a newborn idiot. "Money is a powerful aphrodisiac," she said, sort of dreamy-eyed and distant, her voice suddenly husky. Yet take away his money and put a waiter's apron on him, or a pair of workman's gloves, and he would not be able to hold either a job or a conversation.

I think of the men who have slaved for the corporate master, sacrificed their lives as its foremen, its executives, and its CEOs. Then they retire and go to their reward—one of those air-conditioned adobe affairs in some Arizona retirement village on a golf course.

I think of the phenomenon as the completed circle, from cradle to coffin. No longer do we behold a satin-lined crib, but a satin-lined vault. The helpless babe has been exchanged for the stiffened corpse. The family and friends drop by to pay their last respects. The thought must come to their minds, What does his life stand for? It stands for fifty million dollars, no doubt. It stands for workers squeezed dry like old sponges. It stands for endless haggles over money and profit, the battles for a never-enough market share. It stands for countless hostilities with unions and consumer battles. Perhaps it stands for a useful product given to the public at a price not that the public can afford, but that the competition permits. But in the end, the life was successful. He had money, and because of it he had respect. At the same time I think of van Gogh, who never was able to sell a painting and who yet remains immortal.

—"MAN, THAT'S LIVIN'!"—

I remember the old story of the man who wanted to be buried in his gold-plated Cadillac—for him the ultimate symbol of success. The crane is at the gravesite, the Cadillac is being hoisted up over the waiting hole, the deceased fully dressed in his tuxedo, sitting erect, his hands affixed to the wheel. As man and car are being lowered into the abyss, two gravediggers sitting on top of the pile of excavated dirt are watching the whole affair. Suddenly one of the gravediggers shakes his head in wonderment and says to the other, "Man, that's livin'!"

—THE NEW SUCCESSFUL PERSON—

I am not speaking against the notion of free enterprise. Men and women should be at liberty to engage in whatever enterprise they choose. I am not suggesting that we impose much of a limitation on the greedy. The greedy should be nearly as free to be as greedy as they wish. Their neurosis, so long as it does not threaten the right of their neighbors to exist, is their own, and they must struggle either to incessantly feed it or to cure themselves of it. I am speaking now of *our* view of success. I am speaking about whom we should endow with *our* respect. I am speaking about a new archetype of the *successful person.*

In the Middle Ages as today, money was necessary because without it, absent barter, man could not support himself and his family or help his needy neighbor. But the goal of material riches was secondary. Riches existed for man, not man for riches. In the Middle Ages, it was acceptable for a man to seek such wealth as was necessary, but to seek more was avarice, and avarice was a mortal sin.

Beyond the needs of the businessman, business was to be carried on for the public good, and the profits he took ought not be more than the value of his own labor. Controls were not imposed by the system against the greedy. There was a common value among the people that scorned the likes of our modern capitalist, whose overriding goal is the acquisition of money and more money—money without end, amen. In short, greed as virtue was rejected by our Middle Age forebears.

But by the late Middle Ages that system of values began to change, and by the sixteenth century it had collapsed. Monopolies began to spring up. Martin Luther could have written his words with as much relevance today as when he wrote in his small pamphlet *On Trading and Usury,* "They [the monopolies] have all commodities under their control and practice without concealment all tricks that have been mentioned; they raise and lower prices as they please and oppress and ruin all the small merchants, as the pike the little fish in the water, just as though they were lords over God's creatures and free from all the laws of faith and love."

Success in the Middle Ages was defined in terms of morality. When monopolies took over, power shifted, so that by the sixteenth century success had become redefined in terms of wealth.

Today, money is unquestionably power, and our view of success is therefore principally measured in money. In general terms, those who have money are successful; those who do not are not. Even in today's slightly camouflaged slave state, those who have money, although they may be slaves themselves, are held up as successful; those who do not have money, the lowest of the slaves, are not. Although we give lip service to Mother Teresa and recognize her success as a successful person, and although we may acknowledge Martin Luther King, Jr., as a human being, few strive to emulate either. Although Mother Teresa and Princess Diana each had compassion for the poor, when both died during the same week, the fantasies of the masses were ignited by the rich and sexy, not the poor and saintly.

There remains a paucity of courses in our colleges that teach us how to become successful persons, while many teach us how to make money, how to conduct business, how to beat the law in courts of justice, and how to convert ourselves into commodities so that we may sell ourselves in the labor market for money and therefore become "successful."

—THE APPEARANCE OF MONEY—

Money, or the appearance of money, stands for nearly every virtue in America. If we have money—or at least enough of it to buy a meal at a fancy restaurant—and if we can comply with the dress code of a jacket and a tie, we may enter the dining room and join the other patrons, all of whom appear to be equally moneyed and successful. But consider the words of Thoreau: "It is an interesting question how far men would retain their relative rank if they were divested of their clothes." And Thoreau again: "I say, beware of all enterprises that require new clothes, and not rather a new wearer of clothes."

Recently some friends and I approached the maître d' in a Chicago restaurant for a table. The maître d', with feigned sorrow, said he could not seat us. "The jeans, you know." He pointed at mine with a certain puckered-lemon look on his face.

"May I ask you a question?" I said.

"Of course," he said, his nose tilted skyward.

"If Jeffrey Dahmer—you know, the killer who liked to eat his victims—came in here and he was wearing the required coat and tie, sans jeans, would you seat him?"

"I suppose," he said.

"What would you do if Jesus Christ came in wearing jeans?"

"I hope you will come back," he said. It was the proper thing to say.

Appearance, of course, is not a good substitute for propriety. Yet a snooty world loves its pretenses. Thin garb covers deep deficiencies.

I know a man who is nearly eighty years old. Let us call him Sam Superficial. He dyes his gray hair black. He has had his nose reshaped and retextured. He wears expensive clothes, married a woman young enough to be his granddaughter, drives a Rolls, and wears a heavy gold watch that, along with a diamond the size of a hen's egg, must each day require a major portion of his bodily energy to lug around. I asked him, "Sam, what is all of this show of affluence about?"

"Why," he replied incredulously, "I have to make a *statement*."

"A statement? What do you mean, a statement?"

"Why, a statement—as to who I *am*," he said.

"Well," I asked, "who *are* you?"

There was a long silence. Then he finally said, "You know who I am," and he laughed and patted me on the back.

How we look! I rarely go into a group of people without many saying, as if out of habit, "You're looking good," which is this culture's substitute for saying anything substantial at all. If you *look* all right, you must *be* all right. If you *look* successful, you must *be* successful. If you look like others look, you must be one of them, a member of the club, and therefore all right.

If your clothes are expensive, you must have good taste and therefore be a tasteful person. When clients come to my office and find the attorneys there most often attired in sweatshirts and jeans, they are likely put off for a moment. Power suits with power pinstripes are the uniform of success. You can dress an idiot to the teeth and he is still an idiot. But a lawyer in his office who, in comfortable clothes, is laboring for the rights of his clients can more easily call upon his creative energies when none are focused on how he looks. In such a profession, one needs all possible assistance to *be* competent, rather than to *appear* competent. I never saw a fancy suit that could take the place of a well thought-out argument. But in America, success, being but another commodity that may be purchased, often requires merely that we grasp enough of it to don the trappings of the wealthy. You know the old saw: "Money talks. Bullshit walks." I say, money talks, and it's mostly bullshit!

Most of the wealthy persons I know have, in the pursuit of the dollar, lost their ability to see value elsewhere. I cannot remember having met a wealthy man who was a poet. Most have not even read a poem in thirty years. Large numbers of the "successful" businessmen with whom I am acquainted know something about golf and the condition of their fellow golfers' handicaps. But they know little about the condition of their workers as they struggle to put their children through school, multitudes of whom they have laid off as part of a much praised downsizing. The champion money-maker is viewed as highly intelligent and may adorn the cover of *Time* magazine when, in truth, he may be simply lucky and cruel.

A person may become a person despite the fact that he has made large sums of money, yet nothing is more destructive of personhood—

indeed, of success—than money itself. Although food in the belly and a roof overhead are conducive to personhood, three-thousand-dollar suits, a pearl-colored Lamborghini, and a beach nymph on each arm do not promote personhood. Once we equate the acquisition of large sums of money with success, we have made the fatal judgment.

If you have money, you can join the Burnam Wood Country Club. If you do not, even if you are a Nobel Prize winner and have given all of your prize money to charity, you may not be welcome. If you have money, even if you are evil at heart and so greedy you would cheat the maid out of an hour on Christmas day, you will be greeted with open arms by the church to which you have made a large, loudly advertised contribution.

I remember when I visited St. Peter's in Rome. The cathedral is so huge you could take off in a small plane over the length of the marble floors. I watched the tourists as they exited. The people passed by nuns who held out bowls in support of that great historical structure, and the people dropped their money in the bowls. But they turned their heads from the wretched beggars who, on the steps of the cathedral, extended their empty hands for a penny. Money given into the hands of the church was the way to salvation. Money given into the hands of beggars was a waste.

—Enslavement by Money—

Money in doses disproportionate to our needs enslaves. Man's search should not be for dead money. Man's search should be in the long, winding corridors of the self. How could one lay one's head down upon the embalming table without having explored every niche and alcove, every attic and basement, for the bonanza that is hidden in the self? It would be as if a miser were living in the most wondrous botanical garden filled with every fragrant plant and flower, every blooming tree and shrub, yet he sits in the cellar with his green visor pulled down low over his eyes as over and over he counts his crumpled bills, a stranger to himself and wasted to the world until his yellowed corpse is hauled off, after which it will, for the first time, touch the earth.

In 1863, Thoreau, writing in *Life Without Principles,* saw it. "Business!" he exclaimed. "I think there is nothing, not even crime, more opposed to poetry, to philosophy, ay, to life itself, than this incessant business. . . . There is no more fatal blunder than he who consumes the greater part of his life getting his living." And in *Walden* he wrote: "Why should we be in such desperate haste to succeed and in such desperate enterprises? If a man does not keep pace with his companions, perhaps it is because he hears a different drummer." Finally the sage of the woods said it all: "However mean your life is, meet it and live it; do not shun it and call it hard names. . . . Cultivate poverty like a garden herb, like sage."

—MONEY AND FREEDOM—

I say that when one is too long in the presence of only dead money, one is likely to catch the fatal disease. I have never seen a thing grow that is planted in money. Yet money is a useful tool, and it takes a quantum of money in this money society to free oneself. The great works of the Renaissance likely would never have graced the domes but for the money of patrons. Michelangelo might never have created his masterpieces without the support of the Medici family. Much of the immortal music and the classical literature we so cherish might never have sprung from the souls of their creators but for the stipends of the wealthy. But the artists were liberated, not to pursue money but to pursue themselves.

Today one needs to become one's own patron to free the artist within. I see the struggle everywhere among those gifted in the arts. I see musicians struggling to feed their bodies as they fight to free the muse. I see young painters unable to loose the angels, to affix their melodies on their canvases. Mountain climbers, half starved and ragged, endure the pain of poverty to touch the tops of peaks. Poets wither away on park benches, or along desolate, lonely roads. I know whole crowds of talented people. I know the bucking-horse rider who works between rodeos in the hay fields, and the marathon runner who works nights as a bellhop. Yet sometimes the struggle itself leads to a better journey through the self. I doubt that but for van Gogh's struggle, we would have known his exquisitely tortured art. One thinks of the tragic waste if van Gogh, living today, were to sell himself as a commercial artist to create an ad page for Ralph Lauren's toggies.

In America success has become a painful, endless, enslaving quest for money. But success must, in the end, be acknowledged not in the eyes of others, but in our own. Carnegie cruelly stole the lives of thousands of workers to amass his fortune. But I dare say, until he gave it away to found the nation's libraries, he was not a success to himself. To experience a sense of one's own success is a luxury not offered for sale in the marketplace at any price.

—UNSUNG SAINTS—

On the other hand, one need not be a Mother Teresa or a Martin Luther King, Jr., to be successful. I know men who by virtue of being successful fathers have achieved a status far beyond the riches of the magnate whose usual effort as a father is to hire a nanny when his children are young and to thereafter shuttle his kids off to an expensive boarding school when they become troublesome teenagers. This is a man who can purchase everything, including his fatherhood. Too often his product is empty children who, because their souls have been smothered in money, cannot grow. Too often they are emotionally and experientially deprived children who, in fact, are the objects of pity, not envy. Still, in praise of the paradox, although money is no substitute for fatherhood, in moderate doses it has proven to be a good thing for the health of every family.

I know women who have risen above the saints by reason of their motherhood. No artist's masterpiece can match a mother's creation of a successful child, one who has been freed to explore and to grow. Who is more laudable, a land developer who takes a piece of raw and beautiful land, cuts it up, creates a shopping mall and a golf course, and builds expensive houses around the fairway for the rich, and who thereby becomes rich himself, or a poor mother who struggles to feed and dress her child, who nurtures him with love, opens his being to the boundless possibilities of life, and thereby produces a person? Success is measured not only by who we are, but by what gifts we give. As the old chief said, "The gift is not complete until it is given again." Ah, the mother whose gift to the world is a *person*!

—MONEY, THE ERRONEOUS INVESTMENT—

The enslaving quest for money leads us to the wrong investments. By the end of the Middle Ages, the idea that time and money were somehow connected began to change social values. Concurrently, then as now, the desire for wealth became an all-absorbing passion. The preacher Martin Buber, in the late Middle Ages, complained, "All the world is running after those trades and occupations that will bring the most gain. . . . All the clever heads, which have been endowed by God with a capacity for the nobler studies, are engrossed by commerce, which nowadays is so saturated with dishonesty that it is the last sort of business an honorable man should engage in." Christ probably said it best: "For what shall it profit a man, if he shall gain the whole world, and lose his own soul?"

The "time is money" rule is one that converts life to dollars, which is the most cruel fraud of all. I know a plastic surgeon who figures his time is worth a thousand dollars an hour. One day I asked him, "Do you ever stop to smell the roses?"

"For how long?" he asked, as we hurried by a sidewalk garden.

"Say, a minute," I replied.

"My time is worth a thousand an hour," he said. Then, as if he were a walking calculator, he stated, "It would cost me $16.66 a minute to stop and smell the roses. I can buy a whole bouquet for ten bucks from the street vendor on the corner." That would, of course, put him well ahead of the game.

The new paradigm of success must be the amassing of a different and incalculable fortune—the wealth of *personhood*. We should be investing in the exploration of the self and in opening the gateway to the rich, unexplored frontiers in our children. Ought the wealthy not be seen as presumptively successful, but as presumptively greedy? I would recognize the man who invents a better mousetrap and becomes wealthy. But such success is measured by his contribution, not by the money he has amassed in the process.

—Ultimate Wealth—

Jean Jacques Rousseau, the man who influenced the Founders more than any other, believed in the freedom of the human spirit. That enlightened notion echoed throughout the language of the Declaration of Independence and the Constitution—the right to life, liberty, and the pursuit of happiness. Theirs was a desire to be free of the despotism of convention. To them, the tyranny of politically correct thinking would have been a horror. Their dream was of a nation in which the rights and dignity of the individual—especially the right to unfettered thought—flowered in every season.

Rousseau said, "It is too difficult to think nobly when one thinks only of earning a living." To be sure, the pursuit of money attracted the attention of the great minds of the time. Jefferson, facing bankruptcy, put his slaves to the manufacture of nails to gain a profit. But the primary archetype of success to the Founding Fathers was not the gross accumulation of wealth, but public service and, despite their addiction to slavery, the elevation of the human spirit.

The false symbols of success disguise the person beneath. They cover the evil, the tawdry, the insensitive, and the mundane with what are today socially acceptable symbols of success: the Rolls-Royce, or at least the new Jag; the jet with the gold-plated latrine; the fifteen-bedroom guest house on the beach; a $12,450 Kisselstein-Cord "large trophy" handbag. The trappings of wealth are the costumes of players who refuse to show themselves.

But how will we come to adopt a new paradigm of success? Rousseau offered the solution. It lies in the most risky of all activities, education—risky because it creates the image of possibility, and such an image always precedes change. Said Rousseau, "All that we lack at birth, all that we need when we come to man's estate, is the gift of education."

Education will bring on a time when we shall view a mother who has taught her daughter to dance to the music of the self as more valuable than the broker who played the stock market from the inside and now owns half of the good ranch land in Wyoming—which he hoards for his private fishing.

Education will bring on a time when we shall view a father who has taught his son that true wealth is derived from investing in the self as more valuable than the investment banker who, after having arranged the financing of yet another gambling extravaganza in Las Vegas, shaves off millions for his own account.

Education will bring on a time when we shall view the poor man who flings himself in front of the oncoming bulldozers to spare the trees as more valuable than the corporate executive who has elevated the stock of his company by laying bare the forest and shipping millions of unsawed logs to Japan.

One day, when education has performed its magic, we shall see the unmasked, open faces of people who are proud of who they have become, not proud of the clothes they wear, the clubs they belong to, or the possessions behind which they hide a shriveled self.

—MONEY, THE PARENT OF SLAVES—

Success, then, must be redefined. Our American notion of success being somehow inextricably tied to money is the enslaving deceit that causes the species to give up life in exchange for that which is dead— dead money. Our money-driven view of success causes us to bow our necks in the traces to acquire it, to sell ourselves to our masters to possess it, to become slaves in order to be seen by our fellow slaves as successful. Slavery and money are copulating twins, the progeny of which is the empty man.

If we exist in an enslaving money system—one in which we exchange our lives for money—a formula for achieving our freedom in such a system can be easily constructed: *The less of one's life one must exchange for money, the more freedom one may enjoy.*

This formula, on the one hand, grants the most freedom to the born rich, whose only effort to achieve money is to clip the coupon, and, on the other, to the homeless, who by choice sleep in some doorway and whose only possessions are contained in the small packs on their backs. I do not envy such freedom at either extreme.

But the formula in this raw-money society is worth working with. If we own a home valued at $150,000 and we have a mortgage on it for $120,000 for thirty years at 8 percent, and if we own a car that we purchased for $20,000 with interest at 10 percent for five years and, trading in the old model, we buy a new car every five years, and if we have an average credit card balance of $5,000, on which we pay interest at 18 percent each year, these combined interest payments alone, over our average lifetime (starting at age twenty-five and ending at age sixty-five), will amount to something like $223,987.23. If we are working for a wage of $30,000 a year, over our lifetime we will contribute 7.47 *years of our precious lives to the bank*—just to pay their interest. And that is overt slavery.

—We, the New Indians—

Sometimes I wonder if we are not the new Indians who have given up our land and our freedom and are imprisoned upon the master's reservation in our bunched-up condos and deadly boring jobs in exchange for the master's firewater and beads. How much more of our lives must we deliver to the master for his trinkets, his frozen dinners, his entertainment, subscriptions to his cable TV, his cellular phones, his packaged vacations, his designer clothing, his toiletries that are sold to us to make us smell better and look younger? How much do we sacrifice to drink his Cokes and his Pepsis with their sugar and caffeine to give us false energy that gets us through the day, his beer that we are told we deserve at the end of the workday, his cigarettes that we are told give us freedom but provide us, instead, with the joy of heart disease and cancer?

—Buying Back Our Liberty—

"Work to survive, survive by consuming, survive to consume: the hellish cycle is complete," cried Raoul Vaneigem, the Belgian philosopher. How much liberty could we buy for ourselves if we stopped this deadly cycle of consumption by keeping our own lives, huge chunks of which are delivered to the master for his trinkets? How much freedom could we buy if, say, we owned one car instead of two, one TV instead of two? What if we had a small garden and canned our own produce, like our mothers used to? What if we put away the potatoes and carrots and parsnips and turnips in sand in the cellar as our grandparents used to? What if we entertained ourselves in our own neighborhoods and saw two movies a year instead of thirty? What if all the day care that the family pays for were saved, and the mother or the father, one or both, did at home what they wanted to do most—maybe work as a designer, work with the computer, writing, working in the in-house office?

What if we drove our single family car to the mountains and camped out rather than taking a trip to Disneyland or Marine World? What would happen if we canceled the cable TV and the subscriptions to all of the magazines and, once a week, as a family, visited the local library? Today could we hang our clothes out to dry? Could we darn a pair of socks or iron a shirt? For some it would be a source of pleasure. Could we do our own painting, our own home repairs? Could we fix a car, or trade housework with a neighbor who could?

I was talking with a carpenter the other day. I asked him what his wife did. He said she took care of the neighbor's kids for a wage and was thereby able to stay at home and take care of her own. Together the carpenter and his wife got by and kept *their kids*. Could we not once more live on the salary of one of the parents? Or on the combined salaries of parents who are employed part-time? How much of our lives could we buy back if we cherished our lives instead of our trinkets? How much of our lives could we buy back if our view of success were altered?

And what would happen to the crime rate if America launched into such a program—a parent at home, the violence of TV shut off, the children learning to garden, to sew, to cook, to discover, to wonder, to explore? Would it be a different world if at last we experienced a new success, one in which money became nearly irrelevant, and personhood became nearly everything?

PART III

Freeing the Nation

Overture

What happens to a dream deferred?

Does it dry up

like a raisin in the sun?

Or fester like a sore—

and then run?

Does it stink like rotten meat?

Or crust and sugar over—

like a syrupy sweet?

Maybe it just sags

like a heavy load.

Or does it explode?

—LANGSTON HUGHES

—ABOUT DREAMS—

I say:

Dreams are godly, for without a splendid dream God could not have created the universe.

Dreams can introduce us to the divine.

Dreams precede all human activity whether it be love or war.

Dreams are the seed stock of action.

No one ever dreamed an original dream except God. All other dreams arise out of our genetic memories or our common human experience. In this way, without regard to race or class, we are bound together in a brotherhood of common dreams.

After we have seen our dreams of freedom we can measure the depth of our enslavement.

[An index to my dreams that follow may be found on p. ix.]

—Touching the Absurd—

Dreams are often absurd. But what is wrong with touching the absurd, with *dreaming*? The difference between that which is absurd and that which is not is like the concrete in a cement mixer. When it is swirling around in the drum, all fluid and formless, it is nothing but preposterous mud. But when the dream has been poured into a form and it hardens, it becomes the foundation for whatever we have planned to build upon it.

Together we shall dream new dreams. Our fathers, the Founders, poured out their dreams that might have seemed absurd, but which launched an experiment. Despite its flaws, its inherent hypocrisy, and its enslaving structure, the dream provided the world a vision of a new nation where the human race might find refuge and one day be free.

We are the architects. Architects are nothing but dreamers. They stand on the land. They look around, sniff the air, and see those visions, those harebrained, half-cocked mirages, and then they write them down on paper, and it is called a plan. And no one scoffs at them. No one says the architects are mentally disoriented. No one says they are moonstruck fools.

And then some other fools pour the concrete footings, and still others congregate at the footings and build the towering structure, all majestic in steel and glass, with elevators and lights and alarm systems, and a coffee shop on the third floor. And the people come and urinate in shining marble latrines, and the people work in the skyscrapers and other dreams are born.

Our brains are stretched like taffy. Our brains are pulled apart. The inventive brain. The right brain, they say. I do not care if the invention comes from the left side or the right side or out of vague genetic memories. To reinvent a democracy for America, any dream is acceptable. We can make aspirin out of willow bark. Both diamonds and coal are made of carbon. Any thought is valid, any dream worthy of respect. Dreams precede skyscrapers. Orville and Wilbur Wright had a dream. Martin Luther King, Jr., had a dream. Dreams precede revolutions. Dreams, no matter how innocent, declare war on the status quo.

—THE BLANKET OF SCOFF—

But beware! For those whose dreams attack power, there lies an inherent danger. And the first attack at the dreamer is not that his dream is treasonous or that he is a heretic. That is the second wave. The first attack is even more pernicious. Against the dream, any dream, the scoffer always hurls the *blanket of scoff*.

The scoffer calls himself a realist. He is a know-it-all with his brains alphabetized. The first attack is by those who never in their lives had an original thought and who were taught as children not to dream because their dreams were foolish. And dangerous. They are the ones whose right brains are as atrophied as a grape that has lain out in the sun all summer—one of those hard, brown, wrinkled, unchewable things. And since they cannot dream, they have become scoffers, and throw the blanket of scoff over all dreams, including their own—if, indeed, they should ever dare dream one.

The scoffer, the cynic, the pundit, the critic, usually the most loyal of slaves, searching, searching for something new at which to scoff, shrugs his huffy shoulders, most often from a privileged perch above the muck and the toil. The scoffer mocks the dream, usually in the high, flat, pedantic language of the intellectual. The scoffer proclaims that the dream is not only impossible but silly. The blanket of scoff, like the board dropped on budding daisies, is a destructive, negative thing, under which nothing can grow. It destroys all light. It is thrown over the dream in obsequious service of the status quo, of the master.

Scoffers have always belittled the notion that the people themselves possess more than a pauper's pittance of wisdom. I hear it every day from the easy lips of those who hold themselves superior because they have a degree stuck away in a trunk somewhere and have read *The New York Times* for thirty years and once struggled through Tolstoy's *War and Peace*. At least a slight majority of those who see themselves as intellectuals can show us little return for their space on this earth other than the high tracks of their noses. They often put me in mind of the hen who cackles ceaselessly over her unfertilized egg.

William Ellery Channing, the American religious leader whose intellectual writings and sermons led to the emergence of Unitarianism, is said to have turned his head away in mortification at the "impassioned illiterates," as he called the abolitionists. But Samuel May, an ordinary man, with his deep compassion for the slaves, championed his fellow abolitionists hotly. Said he:

> *We abolitionists are what we are—babes, sucklings, obscure men, silly women, publicans, sinners, and we shall manage this matter just as might be expected of such people. It is unbecoming in abler men who stood by and would do nothing but complain of us because we do no better.*

I think of the ordinary man who fights against diminishment until the pain of it becomes boring. I think of the "little man" who endures the futility that hangs over him like an eternal fog and, despite the dull dread, goes to work every morning. What does the scoffer know of such bravery? The scoffers, the highly perched, do not forgive him for being an ordinary man. The bottom-liners, the Wall Street bankers, the goons of Mammon, do not even ascribe ordinary sensibilities to him but see him as dense and unfeeling, like plow horses who whinny for their oats. Yet the true fools are those who, out of the precision of finely honed minds and facile wits, their incessant questions always on the edge of irrelevancy, shoot down with hair-trigger quickness the inherent wisdom of the ordinary men as the murmurings of fools. But the wise man listens, even to the village idiot.

We have arrived here together, and I say, together we will reinvent democracy. And we will begin it with our dreams. We will revere the old only if it has been proven useful. Let us then take hold of the old, not with the delicate hands of the museum keeper, but with the rough-ened hands of the worker, the educated hands of the surgeon, and if the thing needs pulling apart, let us do it, and if it needs surgery, let us not hesitate. Throwing off the blanket of scoff, let us sit back and *dream,* not lay back and molder. We have moldered long enough.

EIGHTEEN

·•·

The Myth of Democracy

————————•·————————

You can never have a revolution in order to establish a democracy.
You must have a democracy in order to have a revolution.
—G. K. Chesterton,
English author

—The Largest Brothel in America—

We worry endlessly about the blank-eyed prostitutes who sell their wares in skimpy costumes on the streets of our cities. I say that the most dissolute whores in America do not wear skin-tight hot pants and low-cut blouses. They wear business suits with dignified pinstripes, starched white collars, and two-hundred-dollar silk ties. They will sell themselves to whomever and whatever will buy them—usually on the cheap. They have become the most powerful, the most skilled whores in the history of the world, piously, willfully screwing us under the bedcovers of government in the largest brothel in America, the Congress of the United States.

The issue in this country is not whether we should legalize prostitution—an argument that enthralls many and keeps the preachers in high pant—but whether we should continue to permit our congressmen to prostitute themselves and, in so doing, to sell us down the river. We have our priorities mixed up. While we worry about young women turning tricks to eke out a miserable existence, our representatives in Congress are turning trick after trick, year after year, involving billions. While some harlot sells her body for small green to satiate the licentious needs of her john, our congressmen sell their votes for millions to satiate the money addiction of the New Master.

We look down our self-righteous American noses at the governments of the Philippines and Mexico, critical of their payoffs and bribery, which in those countries has become an acknowledged way of life. But our bribery, made legal, is yet more evil, permitting the corporate core to buy and own the Congress and the presidency with pious impunity.

—LIFE IN LA-LA LAND—

If a democracy is rule by the people, then may we not take a few obvious steps to reinvest the people with their rightful power, reinvigorate the elective process, and at once become a genuine democracy? Can we not find a way to elect true representatives of the people who will enact legislation that will finally free us? Can we not find leaders, elect statesmen, and draft men and women to represent us who have not sold out to the corporate mass?

The notion that today we vote for a living candidate, a real person, is itself a delusion of mammoth proportions. We vote for television images—fictional people created by Madison Avenue's advertising gurus, a process that abandons the democratic electoral process to fabrication and myth. It's as if we live in La-la Land and our representatives are its cartoon characters.

Only the New Master can spend the billions required to buy a president and a Congress. And the people? Some of the people, sometimes less than a majority, slavishly still find their way to the polls and, fulfilling their self-image as "good citizens," jerk the levers on the voting machines, for the New Master possesses no hands with which to record the choices it has already made.

But we are not fools. We know that the candidates themselves have been transformed into products, political commodities as fictional as all of the other Madison Avenue fluff and deception that surrounds every product sold on television from cars to deodorant. So apathetic have the people become about matters of state that more people watched the return of the O. J. Simpson verdict in the civil case than the competing State of the Union address by President Clinton.

—A CHOIR OF HYENAS—

The specter is weird and frightening. In place of a Congress of men and women—leaders with wisdom, with ideals and values, leaders who reflect our search for enlightenment and freedom—we are provided talking mannequins who have drawn no moral line, who stand for nothing except their compulsion to hold office, and who enunciate whatever the polls reflect as the mood of the people—often whatever mood the corporate-owned media has itself created. We are provided a Congress that, like a choir of hyenas, yaps at each other endlessly while the New Master laughs. And laughs.

—McDONALD'S OR BURGER KING?—

Although in the technical sense we may elect our representatives and the president by engaging in the physical act of lever-pulling, in fact, the modern election has degenerated into choosing between whomever the power structure has put up for the job, much in the same way that we choose from among any other products offered by the corporate core. Do we want a Ford or a Toyota? Shall we go to McDonald's or Burger King? The master sets our choices. Shall we vote for the Republican supported by the big money, or the Democrat supported by the big money? In short, our candidates are pre-bought by money interests. What we are provided is the illusion of representation.

An easy example: Not so long ago, on my short-lived television show on CNBC, I launched a campaign against the tobacco industry, a worse than criminal business that is responsible for more than 400,000 American deaths a year. This number is about seven times more dead *each year* from cancer, lung and heart diseases, stroke, and fires caused by cigarettes than the American soldiers who were killed in combat in Vietnam from 1959 to 1975. That Americans can be controlled by tobacco money, by the fictions of the Marlboro Man and Joe Camel, who help addict 3,000 of our children a day, is the best evidence that we are as impotent as capons on a chicken farm. Despite the dead and dying who surround us, the media blitz blurs our vision. Incapable of recognizing this plague, we shrug our shoulders and blandly take it as just another day at Melrose Place.

On my television program, I named every senator and representative who had taken money from the tobacco industry—*over 85 percent of our congressmen in both houses*. I began with my own home state of Wyoming. We have two senators and, because of our piddling population, but one representative. All three of our congressmen had taken thousands of dollars from the tobacco companies.

Tobacco farming is as foreign to Wyoming as orchids to Antarctica. The only interest Wyoming has in the tobacco industry is the morbid business it creates for our doctors, who make a fine living treating citizens as they cough out pieces of their cancerous lungs, and for our hospitals, who house, at great profit, those who have ignobly fallen in the battle against heart disease.

—TREASON: *THE WAY OF THINGS*—

Now let us ask: Who prevails with our congressmen? The people who elected them, or the corporations who have purchased them? How is it possible, in a democracy, for Wyoming's representatives of the people to take money from the enemies of the people? When our CIA agents take money from the enemy, we call it treason and demand the death penalty. When our congressmen take money from entities that defile the people and kill them, we call it *the way of things*.

We have been trained not to look, like old horses with blinders affixed to our bridles. We have been trained not to think, not to speak, not to protest. We have been trained since we were children to believe that silence is golden.

To facilitate their lawful purchase, our Congress created political action committees (PACs) and passed laws permitting "soft money" to be given by corporations to the political parties. In America, taking money from those who injure the people is not considered treason, since the treasonous themselves—*our representatives*—have made it legal. Again taking the tobacco industry as an easy example, representatives who are the beneficiaries of tobacco money vote in support of that industry, provide tax relief for it, and subsidize its growers, but they refuse to supply adequate health care for our citizens maimed and killed by it. We are not only enslaved, we are insane.

Corporate America spends more money each year on advertising than the nation spends on *education*. And by such device, Americans are taught various insanities, one of which is that this corrupt government is a government of the people. Still using the example at hand, we condone the tobacco industry's mass murdering of our people for profit in the name of free speech, which, of course, permits Madison Avenue to teach our young the fatal lie—that to use a poison that will eventually kill them is glamorous, smart, and stylish. We've come a long way, baby—a long way, indeed: from freedom to slavery, from sanity to madness. And for what? For the profit of the New Master.

—AMERICA'S PROPAGANDA MACHINE—

We wonder that a whole nation should cheer Hitler's goose-stepping troops as he murdered and incinerated millions of innocent people, and obliterated whole cities of Jews. The German people were taught his insanity. The method, of course, is called propaganda. Continuing with this example, by the same method the tobacco companies of America are murdering millions every decade, intentionally and viciously—for profit. It was Hitler's propaganda that wrought its vile magic on the minds of a whole nation. And it is an equally monstrous magic that renders America helpless to bring about effective reform, including ending the tobacco holocaust.

—MONEY AND DEMOCRACY—

Money, dead money, controls our Congress—not the people, not justice, not decency, just dead and dirty money. Joseph Seagram & Sons is now pushing to end the voluntary ban on broadcasting hard-liquor advertising in America. In 1996, Seagram gave $1.6 million to the two major political parties. The company covered the field—$950,000 to Democrats and $640,000 to Republicans. Philip Morris gave $2.2 million, 81 percent of it to Republicans. Atlantic Richfield, the energy giant that wants Congress to bless its rape of the Arctic National Wildlife Refuge in Alaska, gave more than a million. Anheuser-Busch, a company that faces threats of advertising regulation as well as increased taxes, gave nearly three quarters of a million. The list of the purchasers of our Congress is endless.

Reported *USA Today,* "In 1997, in all, the GOP raised $40 million to the Democrats' $27 million in unregulated 'soft money' (contributions that don't go directly to the candidates) and 1997 wasn't even an election year!" The money didn't come from the woman pounding her computer or the college professor studying the political system. The money didn't come from the "little people." It came, as always, from the non-people.

Do we think it makes any difference how we vote and for whom when Seagram has bought its way into *both* parties? Who do we think has more power, the whiskey people who want to see their ads on television, or those in America who are trying to help their children somehow survive the scourge of alcohol?

We can see the politicians stomping up and down the dais crying, "Your vote counts!" And the politicians cite to us those old worn-out examples of how some election somewhere was won by a single vote. What we don't hear is that on issues in which the corporate master is invested—money and power issues—it makes little difference who wins the election.

—DEMOCRACY IN THE SLAVE QUARTERS—

In America, the New Master generally takes no active part in issues that affect the slaves in the slave quarters. This forbearance contributes to the illusion that the people govern themselves. The abortion issue, as an example, is irrelevant to the master except for its periphery effect on the size of the population the master can eventually exploit. Whether women can join the military or attend Citadel makes no difference to Anheuser-Busch. Kids drink approximately the same amount of beer whether or not they cohabit in the dorms. Let the slaves fight their civil rights issues among themselves. Let them have their fights over religion and morality in the slave quarters. But in the end, who do we think has more power, a conglomerate of television monoliths that wants advantages for its collective profit, or those parents in America who are trying to raise children without the stultifying influence of television that is mummifying the minds of their children?

With rare exceptions, it is beyond possibility to pass legislation in Congress that tends to liberate the slave or the planet upon which he lives. Such legislation as Social Security, medical care, military spending cuts, poverty eradication, minimum-wage increases, and environmental bills can never see the light of day without, concurrently, demonstrating a profit to the master. And why not? The master owns the Congress and the president—bought them and paid for them.

—FOREIGN MONEY: IT ALL SPENDS THE SAME—

In this money nation, everything is for sale, and foreign money all spends the same. The rash of money from overseas into the Clinton campaign coffers in the 1990s created a national disgrace. But the evil knows no party boundaries. The principal spokesperson in George Bush's presidential campaign was himself a paid lobbyist for Japanese electronics and auto-parts makers. A Bush campaign adviser on Asia-Pacific issues was a lobbyist for the government of Iraq. Dan Quayle's handler was also an adviser to the president of Panama. Tobacco lobbyists and tobacco attorneys surrounded Senator Robert Dole in his campaign.

Pat Choate wrote in *USA Today,* "The international money flowing into Washington, money intended to buy influence with elected officials and unelected regulators, is a big part of how Washington operates every day—and the vast majority of it is perfectly legal." According to the Justice Department, there are 1,074 foreign governments, foreign political parties, and other foreign principals now engaged in political activities inside the United States.

The intent of foreign and domestic corporations is as indistinguishable as separating zebras by the color of their stripes. The corporate intent, foreign or domestic, is to buy special advantage for itself or, as if the government were a monstrous Mafia chief, to buy protection for themselves. The Clinton administration has cut tariffs on Indonesian imports by more than $600 million annually. China obtained most favored nation status, which greatly enhanced their $40 billion U.S. trade surplus. Changes in the law governing fishing practices that kill millions of dolphins and threaten their extinction amount to hundreds of millions in annual sales to Mexican tuna fisherman. These and thousands of other decisions made in Washington every year are worth many billions to foreign corporations.

"The dirty secret of Washington influence peddling," writes Choate, "is that it can be done so cheaply and easily." For a mere $900,000 in political contributions, James Riady, on behalf of Indonesia's powerful Lippo Group, visited the president not once but twice annually to go over trade, politics, international relations, and the shift of ex–Lippo employee John Huang from the Commerce Department to Democratic National Committee fund-raising. A Taiwanese entrepreneur visited the Clintons more than forty times in a three-year period, sometimes dragging along his clients, and all for just $400,000 in contributions. Again, who has more clout with the president, the Lippo Group in Indonesia, or America's mothers attempting to support large families on minimum wages? Who has more pull with Congress, Taiwanese businessmen who dumped $400,000 on the president's steps, or the small businessman who is fast becoming a curiosity of times past?

The sale of influence, our national treasures, our clear air, our streams, our jobs, and our security knows no party boundaries. Both parties have been thoroughly purchased and repurchased. So it has always been. As early as 1790, David Rice, a leading emancipationist, was laying his judgment on the failure of Southern abolitionism when he noted that many Southerners supported freeing the slaves, "but the majority [who support abolition] are poor; the rich hold slaves, and the rich make the laws." And of course, Oliver Goldsmith's "The law grinds the poor, and rich men rule the law" has become the first axiom of government.

—THE POLITICIAN'S RARE TALENT—

To acquire and hold a seat in Congress requires a simple twofold talent: The politician must be able to raise large sums of money, and he must be able to read the polls. Accordingly, our politicians make bargains with the moneyed and sell themselves to corporate interests.

Then, to win their elections, they simply try to outspend their opponent on television, hailing in high tautology about whatever may be reflected by the most recent polls. But when the time arrives to vote in Congress, the money that bought the politician owns the vote.

According to the Federal Election Commission, in 1995 a total of $892 million was spent in the House and Senate races, "a battle of money," *The New York Times* called it. Boasted John Heubusch, executive director of the National Republican Senatorial Committee, "I've watched Senator [Al] D'Amato [R–NY] raise $750,000 in forty-five minutes." D'Amato presided over a black-tie dinner in New York that raised $28 million in one night. "Every time Al has one of these dinners, he has an impact on the international bond markets because he's sucking money out of them to here, where it belongs," said Trent Lott of Mississippi, Senate majority leader. And as for "sucking," one fund-raiser for the Democratic Party said, "The giant sucking sound that you hear in this town is the Democratic National Committee soliciting for the president."

In the 1996 presidential election, Bill Clinton, far behind in the polls, simply turned to the power of money. He courted oil and defense, not people. Oil and defense money gave him a war chest to scare off any potential Democratic challengers and to provide for his early advertising blitz. Thomas Ferguson, a professor of political science at the University of Massachusetts at Boston, found that 46 percent of the largest firms in America contributed to Clinton's campaign through either individual contributions from top executives or by soft money to the Democratic Party. As one Democratic strategist naïvely lamented in *The Philadelphia Inquirer,* "Lately we've been cowed into the position of not sticking up for working people because we've been looking increasingly to wealthy interests in order to fund our campaigns. You end up spending time with wealthy people who say, 'Let's not make this a class thing.'"

In the meantime, few Americans even knew that Ralph Nader, who ran with no money, was also a candidate for president. He was the one candidate with integrity, uncommitted to any faction, not bought off, not owned by anyone, a true people's representative who campaigned on issues that would provide us with a reintroduction to democracy. He was the only candidate who addressed the ongoing tragedies in this country—the falling incomes of 80 percent of Americans, the concentration of power and wealth in the nonpeople, the disgrace that in this richest nation in the world, 23 percent of our children exist below the poverty level.

He spoke out against major crime in America, which, as we shall see, is corporate crime, and he told the truth about welfare, that the most expensive welfare program in America is the corporate welfare system—Nader calls it the Aid for Dependent Corporations programs—which, with subsidies, costs Americans $200 billion a year.

Nader pointed out that in the 1950s, corporations were paying 25 to 30 percent in federal taxes, while today the New Master pays only 6 to 8 percent, with many of the corporate monsters paying as little as 1 to 2 percent. But few heard Nader. He had no money to purchase a television image, nor any inclination to cast it ad nauseam into every home in America.

The power Clinton garnered with early money in his campaign permitted him to buy the election. Dick Morris, Clinton's former adviser, bragged that the key to Clinton's victory wasn't his record or the economy or the Republican-led government shutdown. And it wasn't Bob Dole's age. It was Clinton's television advertising: He spent $85 million in the early months. Morris exclaimed that they had created "the first fully advertised presidency in U.S. history."

Big money having been secured, Clinton needed merely to echo the polls. He began each day, not by reading the news, but by reviewing the latest polls. Hence he took on the tobacco industry, jumped ship in favor of a balanced budget, and became a "family values candidate" in order to retake the "family values voters." Morris, unconcerned with the blatant hypocrisy of it, said, "We formulated each ad according to our polling," and often they released the ads on an unsuspecting American public without even consulting the president.

I heard President Clinton field a question from one of the reporters at his first press conference after his reelection:

"Mr. President, do you have any explanation as to why so many American voters have seemingly boycotted the polls?"

He was stumped momentarily for an answer. Then he leveled his kind smile, made his eyes soft, and after a moment said, "I'll have to think about that."

He *will* have to think about that, as will we. The intelligent voter, unencumbered by a conscience dipped in patriotism, has concluded that it makes no difference whether he trots off to the polls or not, since both parties have sold out. The elections are not run for the people, but are ad hoc happenings every four years or so to ensure that the corporate sector remains in power.

Yet, just as every scoundrel wishes to dress up his act, Congress will go about its own face-saving by pretending it is attempting to pass term limits and campaign-finance reform, knowing full well that they are quite safe, that such bills against their vested interests will never pass, and that they can benumb us all with the same worn-out verbiage as they blame each other for reform's perennial failure.

—FREE SPEECH FOR SALE—

The corrupt system of campaign financing is at the heart of our slavery. But effective reform was frustrated in the 1976 decision of *Buckley v. Valeo* when the Supreme Court declared limits on a congressional candidate's expenditures unconstitutional—an abridgment of free speech as guaranteed by the First Amendment, or so the judges decreed. Free speech is to preserve "vigorous, robust debate," the court had said in its 1964 decision in *New York Times Co. v. Sullivan.* But *what* debate, one asks, when argument is reduced to its lowest possible denominator—negative television ads, vicious half-truths, insults, and ugly rumor—in short, when the debate is nothing more than the hurling of the garbage can of politics at whoever passes by?

The free speech preserved by the court has become yet another commodity that can be purchased only by the moneyed sector, by those who can expend a major fraction of a billion dollars in any presidential election. The constitutional fathers did not intend to grant free speech to monstrous corporations who could buy those million-dollar minute spots on television. Free speech was to be preserved for citizens carrying on their dialogues with each other at town meetings and at face-to-face political rallies, for people engaging each other through their pamphlets, such as Thomas Paine's powerful *Common Sense.* Do we really think Jefferson would have been crying out for free speech in order to preserve General Electric's right to sell, through its wholly owned NBC subsidiary, advertisement time to this year's flock of pre-bought congressional candidates?

Today, the same men—and now women—sitting on the same soggy seats of the high court hold that free speech is somehow abridged when we wish to stop candidates from buying elections and destroying the democratic system. It is as if the court, a lover of snakes, perched high up in a sycamore tree in the botanical gardens, cries down to the garden keepers, "Do not touch that boa constrictor!" as the judges watch the snake choke out the life of a child.

The Supreme Court's decision in *Buckley* does not serve the right of American people to speak freely but the right of the corporate media to sell their commodity: *tube time*. In the Philippines, the politicians are brazen and blatant about purchasing their elections; I am told by those who partake in them that the candidate distributes millions of dollars to his precinct workers, who in turn pay the voters directly for their vote. As in this country, the best-heeled candidate usually wins. Naturally, we criticize their system as corrupt. Yet, if we *must* pay someone in the elective process, to whom would we rather see the money go—to Westinghouse, which owns CBS, or to the working man, who could buy the kid a new pair of shoes with the money?

The choice in either scenario is fatal to democracy. But the United States Supreme Court has told us in *Buckley* that corporate interests will still prevail. As we contemplate *Buckley,* we remember the slave master's court in the Dred Scott case holding that the slave is but property. Today we experience the new slave master's court holding that free speech has become the property of the corporate master.

—"DEMOCRACY NEVER LASTS LONG"—

"Remember, democracy never lasts long. It soon wastes, exhausts, and murders itself. There never was a democracy yet that did not commit suicide," said John Adams, the second president of this brave experiment. Deep distrust seems to set in when we begin to contemplate vesting power over our lives in the so-called rabble. We love democracy so long as our voice is the voice of the majority. Otherwise the people are wrong. Some say the people have always been wrong.

Henrik Ibsen, the Norwegian dramatist, neatly summed up the conventional wisdom of democracy's detractors: "When are the people right? Never, I tell you! That's one of these lies in society that no free and intelligent man can help rebelling against. Who are the people that make up the biggest proportion of the population—the intelligent ones or the fools? I think we can agree . . . it's the fools that form the overwhelming majority."

But when have dictators, despots, or kings ever been wiser? When brighter than blithering buffoons? Would we trust the fate of the nation, much less our own, to the board of directors of General Motors? When has a parliament of the effete ever been right? But still, we suspect the masses, impose on them the intellect of the mob, and shy away from their wisdom. There is something about the ordinary man that seems loathsome to those endowed by the accident of birth with either better financial statements or more facile brains.

—AMERICA, YES; DEMOCRACY, NO—

Without reference to the distinction often made between a democracy and a republic, we have never known or enjoyed either in America. As we have already seen, four important groups were not represented at the Constitutional Convention: the poor, women, slaves, and indentured servants (who for most purposes were white slaves). Democracy, that lovely dream of Jefferson and Madison, was supported by a clique of the self-interested, of which Jefferson and Madison and the other Founders were members. Early in this century, the historian Charles Austin Beard claimed in his controversial book, *An Economic Interpretation of the Constitution of the United States,* that beyond the suppression of anarchy, government was intended to protect the property interests of its members, and since the rich had the most to lose, it was incumbent upon the rich to control the government. Thus it was at the time of the Constitution, and thus it remains today.

—SELF-INTEREST IN THE TEMPLE OF DEMOCRACY—

Beard studied the economic background of the fifty-five men who gathered together at Constitution Hall in 1787, and found that most were lawyers, and most were wealthy in land and slaves. In addition, they were engaged in the business of shipping and manufacturing, and half of them were moneylenders. Moneylenders! Forty of the fifty-five held government bonds. This was an all-white country club whose self-interest established the motivation for its rebellion and led to the underlying Constitution we so revere. Benjamin Franklin was wealthy by the standards of the day. Alexander Hamilton was connected to great wealth. Madison was the ruler of a great slave plantation, and Washington was the wealthiest man in the colonies.

Most, according to Beard, had a direct economic interest in establishing a strong federal government. Manufacturers wanted protective tariffs, and the moneylenders sought to prevent the use of paper money to pay off debts. Slave owners wanted the federal government to aid the slave master in recovering the runaway, and the bond holders, of course, wanted a government that could tax the people to pay off the bond holder's bonds. Let us therefore understand that factions, pure factions, fathered the Constitution. Interest, pure self-interest, was its mother.

Yet, as unlikely as one might suppose, we have made great strides toward freedom under the old machinery. Still, despite deluding exceptions that engender hope and foster our toleration, it has also remained the tool of the oppressor. The trick has been to convince the people by myth and propaganda that they are free, indeed to guarantee that they enjoy some of the amenities of freedom, and to cause them to blame themselves when they discover that they are not.

The government of the United States has never been a democracy *or* a republic. It has been an oligarchy driven and controlled by the power of wealth, yet one that exhibits on the surface the ostensible characteristics of a government of the people. Under this mislabeling it took the most heinous war in our history to free the black slave. I do not write in support of another to free the New American Slave, although I would not discount the possibility of revolution, one that arises from a new enlightened consciousness of the many rather than the force of arms of a few. A new enlightened nation will not be empowered by rifle or rocket. The new democracy, indeed, the first, will come of *dreams.*

DREAM 1
CRIMINALIZING CAMPAIGN CONTRIBUTIONS

Under this counterfeit democracy, the people have been prevented from ridding themselves of the prostitutes who have converted Congress from a temple of democracy to a brothel of Mammon. Today, the politician's very survival depends not on a purity of heart, not on a commitment to good work, but on money. Only dirty money. As a consequence, we cannot take the feeblest first step toward an exhumation and resurrection of our democracy until all campaign contributions are made criminal and until, as it were, the johns are driven out of Congress and politicians are forced to give up the oldest of all professions. Then and only then will the people have a choice, for then and only then will people of worth, of honor, people who will not sell themselves for the office, stand for election. But campaign-finance reform is thwarted at every turn, and obviously we cannot beseech the whores to close down the whorehouse.

So let us first dream our way out of this nightmare.

In our dream we have somehow elected a Congress dedicated to the reestablishment of democracy in America. The Supreme Court is no longer the most powerful political body of the nation, one beholden to the master; it has, as was intended, become a judicial body devoted to securing the rights of the people under the Constitution.

Given this dream, we might propose the first and most vital piece of legislation: *New laws would make it a felony for any person, firm, or corporation to pay any sum or to provide anything of value, directly or indirectly, to any candidate seeking or holding public office, and at the same time, it would be a felony for any person seeking or holding public office to accept any money or thing of value from any person or thing whatsoever. Contributions to political parties would also be outlawed. Soft money would be but a memory of putrid things past.*

Since campaigning for public office entails certain minimal expenses in order for the candidate to get his message across fairly, and to ensure that the above laws would not prohibit all but the rich from seeking office, the amount that each candidate could expend in a given campaign, *without regard to the source of the moneys,* would be set by law. As we shall see in a later dream, the people themselves would provide the moneys, for when should we ever ask our citizens to run for office, to contribute their lives to our freedom, and not pay for it?

DREAM 2
COMPULSORY DEMOCRACY: AN OXYMORON

A democracy cannot function unless all of its citizens take part in the process of government. A democracy is not government by the few, but government by the many. It is not a government established by 40 percent of the voters, but a government created by 90 percent or more. Yet we face a seemingly irresistible voter apathy.

Such apathy can be attacked in various ways, the best and surest being to make our voting experience count for something. We, as voters, must, in fact, make a difference. We must be given the opportunity to vote for uncorrupted candidates, the best and the brightest the nation can provide. I shall discuss this issue in later dreams. In the meantime, a stop-gap measure, an easier way to ensure that every adult American takes part in democracy, is the employment of an oxymoron: *compulsory voting for democracy.*

If the government can make the filing of an income tax return compulsory so that the extraction of the tax dollar is made possible, is it not more important that we make voting compulsory so we may keep the democratic process alive? If we can make the wearing of seat belts compulsory for our safety, can we not make voting compulsory for the safety of our freedom?

It is a favored tenet of democracy that on election day we can vote if we wish, or stay at home and keep the old rocking chair rocking if we wish. This notion, of course, suits the "top-rungers" fine because there are obviously fewer at the top than at the bottom, and if those on the lower economic rungs stay at home, those at the top will always remain in power. Today, the courts, as presently composed, would rule that the Congress cannot impose upon the citizen the duty to do his duty. Yet by law we impose upon the citizen other duties—from the duty to sit on juries to the duty to obtain a building permit to add a porch on the house. And in a democracy, the very breath of freedom depends upon the participation of the voter. When voters fail to fulfill their duty to vote, democracy is left in the hands of the few and eventually dies of disuse.

But how would we enforce compulsory voting? At the polls, after one casts one's votes, one would be issued a voting certificate (VC). One would be required to show one's current VC before he could renew his driver's license. Without proof of having voted in the year preceding, one could not apply for any government benefit—for, say, Social Security, unemployment compensation, or Medicare, to name a few. A VC might be a prerequisite to obtaining a passport—minimal evidence of good citizenship, I should think. In short, a VC could be made a condition to the citizen's receiving any government benefit whatever under the theory that if the citizen has not partaken in government he should not be permitted to enjoy its fruits.

DREAM 3
THE ELECTION LOTTERY

Let us dream on. Since a free people uniformly rebels against any compulsion, since we hate taxes for any purpose and similarly would hate a direct assessment against us to supply our candidates with the necessary moneys to carry on their campaigns, might we not devise a scheme that would address some of the negatives usually encountered in our attempt to revitalize democracy? Sadly, in a society in which the principal human value has become money, it may take the attraction of money to bring the people back to the business of liberty. Let us, therefore, consider the use of the infamous lottery to do good work. Let us hold out the chance to win large sums of money as a means by which we may force democracy onto the backs of the people.

Dreaming on, the scheme might work like this: Every person who buys yearly license plates for his automobile, who applies for a driver's license, or who receives any government benefit must first show proof of his purchase of an election lottery ticket (ELT), which costs, say, a hundred dollars (deductible from his income tax). He can buy no more than a single ticket for each member of his family of voting age, but one must be bought for each such member of his family.

By simple math, if a hundred million qualified voters paid a hundred dollars each—a small price for liberty—we would have amassed a fund of $10 billion. The lottery would provide large cash prizes for many winners. The only requirement for the lucky citizen to collect his winnings would be that he present proof that he also voted at the election in question.

The house always wins in lotteries. In this case, the house would become the Candidates' Campaign Expense Fund, from which, after the lottery winners had been paid, a sum would be fairly distributed among the candidates in all federal elections. Candidates could expend only moneys received from the CCEF. Perhaps the idea would catch on and would be extended to state elections so that private money could no longer elect governors and state legislators.

The arguments against this idea are many, the most obvious of which (once its constitutional objections are overcome) is that the candidates who are to receive such public moneys must somehow first be sorted out. In the presidential race, the state caucuses and party conventions are still in place, and if the amount any candidate for public office can expend is limited by the moneys received from the CCEF, then those who enjoy the highest name recognition will likely win their primaries whether they are the best qualified or not. This is not always bad, since worthy people who do worthy things occasionally earn the media's attention. But just as often, the good and the decent are destroyed by the media. At last, this dilemma puts the power back into the hands of the master, since the media still stand as the voice of corporate America. The questions will remain: Who will get the ink? Who will win the airtime? Will the master open up its newspaper columns and its television cameras to those it sees as its enemies? The problem is endemic in the system. Still, is it not better to be involved in the eternal struggle than to lie down in the surrender field? And such a lottery would bring most voters back to the polls and at the same time remove some of the more blatant opportunities for the wholesale purchase of our candidates.

DREAM 4
RETURN TO LINCOLN-DOUGLAS–STYLE DEBATES

Whatever method is used to finance our campaigns, the limited amount of financial aid offered to the candidates should force them to return to the classic Lincoln-Douglas form of debates. The candidates should reach out and touch the people personally, communicate with them face to face, talk to them over the Internet, and present *themselves,* as distinguished from the fictional images that are created by the media.

But, alas, no amount of campaign reform will totally fix the problem. Our election process, having been designed for the village, for sparsely populated colonies in which the candidate could stump for election directly with the people, can no more cover our modern needs than a boy's knickers can be worn to the ball when he achieves adulthood.

George Washington was drafted for both of his terms. At the time of the Constitution, there were no political parties. That we should take this machinery invented to operate in that infant nation where the candidates were the Founding Fathers themselves, men already well known to the people, and attempt to use that machinery, however modified, to operate successfully in today's elections is not a wholly rational idea.

DREAM 5
AN END TO THE CORPORATE SPORT OF POLITICS

To achieve any broad and effective reform, we must take back the media, involve all the people in the elective process, criminalize campaign contributions, cap campaign expenditures, and limit terms. Such reforms cannot be achieved as long as the media are controlled by the master, so long as the master's money elects our representatives and the politician votes for not what is right for America but what is right for his continued residence in Washington. We must, of course, enact term limits. I need make no argument for their obvious need.

This game of government has become but another form of corporate sports, like the National Football League. All the players are the property of their corporate owners. The senators, the representatives, the president, the judges whom the president appoints, all are in one way or another corporate owned. Football players in the National Football League must always play the game in accordance with the rules of the NFL. In the case of our politicians, they, too, must play the game of politics according to the rules laid down by their corporate owners.

Today we, the people, watch the game being played. We are in attendance in person or by television, though we have become little more than spectators. But a democracy is more than a spectator sport, and if we are to retain the limited freedoms we still enjoy, the process of government must soon become much more than it is today—just one more large corporate money adventure dedicated not to the liberty of the people but to the profit of the master.

NINETEEN

·•·

The Benevolent Dictator

———— ·•· ————

*To choose one's victims, to prepare one's plan minutely, to slake an
implacable vengeance, and then to go to bed . . . there is nothing sweeter in
the world.*

—JOSEPH STALIN

—GOD AT DISNEYLAND—

For as long as I can remember, I have heard people whispering that we
would be better off with a benevolent dictator. These are dreamers, too.
Oscar Wilde penned,

> Better the rule of one, whom all obey,
> Than to let clamorous demagogues betray
> Our freedom with the kiss of anarchy.

Such is a dream for a wise and charitable father, I suppose, someone
to make our decisions for us, to care for and protect us and, in so doing,
deprive us of life's greatest gift, the freedom to make our own mistakes
and to thereby grow from them. Those of such dreams wish for God
to descend, to take a throne in Disneyland, and to dictate to us what
is good and what is bad and to punish us when we err. They wish for
God to take away our terrible fear of living each day, to end our damnable struggle to make good decisions, indeed, to have someone to
blame for our failures.

Ah, for a God on earth! We have dreamed of the Second Coming,
and have predicted it with each change of the seasons. Some have

yearned for death, believing that they will then be saved from sin, from pain, from error, from foolishness—that they will sit at the feet of the Father, and all will dissolve into misty perfection while the angels sing. If we could only endow a wise and benevolent dictator with the power of the people, we would be better off. After all, may we not trust one good man better than a mob of the riffraff?

Never was born such a man, or if he was, we have promptly killed him lest he remind us of our own blaring and unbearable imperfections. If history has recorded benevolent tyrants who have led their people to a better world, it has also shown us the Napoleons, Mussolinis, Hitlers, and Stalins, not to mention the eons of brutality and slavery imposed on the world by endless kings, popes, and despots. History has introduced us to the dictators. As a group, these have proven to be the most celebrated fools of all, the most dangerous, the worst killers ever spawned by the species. Yet all took power under the promise of serving the people in total affection and wisdom.

In 1936, Joseph Davies, then U.S. ambassador to Moscow, wrote to his daughter about Stalin: "He gives the impression of a strong mind which is composed and wise. His brown eye is exceedingly kindly and gentle. A child would like to sit in his lap and a dog would sidle up to him. It is difficult to associate his personality and this impression of kindness and gentle simplicity with what has occurred here in connection with these purges and shootings of the Red Army generals."— without mentioning the later discovery of his extermination of millions of Jews and other minorities, which perhaps exceeded even the infamous furnaces of Hitler.

—THE PIDDLING BRAIN—

Very little wisdom is lodged in the man who stands alone as final authority. The poor brain of the best of the species has a piddling capacity to understand the issues growing out of any serious matter. Usually he cannot comprehend the full spectrum of problems arising out of the conflicts in his own family, and even then, one wise spouse provides wisdom and balance for the other, and both can benefit from the native intelligence of their children—and their dog.

A corporate head relies almost exclusively on his department heads.

They, in turn, operate in committees, and scoop up the knowledge and experience of middle management. And middle management, if it is worth a whit in the woodpile, absorbs the wisdom of the workers. The single brain without fertilization and pollination, without feedback and dialogue, is a disadvantaged organ with a potency comparable to that of a dish of cold oatmeal into which the king's stooges dump their poison along with their raisins.

—WE ARE AS WE SEE OURSELVES—

Yet, if it is our turn to govern ourselves, how can we trust ourselves, we, the common rabble? We have been convinced from the beginning that we are not smart enough or moral enough to govern ourselves. The clergy tells us we were born in sin. The teacher tells us we are dumb. The evening news tells us we are criminals. The movies portray us as sex goats. Even John Calvin preached that "[n]o work of a pious man ever existed which, if it were examined before the strict judgment of God, did not prove to be damnable." How then could the likes of us be entrusted with the affairs of our own government? Slaves were born to serve a superior master and to moan in the fields of labor. Yet what despot, what king claiming uncommon sense and uncommon virtue, even infallibility, has not led us into slavery? Those with the green-stained fists and hard eyes, who profess to own the intelligence necessary to rule, have from the beginning forsaken their trust.

DREAM 6
TRIBAL CHIEFTAINS

If we have rejected all others to govern us, and if at last we cannot trust ourselves to self-govern—*a notion I wholly renounce*—then we have no choice but to create our own leaders, to incubate them as the queen bee is hatched by the hive. I think of our own Native American tribes, often governed by a council of wise chieftains who were trained by the tribe, who grew up as warriors, and who had fought many great battles. Some were wounded, and some were captured and escaped. They had suffered the deprivation of long winters in which the people went hungry and long droughts in which the buffalo herds abandoned the tribe's traditional hunting grounds. And they knew the religion of the tribe and its tie to the great spirit and the Mother Earth.

Can we not form a council of leaders of our own, the ultimate assemblage that will embody the complete wisdom of the species and to whom we will delegate those responsibilities we do not have the courage to exercise for ourselves? Let us again call upon our dreams. Are we not able to identify the exceptional among our young? Could we not protect them, at least *them,* from the ruin of our barbaric system of education and provide these few, at least *these,* a special regimen of learning? Could we not introduce them to solitude, to meditation, so that they could become acquainted with themselves? Could we not teach them to embrace the highest qualities of the human race, to allow them to struggle in the fields so they know the aching back of the laborer?

I see these chosen wandering without an agenda, exploring the world, meeting its people, sleeping with beggars, becoming banished and alienated. I see them touching great art, sitting with the sages, cherishing knowledge, and adoring freedom after they, themselves, have experienced slavery.

But to fulfill such a dream we would first be required to gather together a selection committee, itself composed of wise men and women, of artists, scientists, and gurus, of sociologists, humanists, poets, historians, and lovers, of the great and the humble, the worker, the compassionate businessman, the former slave, and great mothers. But who would select such an elitist group of souls who at last would select and educate our council of leaders?

The dream is sublime. But one ought not have passed this way without having dreamed it. And, as we shall see, this dream, like all dreams, will serve us when, within these pages, we will indeed discover a way to select a better government for a new, free America.

TWENTY

·-·-·

The Media:
The Perpetual Voice of the Master,
the Abiding Ear of the Slave

·-·-·

Our liberty depends on the freedom of the press, and that cannot be limited without being lost.

—Thomas Jefferson

—We, the Cackling Chickens—

We believe we have free speech. And do we not? I can say all manner of evil—that the president is a goon for the corporate mafia, that our senators are fat whores in Town Cars. I can arrange to have this book published so long as I can convince the publisher a fair chance exists for profit from it, and although the book is heretical, I have little fear that I will be executed in the morning. But the master has us and knows how to deal with us. The farmer does not attempt to limit the clucking of the chickens in the henhouse. What could be the possible harm? A little annoyance, that's all. Let them cackle. They will lay better eggs.

—Freedom Without a Voice Is Not Freedom—

We cannot find our way out of the zoo or engage in a dialogue of dreams without a voice. We cannot, as a people, remain mute and be free. We cannot rise to action, impelled by logic and justice, compelled by compassion, if we are voiceless. How do we know what is wise, what is even possible, without having heard the many voices of the people? If the people can be silenced by the endless empty sounds of the master selling its cars and its pantyhose, its beer and its fear, how can the people speak to one another?

"This Bud's for you."

—THE ILLUSION OF FREE SPEECH—

The illusion of effective free speech on network radio and television seems to quiet us some. We tune to the talk shows where the master sells the opinion of a few to the many. The opinions, as a whole, are politically correct—slightly controversial within the lines drawn but contentious enough to entertain. If those with opinions do not entertain, they will not be heard.

And the call-ins are screened before they go on the air. What is it you want to say? Say it in a few sentences. A few seconds is all we have. Thank you. Our lines are busy. After commercials, we have but twenty-two minutes—time for three call-ins at most. Hurry up. Speak at three hundred words a minute. Faster if possible. Others are waiting.

The newspapers have their op-ed pages. Send us your opinion. A few are published. Who decides which ones? The people? No, those who receive their daily bread from the master decide. Without a doubt, they do so in all good faith. And those whose reasoned opinions speak of justice and threaten the power structure are, indeed, heard, but it is only as if in passing. One wonders what would happen in America if such opinions were laid upon us as often as we bear the blather concerning the latest-model cars?

That we read of or hear certain dissident talk stems the argument that we do not enjoy free media in America. But it is a matter of focus, of the weight of repetition. And the focus is on the master's side of it, its ideas, its values, its interminable messages—on television, one every seven minutes or so telling us what we should buy and see, telling us what is good for America. Always we are told the master's interests are ours. As a consequence, the master identifies our enemies for us— whom we should hate and against whom we should send our children to fight and die. When the weighing is done, profit, not enlightenment; war, not peace; and violence, not beauty are the nourishment most often fed to us by the media.

Alexis de Tocqueville, after his visit to America in 1832, wrote: "In America the majority raises formidable barriers around the liberty of opinion; within these barriers an author may write what he pleases, but woe to him if he goes beyond them."

—Propaganda in the Land of the Free—

Through the sorcery called television, our children have been transformed from the bright, the inquiring, the creative, to idiot consumers concerned with things. At the same time, we, their parents, comport ourselves like lumpen slobs drooling at the trough over whatever vacuous fare the corporate master provides. In this country we are bombarded incessantly with a *propaganda of things.*

So long as the media, in the hands of the corporate master, convince us that we are free—mostly free to buy, to encumber ourselves to buy, to mortgage the homestead to buy—and so long as the corporate master's propaganda spurs us on to *buy and buy until we die*, we shall remain in the zoo.

Henry Miller wrote of the phenomenon in *The Air-Conditioned Nightmare.* "Tomorrow I will discover Sunset Boulevard. Eurhythmic dancing, ball-room dancing, tap dancing, artistic photography, ordinary photography, lousy photography, electro-fever treatment, internal douche treatment, ultra-violet treatment, elocution lessons, psychic readings, institutes of religion, astrological demonstrations, hands read, feet manicured, elbows massaged, faces lifted, warts removed, fat reduced, insteps raised, corsets fitted, busts vibrated, corns removed, hair dyed, glasses fitted, soda jerked, hangovers cured, headaches driven away, flatulence dissipated, limousines rented, the future made clear, the war made comprehensible, octane made higher and butane lower, drive in and get indigestion, flush the kidneys, get a cheap car-wash, stay-awake pills and go-to-sleep pills, Chinese herbs are very good for you and without a Coca-Cola life is unthinkable."

—A PROPAGANDA AGAINST FREEDOM—

Nearly every day on the television screen the hero cop breaks into the bad guy's house without a warrant and beats a confession from him, and we cheer on the cop. Propaganda smears our clear vision. It causes us to accept the diminishment of our constitutional protections as something to be lauded—after all, the cop was protecting us. Television creates argument after argument for the tyrant, arguments that dishonor the constitutional safeguards against unlawful searches and seizures and self-incrimination. The Constitution was intended to protect us *from the cop*—to save us from the principal weapons of the tyrants who break in our doors and drive bamboo splinters under our nails to force our confessions.

Although I lay much of the blame at the feet of the legal profession itself, propaganda has turned us against our lawyers, whose work in the criminal trial is to require the state to prove its case against us beyond a reasonable doubt. Our lawyers have become the most hated of all professions. But propaganda tends to strike from our minds the crucial question: *To whom will we turn when the master's thugs drag us away?* Who will fight for our rights, for our justice, for our protection, when we can no longer trust our lawyers? Will the brownshirts see to it that we have a fair trial?

In China, no one ever sees a criminal lawyer. They do not exist. They are not needed. The accused is arrested in the morning, tried and convicted by noon, his appeal exhausted by mid-afternoon, and his execution conducted before sundown. I have heard flag-waving Americans say, "That's the way it should be here." It should be that way until it is our child, our husband, our friend, or us. Whenever one of us is wrongfully dragged off, even the mobster in the movies, our rights are diluted, and all of us are endangered and our rights as a free people diminished.

—A PROPAGANDA OF DISTRUST—

Propaganda teaches us to distrust one another. According to the Rocky Mountain Media Watch, local TV news now spends, on average, about half of its news time covering crime and disasters. After the evening news the already frightened public will see the likes of *America's Most Wanted, Cops, Law and Order,* or *NYPD Blue,* programs of fear, violence, and hatred, the central theme of which is that our neighbors will kill us, blackmail us, rape us, and rob us. Today we can trust no one. Not our friends, not even the old lady down the street. Not anyone anywhere. And, trusting no one, the people, of course, can never join together.

How can we enjoy a just nation when the people who make up our juries have been programmed from infancy to believe that our constitutional rights are worthless loopholes though which murderers escape, and that Americans are a population of thugs and thieves? At last, we have become so frightened of one another that we have no place to run except into the arms of the master's police, no place to hide except in the prisons of our homes, where the master continues to shock us into a perpetual state of anxiety with its terrifying propaganda.

—THE PROPAGANDA OF THE DOLLAR—

The power of the dollar stifles free speech. One man, Coleman McCarthy, who for eighteen years was seen as the conscience of *The Washington Post,* dared to habitually advocate for the hungry and the homeless. I liked the way a fellow columnist, Norman Solomon, described McCarthy: "He is preoccupied with compassion as an active principle instead of a passive piety." We can hear it in McCarthy's own words: "What should be the moral purpose of writing if not to embrace ideals that can help fulfill the one possibility we all yearn for, the peaceable society? Peace is the result of love and if love were easy, we'd all be good at it." McCarthy laid it out like a Scripture for journalists:

I've sought out the experts at love—the only expertise that matters. In whichever town or neighborhood I went into, unfailingly I could find someone or some group—usually unnoticed—advancing human possibilities. These were citizens of high spiritual voltage, dissenters from safe opinions who tended not to be picked up on the scan of conventional media.

But after eighteen years, the *Post*'s managing editor said, "We agreed that the column had run its course." The *Post* cited a slow decline in revenue from the syndication of his column. The media is no place for the innocent. McCarthy couldn't understand what revenue had to do with his work. He said, "I can't help feeling puzzled by being ousted over an issue of profitability—especially when profits are high at the paper."

The writer Gore Vidal once remarked, "The corporate grip on opinion in the United States is one of the wonders of the Western World. No First World country has ever managed to eliminate so entirely from its media all objectivity—much less dissent." Such is the power of all propaganda.

But how can we awaken long enough from the anesthesia of those vacuous sitcoms to appreciate the extent of our paralysis? In 1950, during the early days of television, Raymond Chandler wrote in a letter to *Atlantic Monthly,* "Television's perfect. You turn a few knobs, a few of those mechanical adjustments at which the higher apes are so proficient, and lean back and drain your mind of all thought. And there you are watching the bubbles in the primeval ooze. You don't have to concentrate. You don't have to react. You don't have to remember. You don't miss your brain because you don't need it. Your heart and liver and lungs continue to function normally. Apart from that, all is peace and quiet. You are in the man's nirvana. And if some poor nasty-minded person comes along and says you look like a fly on a can of garbage, pay him no mind. He probably hasn't got the price of a television set."

And what of today? We decry the violence on television. But the producers reply that we demand violence. They say we demand trivia and romance as well. Sadly, television provides a life for millions who do not appreciate their own. One wonders if they might not recover their lives if they threw out their television sets. And, in any event, what kind of life do the networks provide? The networks claim they provide only that which the people demand. Ratings, remember? But when television has become the immense power that it has, we ask, what has happened to its corresponding *responsibility*?

—A Diet of Garbage—

If our children beg for a constant diet of popcorn, Pepsi, and hot dogs, do we succumb to their childish wishes and feed them garbage? I do not argue that the people are childish. I argue only that the people are *childlike*—childlike because, like children, we have no power over what is fed to us by the producers. The power is in the hands of the networks. And it is their responsibility to advance America's sophistication, to encourage a healthier appetite rather than blame the people for their sidewalk tastes.

The people have always yearned for something better. Over the ages, Shakespeare's plays have been the most widely read of all works except the Bible. Alexis de Tocqueville, commenting on the reading habits of the American frontiersman, wrote in 1840, "There is hardly a pioneer's hut which does not contain a few odd volumes of Shakespeare. I remember reading the feudal drama of *Henry V* for the first time in a log cabin."

What has changed? The inherent love of good literature, of enlightenment, has not abandoned the human gene. It remains as dormant today as when it was activated to a national frenzy among the masses of ancient Greece. What has changed is the diet the media feed the people. We eat what is presented us. If the programming chefs, the producers, are ignorant and slovenly and feed us slop, it is slop we find on our plates, and eventually we develop an appetite for it. Still, we do not possess the power to dictate the menu.

Norman Lewis Corwin, in his wise book *Trivializing America,* says, "[T]he people have been conditioned to want what they want mainly by years of having gotten what they have gotten." Walt Whitman wrote, "To have great poets there must be great audiences, too." I say, great poets make great audiences.

I know no intelligent person—and America is populated with mostly intelligent people—who can find much on television to watch. We have become a nation of muscular thumbs grown strong from clicking the clicker. We have become a nation suffering from attention deficit disorder brought on by television. The producers of television—the young, mostly frightened servants of the money-makers—are not commissioned to take chances. If a certain sitcom hits it big, fifty more like it are presented. Originality has become a nasty word in the industry because it is too risky to try something new. If *Rocky* is a hit we endure *Rocky II, III, IV,* and *V.* The goal of the producers is to find the gold, after which they rush like the forty-niners to wherever a strike has been reported.

We are fed the stuff that the producers themselves are best qualified to understand—that which entices the lowest possible level of human interest, the most savage remnant in the human animal: Stories of blood, violence, and sex—even if maudlin and banal—are surefire winners of ratings. We rarely see a movie nowadays without its utterly predictable chase scene and its equally predictable in-bed nude wrestling matches between the leads. Our children have been weaned on it. Our people have begun to accept the industry's garbage as the main course, as *the way of things.* How could we possibly express a desire for something better when we have never seen anything better? At last, we want nothing better.

My brother, Tom, operates a small diner in Buffalo, Wyoming, where he offers the best hamburgers in the universe. "What's discouraging," he says, "is that people compare my hamburger and my homemade fries to the Big Mac as the standard." Because people have been fed an inferior diet on television, that which is inferior, be it food or entertainment, has become the measure by which we judge everything.

—We, the Fishes in the Nets—

Our airways, which belong to the people and are the single most powerful instrument by which a free citizenry could govern themselves, have become instead the nets by which we are caught and marketed in packages of hundreds of thousands, sometimes millions, to corporate advertisers.

Whereas this most powerful of all inventions for social betterment could have raised the consciousness of a nation, it has been used instead to degrade and to debase us. A film featuring Beavis and Butthead, a couple of TV cartoon characters, opened as number one at the box office with $20.1 million its opening weekend. It was reported as the largest December opening in history.

Television always plays to the latent, building hostilities of the people. Understanding our need to express our growing anger at our enslavement, the master provides us with more and more violence on the screen, for if our bursting need for violence can be expressed through surrogate victims on television, will not the master always remain safe?

Daily the television industry takes on the role of the father-sage, advising us of the obvious—we must do something about this violence; we must take back the streets and make them safe for America—while during the same evening, the same industry, for its same profit, will feed us and our children the same obscene menu of blood and death.

In sum, as slaves we have been belittled and benumbed by the master's voice until we are no longer able to unleash our genius and, as a nation, discover new paths to liberty. As slaves we listen to the master's voice for our answers—to television commercials that tell us what car to drive, to evening news that defines for us our condition in life, to endless, banal sitcoms and cop shoot-'em-ups that mold our attitudes. The master's voice tells us all. It tells us how to spend our time—on what cruise, at what Disney theme park. It tells us where to have supper. It educates our young as world-class shoppers, advises us with which broker to invest our retirement funds. I have forgotten when it was that we last told ourselves such things.

DREAM 7
A PROPAGANDA FOR PEOPLE, NOT THINGS

Often the issue of free speech is one of weight as much as content. What if the people were heard as often as "Miller time" is heard, as often as shampoo commercials are heard? What if we listened to women and farmers and schoolteachers and laborers as often as we listen to the finance companies tempting us to get second mortgages on our homes at an even higher interest rate in order to buy new furniture or a membership in the country club? What if we heard from the Sierra Club as often as we heard from Dow Chemical? What would happen if educators and philosophers and psychologists could speak to us in those thirty-second commercials in ways that would, over time, enlighten us to new views of ourselves, that would empower us with our own beauty, that would move us to exercise our rights and preserve our freedoms?

Freedom without a free voice is like a fire alarm with the breakers pulled. What if the voice of the people were returned to the people?

As we shall see in the coming chapter, our airways were blatantly appropriated by the networks when the Federal Communications Commission, in one of the nation's most infamous giveaways, violated its trust and delivered the major networks free to ABC, NBC, and CBS. In the law, when our property is wrongfully taken by our neighbor, we can recover it. What if we recovered our airways?

Commencing our dream with a simple truth—that the airways have always belonged to the people—let us then take back what rightfully belongs to us. After we have done so, if NBC wants to operate a network *for us,* we can pay NBC a fee for its service, something like we pay the telephone company to operate the phone lines though we own the phone lines. We do not, however, give the phone company the right to decide whom we will talk to, when we will talk to them, and what we will say to them.

If CBS wants to stay in the business, we can pay CBS a fair sum for operating the network after which we shall ask our questions, carry on our dialogues, educate our people, inform our public, and present the wide spectrum of views and debates necessary for our existence. But the overall revenue from the networks would belong to the people to foster other dialogues among free citizens.

When corporations want to advertise on the public airways, they may do so. That's free speech. But a significant portion of the total advertising time will be reserved for matters of public interest, for those who are concerned with the environment, women's rights, and social reform. Let minorities advertise. Let educators and nonpolluters and people who care about animals have their say. It would go a long way toward rededicating the airways to the "public good," as was the original congressional mandate, if, say, one-third of all advertising carried over commercial radio and television educated us on matters vital to our welfare.

How do we, the people, finance such advertisements? What if an advertiser—say Budweiser—would like to use six minutes of airtime to promote its beer by sponsoring the Super Bowl? This advertiser would be additionally required to provide two minutes of public-interest advertising showing, say, bloody bodies being pulled from wrecks caused by drunk drivers? What if, when Chrysler purchases six minutes to laud its new minivan, it would also be required to finance two minutes of public time to provide the people with information concerning, say, the dangers to unprotected children in automobiles? What I suggest here is neither unreasonable nor un-American. Fairness has always been among our most cherished values.

Ford Motor Company has already voluntarily experimented with such a program. It was the exclusive sponsor of a *Murphy Brown* episode dealing with recovery from breast cancer. Ford aired four thirty-second commercials. But it also provided two public-service announcements from the Susan G. Koman Breast Cancer Foundation, as well as time during which Candice Bergen, the lead actress, talked about breast cancer. The Federal Communications Commission has had the power from its inception to require that our networks devote substantial portions of airtime to the public good, but it is so beseiged by politicians and lobbyists that it has become not the regulator but the servant of the broadcasters.

In short, my dream is of a time when the choices people make in their lives, as touted on television, will be more important than the choice of beer they drink. I dream of a time when the people will retake their airways and use them to achieve a voice to rediscover democracy, and to seek the divine potential of man.

Dream 8
Muting the Monster

If we are permitted to dream, as others have dreamed before us, can we imagine what would happen if on one day, *just one day,* the slaves rose up, not in revolt against the government but in revolt against the master's voice? Suppose a representative from *every* American household on a given day agreed to turn off the family television set *all day,* like a one-day smoking boycott. This is not a new idea. But its complete success would be. Perhaps the suicide rate would jump to new highs. But many would pour into the streets and, given permission and the leadership to do so, might even knock on a neighbor's door. Suppose, let us dream, that some did, and suppose that this, or something like this, is what happened:

The knock on the neighbor's door:

"Hello. I'm Billy Ray Rapport. We live next door. I thought, since we had no TV today, I might introduce myself."

The neighbor peers out from behind the chained crack.

"Yeah?" he replies suspiciously.

"I was just wondering if you would like to meet me at Harry's for a cup of coffee. Since we've been neighbors for twenty years, maybe it's time we got to know each other."

"Well, I don't know about that." He looks at his watch. "I gotta watch *Law and Order* in twenty-two and a half minutes."

"But this is TV Blackout Day, don't you remember?"

"I don't believe in that stuff."

"What are you watching now?"

The door starts to open a bit wider.

"I ain't watchin nothin'," he says like a kid caught stealing his father's condoms. You can hear the TV in the background grinding out a commercial for eyeglasses: "—if you want to really see how things are," the commercial promises.

"Well, then, come on. I'll meet you at Harry's in ten minutes." The door closes.

Maybe he came, maybe he didn't. But some would. It could be a beginning—neighbors meeting neighbors, neighbors discovering that their neighbors are like them, that they are lonely, isolated, and afraid. Neighbors discovering that their neighbors are decent and trustworthy, that they have had many experiences in life and have acquired a wisdom of their own, and—perhaps the most important discovery—that together they can begin to form a new community.

The return to the community is the way out. Tapping the vast wealth of knowledge and intelligence of our people is the way out. The American people possess a collective intelligence. Within our masses are concealed the many whose genius and creativity will one day reinvent America. I dream that someday we will recapture the airways, *our voice*—that we will no longer exist as a muted people but, through our new voice, we will begin to engage one another in the vigorous debates of neighbors as we seek new ways to free ourselves and to stay forever free.

TWENTY-ONE

·•·

The Theft of Our Voice

————— ·•· —————

I detest what you write, but I would give my life to make it possible for you to continue to write.

—Voltaire, French writer,
circa 1770

We live in oppressive times. We have, as a nation, become our own thought police; but instead of calling the process by which we limit our expression of dissent and wonder "censorship," we call it "concern for commercial viability."

—David Mamet,
American playwright

—"Not One of You Dares Write Your Honest Opinions"—

One trembles when one reads the words of John Swinton who as the chief of staff for *The New York Times* was one of the most beloved and respected newsmen in America. When I lay his words on the page, I feel the familiar chill of fear. Here is what a dean of his profession said about the "free press" in America as he addressed a group of journalists:

There is not one of you who dares to write your honest opinions, and if you did, you know beforehand that it would never appear in print. I am paid weekly for keeping my honest opinions out of the paper I am connected with.

Others of you are paid similar salaries for similar things, and any of you who would be so foolish as to write honest opinions would be out on the streets looking for another job. If I allowed my honest opinions to appear in one issue of my paper, before twenty-four hours my occupation would be gone.

The business of the journalist is to destroy the truth; to lie outright; to pervert; to vilify; to fawn at the feet of Mammon, and to sell his country and his race for his daily bread, you know it and I know it, so what folly is this toasting an independent press?

We are the tools and vassals of rich men behind the scenes. We are the jumping jacks—they pull the strings—we dance. Our talents, our possibilities and our lives are all the property of other men. . . .

The Founders understood that the first and most important freedom of all is unfettered speech, and they guaranteed it under the First Amendment. Yet this freedom is on trial every day in this country in what we might call the *Courtroom of Democracy*, and too often freedom loses.

Every day this trial takes place in our living rooms and bedrooms as we watch television, at the breakfast table as we read the newspaper, on the beach when we read the latest *Times* best-seller, at the movies when we have an evening out. As at any trial, there are many questions to ask and many answers in response.

A trial should be a search for the truth, and the trial's ability to produce the truth depends upon the freedom of the parties to ask their questions and seek the answers in a free and uncorrupted forum. But what would be the result in a court of law if one of the parties owned the court, the courtroom, and the jury? Such chicanery would throw us into unabated convulsions of rage. Yet such is the sham of our blessed right to free speech in America, for the right to *effective* free speech is owned, outright, red-handedly, by the New Master.

—AN INDEPENDENT, UNCENSORED MEDIA IN AMERICA—

Despite the fact that many great journalists and producers struggle to bring us honest news, are fiercely proud of their duty to the American public, embrace the First Amendment with all fervor and zeal, and indeed risk their lives to keep us abreast of the important events of the day; despite the fact that America's media are freer than most, more open than most; nevertheless *there is no such thing as an independent uncensored media in America.* John Swinton knew it, and had the courage to say it. Walter Cronkite, too, knows it when he says, "Only a handful of professional journalists make these significant judgments on the news of the day, and it is a lot of power for a few men."

Today, most of the media in America—the publishers of books, magazines, and newspapers; the radio and television networks; and broadcasters across the country—are owned by fewer than twenty giant corporations. Some of these monsters have combined in what in any other decade in America would have been considered gross violations of antitrust law.

Ben Bagdikian, a Pulitzer Prize–winning journalist at the University of California at Berkeley, thinks that in the near future only half a dozen megacorporations will control the media. The conventional response to his prediction was the charge that he was an alarmist. But when Time merged with Warner as long ago as 1989, the merger was defended by one executive involved in the deal, who said, "We took this move because we know in the not-too-distant future half a dozen corporations will control most of the media."

The corporation with the largest stock value in the world, General Electric, owns NBC. A tobacco magnate, Laurence Tisch, took over CBS, which he then sold in 1995 to Westinghouse for the modest price of $5.4 billion. With its already-owned broadcasting subsidiary, Group W, Westinghouse has become the largest broadcasting company in the nation. The same year, Disney bought ABC for $19 billion, and thus established itself as the world's largest information and entertainment corporation. Turner Broadcasting has married Time Warner to form the world's largest news corporation in a stock deal worth $7.57 billion. It is a little nightmarish to understand that two of the three major networks in this country are owned by Westinghouse and General Electric, which, according to Karl Grossman, a communications professor at the State University of New York, are "the Coke and Pepsi of nuclear power."

Gannett, the nation's largest newspaper publisher, expanded its broadcasting properties by buying Multimedia, Inc., for $1.7 billion. Multimedia will furnish Gannett several TV and radio stations, cable franchises, and nationally syndicated talk shows.

Thomson Newspapers owns seventy dailies in North America. And the Public Broadcasting System, the last of the supposed free voices in America, has teamed up with *Reader's Digest*, a publisher known for its conservative values, which is also one of the six corporations that together gross more than half of all book revenues in the nation. Need we proceed with the list? Is it not already clear that our voice is not our voice, but the voice the master provides us?

At the time of the Constitution, the cases of competing factions were presented to the public by pamphlet. Hundreds of such pamphlets printed by many small printers were freely circulated in those sparsely populated colonies, including Thomas Paine's profoundly provoking *Common Sense*, which was to become the voice of the American Revolution. But today, in the Courtroom of Democracy, predominantly only one faction, one interest, one side, one set of facts, one argument, is presented to the people—the facts and the arguments that forward the interests and profits of corporate control. Slaves are not entitled to a voice. Slaves have never had a meaningful voice, and the people have no meaningful voice in America today.

—WHO SPEAKS FOR US?—

In the Courtroom of Democracy, in which our freedom is daily on trial, who speaks for anyone but the master? Who speaks, but in passing, for any other faction? Aside from obscure publications, who speaks for the position of the far left, for socialists, for libertarians, for the Green Party, for people who are fighting for the earth? Who speaks, except in the occasional documentary, for the poor, for the welfare mothers, for the farmers and ranchers, for the children rotting in the ghettos? Who speaks, except in a book published by a university press, for the blacks, the immigrants, the Mexican laborer sweating out his heart in the lettuce fields for starvation wages? Who, except in labor pamphlets, speaks for the factory worker who has lost his cherished rights in the workplace?

Who tells the full story of the de-skilled and unorganized workers in the high-tech sweatshops or the teachers who are hopelessly entangled in the bureaucracy of our urban public schools? I do not argue that the stories of every faction in America cannot be told, or that they are not told, even by the mainstream media. I argue only a proportional argument—that their stories, when told, are lost to the overall collective attention of the people in the mad scramble of the master to present its case for money and profit. We get a quick look at an occasional "people issue" through *60 Minutes* and *20/20*, enough to keep alive the myth that the media are free, fearless, and independent. And in many instances the media are free and fearless. The publication of such books as this adds to the illusion. But if, in any trial, one side spoke a hundred times and the other only once, and then only from the back of the courtroom, might we not conclude that the trial was unfair? In a single night, more people will hear Rush Limbaugh, the people-hater who is adored by people-haters, than will ever likely hold this book in their hands. And more people will tune in to the racist rages of Bob Grant on WOR in New York City during a single airing than will sit down of an evening and give thoughtful reading to the work of any serious writer on this or any other issue.

One wonders anew what would happen in America if the rights of workers who lost their jobs in downsizing received as much attention as the O. J. Simpson case, media's all-time bonanza.

—CENSORSHIP IN AMERICA—

Censorship takes many forms in America. What have we heard, for example, of the staggering subsidies provided by Congress for the corporate group? We hear much from the master bewailing food stamps, housing aid, and child nutrition programs, which cost the nation something in the neighborhood of $50 billion a year. But except for an occasional errant story, mostly in offbeat journals, the facts concerning the subsidies paid large corporations in America have received little notice over the master's airways.

We could go a long way toward reducing the deficit if we eliminated corporate subsidies. The Washington-based Center for Study of Responsive Law has identified 153 federal programs that benefit wealthy corporations and cost the taxpayers $162.2 billion annually, over three times what we pay in welfare programs.

We have already visited one of the greatest subsidies ever delivered to American corporations: the overt, unembarrassed gifting of our airways to the three giants of radio and television. The vigilant eye of democracy hardly blinked when the Federal Communications Commission, the supposed servant of the people, without apologies, and *for free,* handed over the networks to ABC, CBS, NBC, and, later, Fox— networks that are today bought and sold for billions.

How censorship by the networks operates is not much more subtle. Advertisers, of course, buy spots only on programs that do not present views inconsistent with their interests. Sharp-tongued Texas populist Jim Hightower, whose radio show was distributed by ABC, declared after the Disney and Capital Cities ABC merger was announced, "I work for a rodent." He was, of course, referring to Mickey Mouse. He went after Disney for employing homeless contract workers who were required to pay for their uniforms and tools out of their $4.25-an-hour wage, while Disney's CEO, Michael Eisner, dragged in what amounted to $28,400 for each hour of his work, more than what half the workers of this country get paid for a year's work. A few days later, Hightower lambasted ABC News for caving in to tobacco companies in the face of a lawsuit, observing that the network had just "merged with the Mickey Mouse empire of Disney, Inc." The next day he was informed that his show would no longer be distributed by ABC.

Hightower was not the only Cap Cities/ABC personality to be tossed out after criticism of Eisner. Robert Sam Anson was dumped as editor of Cap Cities's *Los Angeles* magazine after he had written an unflattering profile in which the Disney CEO was called a "wimp." In the meantime Disney, the much-celebrated family-oriented organization of Mickey Mouse and Bambi, found no trouble in carrying Bob Grant's virulent attacks against blacks and gays, as is his constitutional right, though Hightower's defense of the working people of the nation, equally protected by the Constitution, was held by Disney's management to be unacceptable.

Even the greatly respected *60 Minutes* is not immune to network censorship. On the advice of its attorneys, it pulled an interview with a former Brown & Williamson Tobacco Corporation executive who was critical of the industry—because it feared lawsuits. CBS News complained. Joan Konner, Columbia's dean of the Graduate School of Journalism, said, "The conflict of interest between business and journalism was naked on the stage. I felt very bad for the *60 Minutes* crew because they're great journalists, but they were embarrassed and it showed."

But Don Hewitt, who was executive producer of *60 Minutes,* charged that the major network executives view news programs as money-makers the same as entertainment shows such as *Home Improvement* and *ER.* "I blame networks for using information as entertainment. No one who isn't willing to turn TV news into a gold mine is welcome in TV news anymore," he said. If news is only entertainment, then the voice of America will finally become, if it has not already, little more than Donald Duck quacking for dollars.

Walter Cronkite, the dean of television journalists, said, "Those who permit such pressure to be exerted clearly are thinking purely of their pocketbooks and that alone—not of the people's right to know or necessity to know—and I abhor it."

—Ratings, Dollars, and Censorship—

In the end, network producers answer not to the people, not to Congress, not to a democratic system, not to truth or justice, but to the demands of the corporate owners and their corporate advertisers. Ratings, of course, mean dollars. And the networks, like all corporations, are money-addicted and money-driven. Says Carl Jensen, in the preface to *Censored: The News That Didn't Make the News—and Why,* "Corporate media executives perceive their primary, and often sole responsibility to be the need to maximize profits, not, as some would have it, to inform the public." At the end of the day, the dollar, not the people, enjoys free speech.

Advertisers, by exercising the power of their dollars, not only censor the news and network programming, but drive off competing interests as well. When boycotters, employing cherished democratic strategies, bought TV time on a Boston station to air a commercial attacking Folgers for its economic connections to the war in El Salvador, Procter & Gamble knew how to handle the matter. It simply canceled all of its advertising on the station that carried the boycotters' ad, sending a chilling message to every other broadcaster in America. Since then, we are told, no other broadcasters have been willing to run the anti-Folgers spot and risk the same treatment.

—MR. SPEAKER TELLS US HOW TO STOP FREE SPEECH—

On March 6, 1995, the Speaker of the House, Newt Gingrich, spoke to corporate leaders at a closed-door Washington dinner. This is the man who leads our House of Representatives, influences our congressmen's thoughts, garners their votes, and, in the end, is charged with guarding the freedoms of the people, the most important of which is freedom of speech. He has, instead, become a shameless apologist for the nonpeople, the corporate oligarchy that often chills that freedom.

At this affair, Gingrich told his audience that corporate leaders should consider advertising boycotts of any newspapers that oppose their views. Later in the same year, when he was interviewed by *Broadcasting & Cable* magazine, he said, "If you are prepared to be tough-minded about it, the major twenty advertisers in this country by themselves could impose a standard, because among them they are such a dominant force in the market." What we are hearing from the venerable Speaker is that the First Amendment, too, has become the property of twenty major corporations to dispose of as they please.

In the old slave days, the masters kept their slaves uninformed in much the same way Americans are often left in the dark today. So long as the slaves of the various plantations could not communicate with one another, the power of the master was safe. In the book *Advice Among Masters,* one slave master wrote, "Servants that are strictly managed, and closely watched by a good overseer have no possible opportunity of communication with abolition incendiaries, and they cannot of themselves organize any diabolical arrangement. . . . In fact, they do not know what is going on beyond the limits of the plantation, and feel satisfied that they could not, if they were disposed, accomplish any thing that could change their condition." As it is often said, the more things change, the more they stay the same.

—Censorship in Public Television—

But what about public television? Is it not the free voice of the people? Some claim that this is nothing more than an appearance. A bone. A gesture. "Here's your network," Congress says. "We will fund it for you. Now go away." Some say public television is like the master giving his slave a small garden spot in which to raise his turnips and sweet potatoes.

Public television was to be the new, exciting frontier, a place where journalists could attack the important issues of the day and artists could present their work unsmeared with the mundane brush, a garden where, as it were, the slave could raise whatever he chose, as he chose, without interference from the master.

But those with the power of the purse had different ideas. Bill Moyers has said that corporate sponsors called many of the shots in making his TV documentaries. He spoke to *Variety* concerning his series *A Walk Through the 20th Century,* which was funded by Chevron. "I should have been able to air controversial views," Moyers said. "I wasn't." He said that another of his shows, *Bill Moyers' Journal,* suffered the withdrawal of its corporate support after three such "controversial" programs. S. L. Harrison, former director of the Corporation for Public Broadcasting (CPB) and an adjunct professor at the American University, has said that public television is a myth. He said that while he worked for CPB, public TV producers regularly previewed their programs for underwriters to make sure they would not offend the sponsors.

Year after year, conservatives in Congress have been threatening to cut off funds for public broadcasting, and according to Jeff Cohen of FAIR, a national media-monitoring group, every time the threats come, public broadcasting moves further and further to the right. Cohen says that the money sought for public broadcasting is "little more than the government spends on its marching bands. It amounts to about a dollar a person in this country."

What has happened to a free media in America, and what dreams do we dream to free it?

DREAM 9
TWENTY CHILDISH QUESTIONS TO THE MASTER

Let us dream that we have the master in our presence. The door is locked. The master cannot escape, and for once the master must listen. We pummel the master with our questions. We have the right. Freedom of speech. The First Amendment. Perhaps our questions are childlike, simplistic, naïve. But the questions are ours. Perhaps some of our questions do not have answers, not simple ones. But the questions are important to us. The questions set us to dreaming. The answers help us form new dreams.

So let us ask:

1. What has happened to our self-esteem, to the self-reliance of our people, to the independent spirit that once defined us as Americans?

2. How have we melted down from the proud middle class to a majority that is now the impotent "little man"?

3. Why, in an alleged democracy in the richest nation in the world, do the people grow poorer?

4. Why is the planning of our economy undertaken for the enhancement of corporate profit and not, instead, for the general good?

5. Why are we no longer capable of educating our children?

6. Why do we habitually lose our liberty to bureaucratic regulation and to laws that increasingly skin us of our constitutional guarantees?

7. Why is the voice of responsible dissent effectively suppressed?

8. Why, when we have the resources to cure hunger, to educate our young, to care for the homeless, to repair our roads, bridges, and waterways, when we have the wisdom to save our earth and to cure

most of our health problems, do we instead, in times of peace, build more bombs, more bombers, and a greater navy?

9. What would happen if we took the profit out of war?

10. Why are we so afraid? So depressed? So angry?

11. Why have we lost our role as parents?

12. Why are we losing our children to crime and drugs?

13. Why are we imprisoning our minorities and despising them more, not less?

14. What if the people knew who really pays the taxes in this country— how the burden is heaped on the backs of the middle class, who get poorer while the corporate nonpeople simply buy their tax relief from the people's own representatives in Congress?

15. What if the people knew about the epidemic of corporate crime in America, which drains the life blood of the nation like ten thousand ticks on a dog's back?

16. What would happen if we stopped to consider the devastation wrought by the vast, impersonal corporate chains, the Wal-Marts and K marts that run over and run out the struggling small businesses in America?

17. Why are those who care about other human beings scorned and those who fight for the rights of people mocked?

18. Why have free Americans become mere things, expendable commodities that are bought and sold in the human marketplace?

19. Why can't we get justice in America?

20. What would happen in America if the public were as often informed on the issues raised in the foregoing questions as they are about, say, Domino's Pizza or Budweiser beer?

I think of Nero fiddling while Rome burned. I think of America staring mindlessly at celebrity-fueled palaver, mindless violence, mindless canned laughter, mindless games of every description while the clothes of a free nation are on fire.

I dream of a time when we can ask these questions with our own voices on our own airways and demand answers. I dream of the time we can freely turn to our own people, to the best and the brightest among us, to find our way out of the zoo.

DREAM 10
ADVERTISING THE CRIMINAL RECORD OF
CORPORATE OFFENDERS

Have we not had enough of those pretty-faced, smiling institutional ads that make the giant polluters, the corporate frauds and thieves, appear as the best friends the people ever had? Have we not had enough of the undiluted lies that present the corporate swindlers, the cheating insurance companies, and the greedy banks as the first assistants to Mother Teresa?

If corporations have violated the law, their criminal record ought to be fully, *clearly displayed on every one of their advertisements,* like cancer warnings on cigarette ads, so that the people will know with whom they are dealing. We insist on knowing when the rapist moves into our neighborhood. Are we not entitled to know when the dishonest corporation beckons us to trust it once more?

I should think that whenever a corporate criminal advertises anywhere, a warning should be placed on the advertisement setting forth in large, easy-to-read letters the corporate criminal history. It would look like this:

BEWARE
This corporation has been charged and convicted of the following crimes, violations of the following regulations, or has entered into consent decrees when charged with the following: [Here list in easily understandable language the crime or violation and the date of the same]

DREAM 11
THE DREAM THAT'S COMING TRUE

The demise of traditional network television as we know it is predestined, its passage a built-in phenomenon like a fatal genetic defect. The gathering of dead money being its chief purpose, and without the renewal of virtue, already it has lost its vitality. It has played too long to the lowest level of the human experience, and having long ago fallen irretrievably below the median tolerance of the people, it will die of its own cultural malnutrition. Traditional network television will die because it has created its own low-life limits. It can no more burst out with glory and enlightenment than a toad can, by its greatest leap, take wing.

The human mind is a living organism like any plant, like any beast. It requires nourishment, exercise, care. It requires that its potential be addressed. Like the body, it can endure only limited abuse until its inherent survival mechanism screams the irresistible warning that its limits of tolerance—let us call them *the outer boundaries of the mundane*—have been reached.

Having reached the outer boundaries of the mundane, the mind is impelled to revolt. Already a population nearing the breaking point is turning from the traditional source of electronic news and entertainment—namely, network television. The television industry, ever attuned to each commercial quiver, has begun to respond. And unwittingly, its response to the people continues to reduce the power of the master.

More and more channels are being provided—educational, adventure, history, science, and nature channels, to mention but a few—and still we demand more, for we are more. We view several channels of C-SPAN, and many local channels are devoted to the concerns of the community, and still we are not satisfied. But these are only a beginning in a grassroots revolution to recapture the voice of the people.

Endless space in space invites the unlimited launching of communication satellites, and their cost has become correspondingly less. In the new cyberspace age, Americans will continue to abandon commercial television as the sole source of the export and import of ideas. Increasingly, the new Americans will demand the opportunity to receive from an expanding television library information concerning that which is vital to their well-being, which includes, as the first order of life, their liberty.

Today, channels for minorities are emerging. We shall see assembly-line workers and environmentalists and women and gays become a predominant influence in the formation of yet more new channels of communication. Various movements, be they popular or unpopular, herald a new movement. The current surge of the religious right; the Promise Keepers; and the Nation of Islam, led by Louis Farrakhan, are all grassroots responses of a people yearning for community, demanding the right to be heard, and seeking, sometimes at great cost, a sense of the tribe.

The networks, having been stolen from the people, will continue in their decline. The decadent voice of the master, already distrusted by the people and held disdainfully at arm's length, will continue to weaken and at last will be recognized as the quivery voice of an old man who has lied too long and too often to his neighbors.

—THE INTERNET—

Indeed, the Internet has become the phenomenon of the new century. It has become the voice of the people in the first genuine experiment in democracy yet conducted in America. It stands ready to serve every facet, every faction. It creates neighbors where once we were foreigners. It carries our individual voices to new communities formed through the magic of electronics.

The new electronic village has been born, and the village voice, via the Internet, is again being heard. The Internet's new town meeting provides a forum for those who live in the same life-spaces. In this resurrected village, we are already beginning our dialogues with one another. The electronic village has become a place in which the new, freed American can reside, and which others, when they discover themselves, can join. The new pamphleteers, today's Thomas Paines, will take to the Internet, which will expand to become the rising voice of the people, and there a new constitutional convention that will free all Americans can be organized. The dream of a new voice for Americans is a *happening*. Whereas we once felt the helplessness of a people without a voice, we have begun to shout at the master. The Internet leads the way.

The time is upon us when the people will no longer rely on commercial television for the news. The news will come directly from the people to the people as it happens. The middleman, the network newsrooms, where the news is sorted and filtered through the censorship of ratings and money, will shrivel up. Where once only the master's voice could be heard, the voices of the people are beginning to ring out, and the volume will expand across the land. And then the people, hearing one another and beginning to trust one another, will at last become a vast conglomeration of new communities, as different as the parts of any body are different, but with identical cells, cells dedicated to the survival of the body, which requires nourishment. And that nourishment is always liberty.

I welcome all of you to share your voices with me on the Internet at www.givemeliberty.com

TWENTY-TWO

·-·-·

The Death of a Constitution:
Pancake Democracy

————·-·————

Our new Constitution is now established, and has an appearance that promises permanency; but in this world nothing can be said to be certain, except death and taxes.

—BENJAMIN FRANKLIN, 1789

—HERESY!—

To many, it is un-American to even whisper the suggestion that we abandon this venerable Constitution of ours, providing, as it does, many of the safeguards of our liberty. But such is always the mental state of those paralyzed by any religion. The Constitution is not the Bible, and the Supreme Court justices not our high priests. The old Constitution, if once the proud new robe of freedom, has been torn, patched, dyed, ripped, sewn together, and ripped apart again so often that it looks like a tattered sack on the back of an urchin. We give it false reverence because within it we can still observe the last thin threads of freedom. Yet many of the judges who interpret it, the subject of a later chapter, are the unabashed acolytes of the New Master. With great art and artifice these judges continue to stretch the remaining threads of this once proud garment to cover whatever maleficence they choose to impose upon us.

The Constitution was not meant as an article of worship. It was meant as a contract among the people to secure our liberty. When it fails to work, when it has become a mere vestige of itself, in a democracy, we have the power to discard it for the new. Indeed, remember the language of the Declaration itself:

We hold these Truths to be self-evident, that all Men are created equal, that they are endowed by their Creator with certain unalienable Rights, that among these are Life, Liberty, and the Pursuit of Happiness—That to secure these Rights, Governments are instituted among Men, deriving their just Powers from the Consent of the Governed, that whenever any Form of Government becomes destructive of these Ends, it is the Right of the People to alter or to abolish it, and to institute new Government. . . . But when a long Train of Abuses and Usurpations, pursuing invariably the same Object, evinces a Design to reduce them under absolute Despotism, it is their Right, it is their Duty, to throw off such Government, and to provide new Guards for their future Security. [Emphasis added]

DREAM 12
FOUNDING FATHERS FOR THE TWENTY-FIRST CENTURY

Suppose one apocalyptic day we gather together and, in the way of our forefathers, commit ourselves to creating and adopting a new constitution. Like them, we have committed ourselves to spending whatever time as may be necessary to author and ordain a new government. The minds that came together at the time of the Constitutional Convention were no more insightful, no more creative or bounteous than those among us today. Washington, Jefferson, Madison, and Monroe all came from a single state with less than half a million people. I dare say we could duplicate the extent of their genius from any city the size of Cleveland, one with a population of a similar size.

The Worship of the Dead
We have been taught that never in the history of the human race has there been gathered in one place at one time such a group of angels of liberty whose spirit, sifting down from the firmament, created that holy document, our Constitution. The problem with us living human beings is that we tend to enshrine the dead. Think, if you can bear it, of the deity we have made of Elvis.

When we endow the dead with supernatural power and then compare ourselves to them, we deprive ourselves of our own unique power. The continuing myth of the Founders' exclusive genius inhibits our ability to recognize the likelihood of a similar genius among us. When we see our founders as other than people (albeit extraordinary people) we, who today count among ourselves thousands of extraordinary people, feel helpless to try our hand at self-government. We ask, how could we match the Founders' eternal work? And since we conclude that we cannot match it, must we not struggle under the Constitution's moldy cloak, forever playing this senseless game of interpreting its plain and simple language as if it were holy scripture?

Constitutional Religions

A religion has sprung up around this paper. The political parties are like denominations, each with its own interpretation of the Bible. With the Ten Amendments, the Constitution was to provide a guarantee of liberty—at least, for the chosen class. Everyone understood the plain meaning of its words. The colonists needed no judges to raise their nifty brows and gaze heavenward for guidance. And they suffered no need to pack the courts to assure themselves that the paper they had signed would be read in some special way.

But factions were soon to develop into political parties, much like the Baptists and the Methodists. Whigs and Federalists, and later Republicans and Democrats, each with its similar but often different interpretations of the Bible, made their pronouncements as if their interpretations were the infallible word freshly filtered down from the holy spirits of the Founders themselves. But the interpretations we endure have nothing whatever to do with what the Founding Fathers intended, but only with what any given interpreter seeks to accomplish, whatever special interest he seeks to set in concrete as the inalterable status quo.

I have often observed that there is nothing logical, reasonable, or solid about the law. When we enthrone nine head-encapsulated antediluvians on the court, three of whom interpret the Constitution in one way, four in another, and two in yet another, how can we say the law is based on reason and logic unless we admit, as perhaps we should, that reason and logic do not exist but are only the fickle tools of argument?

When these wizards, employing their venerable reason, cannot agree on the simplest proposition, how do they expect anyone else to understand the law? The Constitution is what we want it to be, the intent of the Founding Fathers notwithstanding.

The Founding Fathers, men like thousands who live and work and contribute today, had no idea their progeny would create hydrogen bombs, traverse space, and dominate the world with rockets. If they were to revisit America, they would be instantly thrown into incurable apoplexy and fall prostrate at the feet of the first pimple-faced high school kid who could punch a computer and turn on a television set.

I hold the Founders in no disrespect. I admire them greatly. I simply denounce our worship of them, which, in the end, reduces us to a mindless congregation unable to garner respect for ourselves. The difference between them and us is mostly a difference in time. They climbed a different mountain, perhaps an easier one. And, despite our modern equipment, they were, in many ways, better advantaged. They recognized their servitude to King George III, denounced it, and committed themselves to be free of it. They were not sold out to the master. They suffered from few myths concerning their freedom. And they gave themselves permission to create, and gathered up the courage to act.

Ripping Up the Slave Quarters

Continuing in the dream, suppose a similar group of intelligent, thoughtful citizens, with a commitment to liberty equal to that of our founders, were to meet for the purpose of reinventing American democracy—one relevant to *our* times. Although some would immediately label the group as un-American (and it would undoubtedly be infiltrated by the FBI), nevertheless, suppose the integrity and courage of its individual members were such that they could survive the numerous assaults that would be launched against them. This group's assignment would be simple—to rip up the slave quarters wherever they are found, to break the chains, to defeat the master, and to free the New American Slaves.

Their assignment would be to form a new government of the people, by the people, and for the people. Do we not think that such a group, given such a commitment, could, out of their collective genius, create and put into place a new government designed to fulfill the needs of a modern free society, a government with a new constitution as wonderful and enlightened in this day as was our original Constitution in its?

None of us alone is able to provide all of the answers. Nor could Washington, Jefferson, Madison, Monroe, Hamilton, or Franklin have created our Constitution by himself. But each of us is the mother of ideas and the father of dreams. So, together, let us exchange and examine them and argue and reform them with a love for liberty to the end that we at last invent a new democracy for America. Freedom is an eternal seed that must be tended by many caring gardeners. The planning and tending of this garden will be the work of the *Constitutional Convention for the Reinvention of America.*

DREAM 13
PANCAKE DEMOCRACY

Before we begin to think about creating a new government for America we need to *simplify*. The way to freedom is, in theory, as simple as pancakes. The problem is that we are kept out of the kitchen. But if we understand the easy recipe for pancakes—flour, baking powder, buttermilk, an egg, some sugar, a little oil, a pinch of salt—we can one day fry up a tasty stack.

I asked my friend the other day if he knew how to make pancakes from scratch.

"I don't know," he said.

"Surely you know how to make pancakes," I said.

"No, I don't. Never did make 'em from scratch. I always use pancake mix."

In the same way, the people of America no longer understand the simple recipe for a democracy. They have forgotten the ingredients and no longer know how to experience freedom from scratch. They are given, instead, the Bisquick of democracy, a prefabricated mixture sold to them in a box.

The equally simple recipe for democracy is in the definition of democracy itself: *rule by the people*. The first and the simplest means by which we can return to a pure democracy is to *eliminate the elective process altogether*. As we have seen, the elective process, as exercised in America, is fatally defective as a tool of democracy for the three reasons we have already examined: 1) It allows our representatives to be purchased, 2) it encourages those to seek office who most often are the least qualified to hold office, and 3) it sets our representatives in conflict with the people's interests when they seek successive, unlimited terms of office. Although the first of the fatal defects—the commoditization of our representatives as purchasable property—might be solved by legislation or a constitutional amendment, the second cannot. So long as we elect our representatives, we shall most often be given a choice only among those whose neuroses impel them to public service.

Abolishing Elections

But let us dream on. When we *abolish elections,* we will no longer be required to endure the indignities, the lies, the cheating, the unholy compromises of candidates who, because of their neuroses, crave power, and who must, at any cost, keep power. Once we have abolished elections, we shall be relieved of the obscene specter of those who would satisfy their lust for power by promising anything, spending any amount and committing any act to obtain power. Under the new *pancake democracy,* our representatives will simply be chosen by lot.

Drafting Our Representatives

Every qualified citizen's name will be put in "the hat"—that is, the computer hat—and our representatives from each state will then be drawn from the hat in accordance with the population of the state—by chance. Those whose names have been drawn will constitute our House of Representatives. Those representatives will serve for a single term—say, six years—and if their name is drawn they *must* serve. The terms will be staggered so that some experienced legislators will always be serving in the People's New House of Representatives when new legislators are selected and join them.

The selection of our representatives will be made according to the demographics of the state—county by county, township by township—so that a farming community will likely draw farmers, a laboring community will likely draw working people, a black neighborhood will likely draw blacks. Those drawn will be paid an adequate salary and provided the necessary amenities to do their work. To qualify, one must be at least thirty-five years of age, should have no felony record, possess their normal faculties, and be a resident of the community from which they are selected.

When a citizen's name is drawn who will, as a result, be grievously damaged by being drafted, the Grievance Commission will hear the case and provide just compensation, but in only the most extreme cases would any person be relieved of his or her duty. If our young people can be drafted to serve their country, to even give up their lives, sometimes in senseless wars, all citizens, if called upon, can contribute a part of their life in service to democracy.

I can imagine, for example, the hardship of a farmer whose name is drawn and who must leave his farm for six years. The usual recesses of Congress will, of course, free him for brief periods, but in his absence from the farm, he will be provided with sufficient funds to hire a competent manager. A doctor may apply to the commission for the loss he will likely endure as a result of his absence from his practice for six years.

At first blush it might appear that such a government, as it attempts to justly compensate the citizens who serve it, would be expensive. But when one considers government-financed elections, which would cost hundreds of millions, or when one considers the hundreds of millions spent by special interest groups to gain, as they claim, "access" to our representatives, pancake democracy will prove to be cheap.

To put the matter in perspective: Today's House of Representatives has fewer than five hundred members. The People's New House of Representatives might have twice that number to ensure a proper demographic mix. Considering the fact that there are about 260 million people in this country, one's chance of being drawn would be about one in 260,000, somewhat less than one's chance of being killed in an automobile accident. And to serve as a representative of the people will be considered the noblest service that a citizen can perform for his country.

Pancake Government

The advantages of such a system are many, and powerfully favor a true democracy. Selecting our representatives by lot establishes a government of people from all walks of life, from all classes, from both sexes, from every race, and over its long term, it will fairly and accurately, for the first time in the history of America, represent the makeup of the nation. There will be as many women in the legislature as men. The races will be represented roughly in proportion to their percentage of the population. No longer will this be a nation ruled by wealth or corporate power. Class distinctions in government will be eliminated. Egalitarian principles will prevail. The airline ticket agent so chosen will have power and respect equal to anyone who heretofore held office by reason of a different drawing of lots—fate's lot of wealth or name.

On the other hand, the arguments against such a system are flimsy. "How can we entrust government to the rabble?" is the question most often posed by those who do not consider themselves as members of the rabble because, by the luck of the draw, they were born to an elevated class of money, power, education, or intelligence. How can we let the cleaning lady pass laws for her mistress? But across the board, those who have experienced humble beginnings are as likely to be as qualified to represent us as those who were born, also by luck, into wealth or power. And who knows the human condition better—the cleaning woman who works until her back is stiff and her legs quaking, or her mistress, who plays nine holes of golf, has a massage, and thereafter sips cocktails all afternoon at the country club?

I doubt that the composite IQ of those already in Congress is higher than any across-the-board group of ordinary American citizens. And regarding those in Congress who belong to the moneyed class, let me reveal once more my jaundice: Exceptions admitted, I have never met such fools as the economically advantaged. Most couldn't plant a garden or distinguish a songbird from a crow. As a class they have little knowledge of history or literature; in fact, they have rarely read a book from cover to cover. And they know practically nothing about relating to people in a genuine way. Their lives, as a whole, are skewed so that nearly all important values are translated into money.

Under the pancake system of government, our representatives will no longer be able to buy their way into office. We will not be forced to vote for a congressional or presidential candidate because he or she happens to have achieved an election war chest by hook or by crook or a famous family name. I believe that it can be demonstrated scientifically that people with as plain a name as Jones are, on the average, as intelligent, human, and qualified to represent us as people with the name Kennedy.

Moreover, as we have seen, the best-qualified citizens in this country do not seek office and are rarely found in the halls of Congress. At every election, we hear the citizens' lamentations: As one of my friends said recently, echoing the sentiment of most Americans, "They are always the same old political hacks who I wouldn't hire to operate a cheap motel." The most qualified among us suffer no neurotic bug biting at our entrails compelling us to run for public office. Instead we are running businesses, or teaching or performing other beneficial functions in our society rather than submitting ourselves to the obscene effrontery of today's politics. The so-called best and the brightest will be subject to the draft the same as everyone else. And speaking of today's system of purchased lackeys, who would want a person to represent us who has no more self-respect than to run for public office?

DREAM 14
THE PEOPLE'S NEW SENATE

I dream of a Senate composed of the best talent in the nation selected by the representatives of the people themselves. The drafted representatives from each state in the People's New House of Representatives will caucus, and from their group they will choose, say, seven persons who will serve as that state's Senatorial Selection Committee. In the event a state such as Wyoming does not possess a large enough population to warrant as many as seven representatives, additional persons will be drawn by lot in the same manner as the original representatives were chosen, and with the same qualifications, until a caucus of at least seven persons has been drawn, those additionally drawn serving only long enough to select the state's senators.

The Senatorial Selection Committees from each state will then undertake a search from among the citizens of their states for *the two most qualified persons* to represent the people in the People's New Senate.

A senator so drafted may be a scholar, a university president, a scientist, a poet, a businessperson, an artist, or a humanitarian. The person might be a philosopher, an author, or a civic leader. But in every instance, the person will have the exceptional and proven ability and experience that have permitted the person to excel in his or her life's endeavors.

The search will be conducted in much the same manner that corporations set about seeking a CEO. And when drafted, the two persons from each state so selected must serve. They, too, will serve but one six-year term and may be granted relief for their financial loss, if any, by the Grievance Commission. In the first year, the senators so chosen will be chosen for two-, four-, and six-year terms so that at any given election thereafter, experienced senators will remain in office.

DREAM 15
THE PEOPLE'S PRESIDENT

And how shall we select the president under the new constitution? The People's New House of Representatives will choose a Presidential Selection Committee of perhaps twenty persons. Each member of the committee will nominate his or her choice of the best person in the nation to serve as president. Presumably twenty or fewer persons will thus be nominated. The entire House will then vote on the persons so selected, and the two receiving the highest number of votes will stand in a runoff, again in the House, and the person receiving the highest number of votes will become the president of the United States and will serve for a single term, also of six years.

DREAM 16
COMING HOME WITH POWER

Under any system by which our representatives are selected, we must recognize that the nation has become much too large and too diversified for a single centralized government to any longer function intelligently, efficiently, or justly. How can Washington understand the needs of the rancher in Oklahoma or the schoolteacher in the Bronx? The strength of America was born of our disparate mix, from a variety of lifestyles, ideals, religious, business interests, races, and political philosophies and from a widely divergent genetic pool. A single, powerful centralized government tends to standardize people, to make uniform the way we think and work and live.

Furthermore, a single, powerful centralized government has proven itself too large and inhuman to fulfill the varying needs of such a widely divergent population. Looking to such a mammoth government to provide for the general welfare and happiness of the people is like trying to make love to a face on Mount Rushmore, and approximately as satisfying.

Return to the Tribe

Genetically, we are tribal animals who from the beginning have prospered and spread over the face of the globe in small groups. When the tribe becomes too large, like a beehive that has grown beyond its capacity, the tribe separates into two tribes—usually at about two hundred people, although tribes often were joined in alliances of common origin. Governments of large populations—in our case one of more than a quarter of a billion people from a centralized cell in Washington—have expanded precariously beyond the genetic plan.

Compared to government today, the government of our founders was a very decentralized, easygoing, cheap-to-operate, almost informal confederation of good ol' boys. As we have seen, Thomas Jefferson worried that a stifling concentration of the power in Washington might occur through the auspices of an irresponsible judiciary. And today his fear has become the reality of our judicial oppression.

The city-states of ancient Greece and Rome were small compared to the average metropolitan community today. And in America, the best example of democracy at work was the town meeting of the New England colonies, a direct democracy in which each member of the community took part in the passage of the laws of the village, much like a classroom operates when the students vote on where they will hold an outing. The machinery provided by the Constitution itself was designed for a society of small villages, not for a mega-nation that encompasses a continent and attempts to govern over 260 million people—and even the world.

Without regard to the means by which we select our representatives, the major power of government must be vested locally. Communities must be provided the wherewithal to educate their children as they see fit and to provide for their people as the community assesses the needs of its people. Reserved for the federal government will be matters beyond the ability of the community, such as national defense, a national system of roads, the protection of the citizens' civil rights, and the like. And in passing, we ought to observe that it does not follow that merely because the federal government has the power to tax, it should have the corresponding power to dictate how the tax dollar should be spent. The power to tax was derived from the people. All power, lest we forget, including the right to spend, is derived from the people.

DREAM 17
LIFE UNDER THE NEW PANCAKE GOVERNMENT

Under the new pancake government, campaign reforms will not be required, since our representatives, chosen by lot, will never stand for election, will never need to utter a false word to hold office, will never take bribes or payoffs in the form of campaign contributions, will never have to hire pollsters to read the mind of the electors, and will never hire Madison Avenue to create fictional characters that, so far as truth is concerned, bear only the name of the candidate. Nor will our representatives ever vote in such a way that will assure their reelection, because they will serve but one term and will never stand for reelection.

Free College Education

Such a system of government requires that all of our people be educated and, as in the old Greek city-state, taught the nearly sacred obligation they bear in taking an informed part in government. Education, including college, will be free. Citizen commissions will oversee the administrative agencies. Government will be inexpensive, efficient, and directed toward the needs of the people so that the people themselves will finally become the New Master in this new pancake democracy. The ugly game that has castrated democracy and left it impotent will have ended.

The deep wisdom necessary for the formation of a new government to free the New American Slave will, of course, become the collegial efforts of many minds. Such was our experience at the original Constitutional Convention. As we have seen, we do not suffer from a paucity of wisdom and creativity. We suffer only from a scarcity of hope that someday we shall find our way to freedom. We suffer only from a lack of permission—the permission we must bestow upon ourselves to release our own creativity and discover new ways by which we may become liberated.

Life Without Dreams

It must be clear that the notion of a pure democracy is nothing more than a dream in itself. But without a dream, we have no destination. No light gleams beyond the cage. Without a dream, we cannot measure the small steps, one at a time, we must take in our long trek toward liberty. Without a dream, there is nothing against which we may test our presence in history.

That nonliving corporate monsters should be entrusted with the power to control the lives of human beings and that these human beings should be destined to live out their lives in servitude on this planet is the nightmare we have come to accept as *the way of things*.

I think once more of John Quincy Adams. After his term as president, Adams returned to Congress, and there had to defend himself against a motion of censure. His crime? He had persisted in laying before the House, under the guarantee of the Constitution, the petitions of the people in protest against slavery. The Southerners in the House claimed that by his continuous introduction of such petitions, along with the various and ingenious strategies he devised in support of their presentation to Congress, he was inviting treason.

The retaliatory motion of the old South's spokesman was to inflict the "severest censure" on the ex-president, and his presentation had been filled with language of "the deepest indignity" and "insult" and "wound" that he should suggest that the slavery issue should even be discussed in those hallowed halls.

The scene, however, was differently reported by Joshua Giddings, a "big, stocky Midwesterner" from the Western Reserve of Ohio, who before he was to leave the House would earn the title "the Lion of Ashtabula."

His [Adams's] appearance was venerable; he was dignified in his bearing. He looked around upon his peers, who sat before him as judges, with a countenance beaming with kindness; he had long served his country, had filled the highest office on earth with honor to himself and friends; and now, at the age of seventy-five years, he stood arraigned on a charge of treason to that country to which he had so long devoted his labors, to that people whose rights he was seeking to maintain.

When his time came to speak, Adams merely called for the clerk to read the first paragraph in the Declaration of Independence. The clerk began to read as requested. He read on, at Adams's insistence, through the part about the inalienable rights to life, liberty, and the pursuit of happiness, and through the part that says that "to secure these Rights, Governments are instituted among Men, deriving their just Powers from the Consent of the Governed, that whenever any Form of Government becomes destructive of those Ends, it is the Right of the People to alter or to abolish it . . ."

The clerk is reported to have hesitated. "Proceed! Proceed!" cried John Quincy Adams, and at his insistence the clerk read on: "But when a long Train of Abuses and Usurpations, pursuing invariably the same Object, evinces a Design to reduce them under absolute Despotism, it is their Right, it is their Duty, to throw off such Government . . ."

So argued John Quincy Adams, the sixth president of the United States and the first president to take on the Congress in our relentless fight against slavery, a struggle that would continue thereafter through the great Civil War and on to this moment. One wonders with trembling what a man of equal courage and love for his country would say into the face of the New Master today.

TWENTY-THREE

·•·

Creating the Corporate Conscience

———·•·———

What's good for General Motors is good for the country.
—CHARLES WILSON,
SECRETARY OF DEFENSE AND FORMER PRESIDENT OF
GENERAL MOTORS, 1953

—REVISITING JURASSIC PARK—

Let us revisit a place like Jurassic Park, where the soulless monsters graze on the people. You can see them, tall as the skyscrapers, the earth shuddering under each step, their cold eyes surveying the landscape for something to devour. They are not hungry. But they will gorge until they stagger in their tracks. They will regurgitate and eat again for only the sake of eating.

These monsters are called American corporations. They are called American corporations only because they were formed here and have their history here, like a particular dinosaur is an American reptile only because the awful egg was hatched in the primordial ocean shores of Wyoming. But the creatures know no boundaries and they know no loyalty.

As we have already seen, the people are enslaved to this culture of behemoths. The people are its fodder. No human is safe in this land-scape. Most cannot hide. Most will be eaten. And the beasts do not graze upon the dead. Like their ancestors in the sea, they eat only the living. They consume the people in great mouthfuls, and often consume others of the beasts themselves. When the easy grazing is over in one land, they scour others—first China, soon Russia, then the small islands in the Pacific, Indonesia, and the Philippines. They trample over Mexico and South America, digging great gaping holes in the land, mindlessly gluttonizing on the people wherever they tread.

And the devoured are swallowed up without screaming. As the people are digested in the belly of the creature, they accept their destiny as *the way of things*. And the people exhibit a strange resignation. They call the process "life," this emptying of their energy, this dissolving of their blood into the creature. And then the people die and are said to have lived a good life.

What if we were to ask the childish question, who created these creatures that roam the earth and forage on us? What if we heard the answer, that the creatures that devour us are leviathans of our own making? What if we understood that they are not the creations of God but the freakish monster of man himself? It is an eerie scene of madness, these invisible, soulless beasts standing over us as our masters, and we, the slaves who created them, helpless to save ourselves.

—UN-making the Monsters—

But what if a child, isolated from the madness of this world, were to toddle onto the scene and ask, "If we made them, *can't we UN-make them?*" As it is said, there is a time for all things. And the time has come for the slave and the master to change places. Since the master is the creation of the slave—since we have created the corporate state—may not we, the slaves, as the child suggests, UN-make the master?

—The Good Corporation—

I do not argue, of course, that there are no good corporations. Most charities are corporations. Many smaller, closely held corporations show us the possibilities. I think of a closely held small corporation that designs, manufactures, and markets outdoor clothing and that gives a percentage of its profits to environmental causes. As some corporations do, it provides its workers with day care services at the place of work so parents can be with their children during the workday. It authorizes both paid maternity *and* paternity leave. When the surf is good, it is understood that some workers will be gone to hit the waves.

I have seen Yvon Chouinard, this company's crusty yet loving CEO, out in the back shop, slouching in a dirty T-shirt and wearing his holey running shoes, laboring over the construction of a surfboard his company has designed. It is a large family, a tribe, a people-oriented, people-concerned place. Yet even this enlightened company must resort to Third World labor to manufacture its clothing. "Can't find American factories that can compete, either in price or quality of work," Chouinard complains. Looking sad, he goes back to the surfboard he's working on.

—THE NEED FOR THE BEAST—

We are told by reading the scriptures of capitalism that by the device of the corporation, large sums of capital may be gathered to perform business functions that might otherwise be impossible through the resources of a single person. No one person could have put together the capital necessary to launch a world producer of automobiles, to build an intercontinental railroad, run an airline, or provide the funds necessary to operate commercial banks. America, now the most powerful corporate oligarchy in the world, itself a gargantuan hairball of corporations, could not have achieved its position of world power and could not have provided the material wealth we daily take for granted without the corporation. But what if such colossal power has no conscience?

No human being with a conscience would have burned, as some estimate, a million women at the stake as witches. But in the corporate form, the church, the first and most powerful of all corporations, could order the witches burned, the heretics skinned alive, and holy wars waged, all in the name of Christ, whose simple admonition was to love one another. In modern times, the corporation, still infallible, continues to commit nearly every conceivable social atrocity under the shelter of the corporate tarp. One wonders if the corporate form itself is inherently evil.

Most often no identifiable person can be held responsible in the corporate structure. No individual with a conscience would sell mothers an oral pregnancy test that caused children to be born without arms or legs or a tongue. But one of America's pharmaceutical corporations, with full knowledge of the possible hideous consequences, dumped its excess stock on welfare mothers in New York City when the drug was about to be banned by the FDA.

Honorable men and women own stock in corporations that do dishonorable things, usually for profit; that commit fraud, usually for profit; that bribe public officials, usually for profit; that foist products on Americans knowing they are unsafe and that many will die, usually for profit. Most dishonest, amoral corporations are not only owned by honorable people, they are managed by honorable people. The problem is, of course, that no individual bears responsibility.

—THE ETERNAL SEARCH FOR RESPONSIBILITY—

When the dead girl is dragged from the wreckage of the automobile that her father bought her for graduation, and he discovers that the brakes on the new automobile failed, he complains to the dealer. The dealer, looking sad, says, "I'm sorry, sir. We don't make cars, we only sell them. You should speak to the manufacturer."

When, after an inventive and exhaustive effort, the father is finally permitted to talk to the division head of the corporation that made the car, the division head says, "We didn't design the braking system over here. But, confidentially, I have heard rumblings about those brakes. Hope you get to the bottom of it. I'll set you up with the design department."

When the father speaks to the chief engineer in the design department, he responds, "We are certainly concerned. But really, brakes are out of my area of expertise. I deal with thousands of designs. I've had a few inquiries, all right. But it's really out of my jurisdiction. Let me get you in touch with the brake people."

When the father, still bent on finding the person responsible for his daughter's death, speaks to the section engineer who was in charge of the design of the faulty brakes, the man says, "I didn't design those brakes."

"Who did?"

"Who knows? This design has been in use for years. Modifications are ordered from time to time, of course." He fingers a file. "But nothing significant. We've had some complaints from time to time, and we look into them. We try always to improve our product. But you know how it goes. Some guy gets drunk and kills himself, and his family hollers that there was something wrong with the brakes. The system has been fully tested. Those brakes are on millions of cars. Perhaps you should talk to the testing people."

When the father finally runs down the chief of testing, he is told in a friendly, helpful way, "All of our brakes comply with government standards. Perhaps you should talk to the government people over in DOT. They are real sticklers on safety."

"DOT?"

"Department of Transportation."

"Before I go, could I see your test results on the brakes?" the father asks.

The chief of testing smiles a kindly smile. "All our testing is confidential. Company policy."

When the father finally corners the CEO of the corporation, he meets a cheerful, open type. But the CEO says very candidly, "I don't set policy. Policy is set by the board of directors. I'm merely the chief executive officer. The chief flunky." He laughs. He smiles a good deal. "I suggest you talk to the board of directors."

When the father gets to the board of directors, he speaks to several of the board members individually. One is the CEO of a computer company, another is on the board of a huge bank. Still another is a respected and retired former secretary of commerce. Most have never seen a brake in their lives. They rely, they admit, on what the chief executive officer tells them.

When the father speaks to the CEO once more about the fatal brakes, the CEO says, "I, personally, have no information whatsoever."

"Have you had any complaints about the brakes on this car?" the father asks.

"I wouldn't know. In this business you get complaints all of the time about something. You could manufacture the perfect machine, one designed by God Himself, and, by God, some jackleg shyster would find something wrong with it." He laughs to show he is really a good-natured man. "But hold on. Let me get to the bottom of this for you right now." He cocks an eyebrow and speaks into his intercom. In one moment, in a display of efficiency, he has the file in his hand. He glances at it, clears his throat, and turns to the father. "Just as I thought," he says. "The brakes on that model were manufactured by another corporation. I know the chief over there. I can make an appointment for you if you like, or would you rather speak to our lawyers?"

The very nature of the corporation itself is to concentrate power, to defuse responsibility, and to avoid individual culpability for the corporation's acts. If I seek limited liability, I can form a corporation. My creditor may take my office desk and chair and anything remaining in the corporate bank account, but my creditor cannot touch my personal car or attach my personal bank account.

Because of limited liability, the corporation is the best structure ever yet contrived by man to accomplish the most evil acts ever yet conceived by man without incurring individual legal responsibility for the same. Despite the fact that the corporation may have killed for money or cheated millions of old people of their life savings, despite the fact that corporations may have thrown us into world wars for their profit, bought and sold presidencies, and, at last, become the dominating force in a master-slave society, I have never seen or heard of a corporation that has been put in jail or against which the death penalty has ever been imposed.

—CRIME WITHOUT PUNISHMENT?—

We have seen fraud charges brought against Prudential Insurance Company of America involving 10.7 million policyholders in which that company agreed to pay $410 million to settle the lawsuits. The chairman apologized to policyholders and agreed to pay a record fine of $35 million. Burger King has paid half a million to settle child-labor-law charges against it; a Dunkin' Donuts shop was using hidden microphones to spy on its employees; Laboratory Corporation of America Holdings has paid $182 million to resolve allegations that it submitted false claims for medically unnecessary laboratory tests in government programs; Texaco settled racial discrimination charges for $176.1

million. American corporations reap the spoils of sweatshops in poverty-stricken Haiti, including J. C. Penney, K mart, and Disney, to mention only a handful in the grab bag of recent revelations of how corporations are conducting their business. But I have never seen a corporation put in jail.

The charges of corporate greed and malfeasance are endless and perpetually self-renewing, like a malignancy gone wild. Dangerous products kill something like 30,000 Americans a year, and 150,000 workers incur serious injuries annually. And corporate crime is not a recent phenomenon. A twenty-year-old study conducted at George Washington University revealed that in the ten years preceding the study, at least one in five of America's five hundred largest corporations had been convicted of at least one major crime or had paid civil penalties for serious misbehavior. In another respected inquiry reviewing the criminal administrative actions brought by 25 federal agencies against the 477 largest publicly owned manufacturing companies in the United States, completed over two decades ago with the assistance of the Department of Justice, 60 percent of America's biggest and best had been filed against at least once, 42 percent had been charged with more than one violation, and 25 percent had been charged with "multiple cases of non-minor violations." *Fortune* magazine once reported from its own studies of 1,043 major corporations that 11 percent had committed at least one major crime since 1970, leading the magazine to blandly conclude that "a surprising number of [major U.S. corporations] have been involved in blatant illegalities." Corporate crime has not diminished. We are fearful of the well-publicized crime in the streets, but we are being plagued by the under-publicized crime in the corporate suites.

—Grafting a Conscience onto the Corporate Beast—

In the same way that the sociopath cannot be cured by our sermonizing, the corporation cannot be converted into an upright citizen by our preachings. But there is hope for the corporation. Because it is a man-made creature, it is subject to a mutation brought on by man-made law. *We can graft a conscience onto the corporation.* As we have created the irresponsible corporation, we can also create the responsible one. We can give it an awareness of its social responsibility; we can make it care; we can convert it into a good and productive citizen.

Man, acting as God, has created the corporation. But man has not created the corporation in his own image. Man is capable of love and is governed by a deep sense of that which is right and wrong. Man has a soul, a spirit, a sense of his attachment to the earth, and since he embodies these wholly human traits he can also, at his will, impose them on his fictional creations. The first step toward the creation of a corporate conscience, then, is to impose on it *human* responsibility.

I remember the trial of the Silkwood case, in which I represented the heirs of Karen Silkwood against Kerr-McGee. We heard of a toxic spill from the Kerr-McGee plant that purportedly polluted the river and killed many fish, which washed up on the banks. We were told how the workers as well as the managers were sent out to gather up the rotting fish, supposedly to prevent an incident with regulators. Little chance of one, I should have thought, since Kerr-McGee had been cited seventy-five times for violations of various government regulations but had never been fined a penny.

Be that as it may, the above example is useful in understanding that few wrongs occur in the corporate milieu that are not known at several levels of corporate authority. Often, corporate misconduct is a secret shared by many. The secret remains a secret because employees value their jobs and are afraid of being branded as whistle-blowers for fear that other companies will not hire them.

Dream 18
The New Responsible Corporation

The first step toward corporate responsibility is to require under penalty of law that *every employee* report dangerous or suspected criminal activity to corporate managers, who in turn must report the same to the board of directors. And such employees must keep records that prove their reporting.

Next, every corporate employee, from the laborer to the chief exec-

utive officer and including the board of directors, would become criminally liable for injuries or death resulting from known but unreported
illegal acts, from known but unreported dangerous conduct or dangerous products, from improper testing, cover-ups, fraud, and conspiracies.
The key to criminal culpability would be the person's *knowledge* of the
wrongdoing.

If, for example, a worker knows that brakes fail in a test, he must
report it, and the reports must go on up the line. Since corporations
"are only people" (as corporations like to assure us), *people* must be
made responsible. If any corporate employee with knowledge can be
held responsible, corporate crime will soon end, because corporate
crime cannot be committed without corporate employees willing to
commit it under the cover of corporate immunity.

The plan works this way: Let us say the corporation is dumping
poisons into the river. The worker who, on order of a superior, turns
on the valve can protect himself from liability and criminal sanctions
by reporting the misconduct in writing. He keeps a copy of the report
himself and the misconduct is then reported up the line. If the reporting fails along the way, the person at the breach becomes both civilly
and criminally liable. When the report gets to the decision-making level,
the company executives either take the necessary steps to permanently
correct the wrongdoing or they themselves become personally responsible for the wrongdoing.

That means that the vice presidents, the president, the CEO, and
the board members can no longer hide behind the corporate veil. It
also means that if the worker does not report the wrongdoing in the
first instance, he will be exposed to criminal and civil penalties himself.
The secretary who becomes aware of the illegal activity, the janitor who
discovers evidence of it, the coworker who witnesses sexual harassment,
the CEO who ignores racial discrimination, all are criminally and civilly
liable if they do not report the wrong. And if they occupy a decision-
making position and fail to take the necessary steps to rectify it, they
too will be personally liable. As it should, wrongdoing becomes a vital
concern of everyone.

At the same time, it will be a crime that will also bring on civil
liability for any person in the corporation to take punitive action against
the worker who reports wrongdoing.

The recidivist corporation, whether it be General Electric or the pea-sized local construction company would be barred by law from government contracts until the miscreants at the top have been permanently replaced (without golden parachutes) and the management of the corporation has been reorganized in such a way as to assure the government that such wrongdoing will not again occur. By law, managers fired for serious wrongdoing ought not be reemployed by companies doing business with the government for a period of years—let us say five years, for starters.

DREAM 19
THREE STRIKES AND YOU'RE OUT

The widely acclaimed "three strikes and you're out" idea seems to be vigorously supported by corporate managers as a wonderfully innovative means by which to take common criminals off the streets. One wonders what view corporate managers might have of it if this same law were made applicable to corporations as well. Justice is justice. In court, corporations demand the same right to due process as citizens. How can it be that corporations should enjoy these constitutional guarantees but not be charged with the same responsibilities as citizens?

To be sure, individual criminals can and do cause us egregious harm. But their harm is petty compared to the devastation wrought by powerful corporations. For example, burglars cost the nation upwards of $3.4 billion during the same period of time that the savings and loan scandals were costing the nation something *between $300 and $500 billion.*

Citizens should be protected from any corporation that has intentionally committed a felony on three separate occasions. If we take the three-strikes-and-you're-out felon off the street permanently, let us put the habitual corporate criminal out of business permanently. Three strikes and it's out as well. But since the corporation is immortal, let us give it the benefit of a temporal life in logging its crimes. Most criminals commit most of their crimes between the ages of seventeen and fifty, a span, say, of about thirty years. Let us therefore apply the three-strikes-and-you're-out proposition to corporations so that if, within any thirty-year period, the corporation is convicted of three felonies, the corporation would simply be dissolved and its assets distributed among the shareholders.

Nor could the corporation save itself by a merger with another corporation. Any merger, like a blood disease, would infect the new entity with the old record. Nor would reorganization wipe out the stain. I should think that the threat of such a penalty would impose a wonderfully sensitive conscience on the beast. Employees, too, will have a stake in seeing that the corporation stays within the law, since their jobs would be lost if the corporation were dismantled.

These are not radical ideas, although radical ideas to meet the crisis seem called for. Until the Civil War, most states enacted laws holding corporate investors and officials responsible. Governor Henry Hubbard of New Hampshire made the point in 1842:

> There is no good reason against this principle. In transactions which occur between man and man there exists a direct responsibility—and when capital is concentrated . . . beyond the means of single individuals, the liability is continued.

The penalty for the abuse, misuse, or violation of a corporate charter in those days was the revocation of the corporate charter and dissolution of the corporation. Citizens believed then, as on consideration we must believe now, that it was society's absolute right and duty to abolish an evil. Revocation clauses were written into many of the early charters. In Pennsylvania, such provisions appeared as early as 1784. They were added to insurance charters in 1809 and to banking charters in 1814.

In 1815, Massachusetts justice Joseph Story ruled in *Terrett* v. *Taylor*:

> A *private corporation created by the legislature may lose its franchises by a misuser or nonuser of them. . . . This is the common law of the land, and is a tacit condition annexed to the creation of every such corporation.*

Back then, people were suspicious of corporations, afraid of their power, and jealous of the people's right to control them. But corporations in the Reconstruction years paid "borers" to take over Congress and state capitals. They flaunted new money, bribed elected and appointed officials, and grabbed public land, minerals, water, and timber. Railroad corporations themselves wrested from the public some 180 million acres along with millions of dollars in direct subsidies. Gradually, as the corporate tides enveloped the land, the legislators granted limited liability to corporations and decreased the rights of citizens to control them, leaving corporations themselves to rewrite the laws that would govern them.

DREAM 20
DEATH FOR THE KILLERS

Corporate executives are almost unanimous in favor of the death penalty for humans who intentionally kill. If we are concerned with justice, may we not now properly impose the death penalty upon the corporation that knowingly kills for profit as well?

Again, for the easiest example, I think of the tobacco industry, which kills more than 400,000 of our people every year for profit, knows it, and lies about it. We are understandably enraged when a dope peddler on the street lures our children into addiction and death. But when the tobacco industry, with the use of the most skilled and subtle psychological means, induces our children into tobacco addiction, we often end up arguing for the tobacco company. "The kid knew what he was doing," we argue. How is it that we acquit the tobacco corporation that kills millions, yet convict the dope peddler whose crime is limited to his neighborhood? The kid who uses crack and the kid who smokes cigarettes, in each instance, knew what they were doing.

We are outraged when some hired killer murders for a few dollars, and if he is caught, we argue that he should be put to death. But when an entire corporate industry robs our youth of their health and intentionally kills our people for billions in profits, ought we not have both the courage and the power to rise up and protect ourselves? Ought we not disband such corporations and confiscate their assets in the same fashion that a drug dealer's boat or car or real property is confiscated?

—A World of the Ants—

Today, many corporations are too large to be held responsible by any regulatory body. How, for instance, can a corporation the size of GE be held under rein? Not only is the corporation too large for the government to effectively regulate, it has become too large to regulate itself even if it were so inclined. Indeed, the American megacorporation, like the government itself, has become a massive structure of many corporations, many smaller structures within structures—kingdoms within kingdoms.

Jack Welch, CEO of General Electric, reigns over the numerous corporations it controls in much the same way that the pope of the Middle Ages sat as the king of kings—all the nations of the Christian world being loosely held together under their allegiance to the church, but each with its sovereign in his own domain. GE employs 276,000 people, operates 250 manufacturing plants, owns and operates the largest radio and television network in the world, owns 10 television stations in the 10 major American cities that reach 27 percent of U.S. households, operates in 100 foreign countries, has revenues of $90.8 billion and earnings of $8.2 billion, and at the end of 1997 was worth $246 billion. Such a corporation is beyond the pale.

Anyone who suggests that General Electric can be managed, except superficially, is dwelling in fantasy. It cannot be steered in one direction or another any more than one can change the course of the glacier. The entity has expanded beyond the control of any government agency, although it employs many former government regulators, while at the same time it deals with scores of government agencies that attempt to regulate it. In the end, it concentrates more power than the government itself.

The FCC has as much ability to control NBC or any of the other giant networks as it does to change our weather patterns. It can only open up its regulatory umbrella occasionally and shiver in the rain.

The Securities and Exchange Commission is substantially powerless over the giants on Wall Street and can do little more than shrug its shoulders through the use of essentially meaningless fines and consent decrees.

The Federal Food and Drug Administration can cause bureaucratic trouble, but it cannot perform its mandated duty to protect the people from the drug companies, their monopolies, and their conspiracies with the medical profession. The revolving doors between corporations and the regulating agencies continue to spin wildly, so that he who is a regulator will tomorrow be a highly paid employee of the corporation he regulated only yesterday.

Too big, too powerful, too diverse, the American corporation cannot respond to its employees or the communities whose fortunes are tied to it. If you have ever seen the worker ants, and if you were careless enough to have stepped on them or shuffled through their anthill bringing on an immense cataclysm to their village, the relationship of the individual to the giant corporation is put into some perspective. The individual ant has little chance of infusing our souls with any sensitivity to its plight, its life, its interests, its world. Such is our attempt, without the aid of the law, to sensitize the corporation to ours.

But corporations have responsibilities not only to their shareholders but to their workers and the communities in which they operate. *The New York Times* tells of the effect the downsizing of National Cash Register Corporation had on the city of Dayton, Ohio. NCR was part of Dayton's soul. After the downsizing, the *Times* reports, "[e]verything, seemingly, is in upheaval: not just the jobs and lives of tens of thousands of people, but also the big corporations, the banks, the schools, the religious and cultural institutions, the old relationships of politics and power, and especially, people's expectations of security, stability and a shared civic life."

In Japan, when corporate downsizing decisions are made, the rights of the workers, who are the source of all wealth, are considered first. Then the Japanese decision-makers look to the community and ask, how will our decision affect it? Only then is the profit of the stockholder taken into direct account. Strange that the Japanese, this reputedly ineffable culture, should trouble itself with the rights of workers and the health of the community. Yet the Japanese, also bottom-liners, have learned what modern American managers are slowly beginning to realize—that the flow of profit is inhibited when workers are exploited and communities sucked dry.

DREAM 21
DECENTRALIZATION, NOT ANNIHILATION

Corporations are not just money-making institutions. By law they are citizens, these leviathans sitting among the ants. And as citizens they must be made responsive to the interests not only of the people who produce their wealth, but also of the communities where their operations impact entire populations.

Today, most corporate boards are an exclusive club of executives who also sit on the boards of other giants; former government regulators and politicians who have done favors for the corporation in the past and who still retain governmental connections; bankers, and other insider money types. And this corporate culture mostly spurns any social concern unattached to profit.

The solution is not to dissolve large corporations but to decentralize their power. By law, corporate boards of the megacorporation whose operations impact on the environment, the community, health, and other concerns of general welfare should be expanded to include representatives of the workers, of environmental organizations, of women, minorities, and other major interests in the community. A coalition of minorities could, for example, prevent a corporation from engaging in business practices that are destructive to the environment. It could weigh the detriment to humanity as a whole against the profit of the corporation. Such a coalition could go a long way toward grafting a conscience onto the corporation.

Business leaders complain, and I think with great justification, that there are already too many regulators, too many laws, too many restrictions placed upon them. But in practice, corporations exist in an environment of anarchy. They are like bullies running wild in a nursery. And so long as corporations misbehave, there remains the need for regulation. Sadly, without regulation, we shall never see the day that most corporations on their own will be anything but rampaging, greedy, profit-seeking constructs. Until that day, the people's first duty is to themselves. A reined-in horse can pull a carriage. A runaway horse can wreck the carriage and kill its passengers.

DREAM 22
LOCKING THE REVOLVING DOOR

We will, sooner than later, make it unlawful for any governmental regulator to go to work for any corporation it has regulated. This will make government work not a stepping-stone but a career for our bright young people. It will cause us to hire the best, to pay them well, and to honor them as, indeed, high government officials in Japan are held in higher esteem than even the top corporate executives in that country.

DREAM 23
RETURNING CORPORATE POWER TO THE SHAREHOLDER

The Achilles heel in the corporate structure is the ownership of stock. Therein lies the ultimate power of the people. To the same extent that corporations can consume the people, people can once more put the corporation under the power of the people. Teachers' pension funds, state employees' retirement funds, union pension funds, and other giant coffers of money own billions in common stocks that the individual contributors to these funds do not vote. Legislation should make it possible for individuals to vote their pro rata shares of stock owned by their funds.

More effective still would be stock-voting collectives that could be formed to hold the individual's proxy to vote his stock for reform and responsibility. For example, the Sierra Club could become a voting trust, owning the proxies of millions of individuals who have chosen that organization to vote their stock for the betterment of the environment. Unions could become voting trusts to vote the proxies of millions of worker-shareholders in support of corporate business that returns jobs to America. Teachers' voting trusts could vote millions of proxies in the corporations in which their funds are invested requiring such corporations to take part in designated projects for the betterment of communities.

The distinguishing characteristic of slavery over freedom is that in the slave state the master joins with other masters in imposing the will of the few over the many. Today, our cry for liberty is a small whimper into the void unless, at last, the master becomes the servant of the people. Corporations can be made to serve the people. Such is my dream.

As good citizens, corporations can become a source of immense good for the world. They can become the power that elevates our species to new realms of accomplishment for the betterment of ourselves, the earth, and its other inhabitants, and by doing so increase their profits. The potential of a world of responsible, caring corporations is nearly beyond dreaming. Still, corporations with a conscience can become the valued friend of man. On the other hand, the terror of continuing to live in a world in which these monsters rage out of control creates a nightmare from which we all must soon awaken, or die in our sleep.

TWENTY-FOUR

—•—

The Death of Our Warriors

———•———

The law is like a spider web where the little flies get caught and the big flies fall through.
—Aristarchus, Greek philologist and critic, circa 150 b.c.

If one really wishes to know how justice is administered in a country, one does not question the policemen, the lawyers, the judges, or the protected members of the middle class. One goes to the unprotected—those, precisely, who need the laws' protection most!—and listens to their testimony.
—James Baldwin, African-American author,
"No Name in the Street," 1972

—Plug the Loopholes, Kill All the Lawyers, Scrap the Justice System—

We have too many lawyers and not enough judges; too many lawsuits and not enough justice. Such is the conventional wisdom of a people skidding down the greased slide to slavery. When the people have been taught, as children are taught their catechism, that the sacred writ of habeas corpus is a loophole to set murderers free and that our constitutional rights are merely tools used by clever lawyers to get the guilty off, when major portions of the people believe that criminal defense lawyers are as evil as their clients, we have thrown away freedom's key.

When the people believe that juries are stupid, that they cannot be trusted, and that legislators should be permitted to cap jury awards and substitute the law for the judgment of our neighbors, we have been duped by the master's propaganda.

There are not too many lawyers. There are too few lawyers who represent the people.

There is not too much litigation. There are too many laws that burden the people.

The courts are not crowded with fraudulent litigation brought on by an avaricious populace. The courts have, instead, become the clearinghouse of large corporations doing business against the people.

There are not too few judges. There are too few judges who have become *persons* before they ascended to the throne to judge people.

There is, indeed, too little justice in America. It has become a commodity that is too costly for ordinary people. It is nearly the exclusive property of the wealthy, an asset on the unpublished balance sheet of the New Master.

Justice is as much the right of the child as the right to breathe. Indeed, we can kill the species by many devices, but the most cruel death of all is the slow, painful death suffered by people who have been starved of simple justice. But justice will always be lost to us unless there are just laws, just lawyers to fight for their enforcement, just judges to interpret them, and just juries to hear the cases of their neighbors.

We can overcome the poverty of justice in America as easily as we can feed the starving and house the poor. We need only want to. When we have endured injustice long enough, when we have suffered the contumelious snarls of the judges long enough, when we have had enough of it—quite enough—we shall have justice.

I was sitting recently in the airport waiting for my flight home to Jackson Hole. A woman who recognized me came up, stuck her face in mine, and said, "What are we going to do about all of these lawyers?"

"What would you like to do about them?" I asked.

"Get rid of them all!" she screeched.

The man sitting next to me joined in. "You said it, lady. There may be a few good ones around"—he gave me a wink to assure me that he meant no insult—"but the most of 'em are a bunch of lyin' thieves. We oughta take 'em all out and shoot 'em. No offense intended," he added with another wink.

"You got it," she said to the man. "We oughta run you for president."

"Well," I asked, "what would we do if we woke up one morning and there were no lawyers?"

"Wonderful!" the woman said in a loud voice. She stuck out her chest and surveyed the waiting crowd to see if she had mustered any support. Numbers of people were listening by now, and several were nodding in her direction.

"Suppose one day you hear your front door being kicked in. What will you do?"

"Call the police," she said.

"What will you do when the dispatcher tells you that those kicking in your front door *are* the police?"

"That's ridiculous," she said. "I would never do anything that would cause them to kick in my door."

"You trust the police, then?" I asked. She was silent for a moment. "Have you ever had anyone in your family charged with a crime?"

She looked at me as if I'd asked her if she had AIDS. Then she said, "Well, my son was charged with DUI. Of course, he wasn't guilty. You know those cops. They have a quota. Emery had had a beer or two. Nothing more. I have never known him to lie. But he pled guilty, and that was that."

"If the police had had a quota for arresting people on charges of treason when they arrested your son, would he have pled guilty?"

"That's ridiculous," she said.

"What if there were no lawyers to defend him or help him get out of jail on bond? Would you think the judge would release him on your statement that you have never known your boy to lie? Think you might need a lawyer?"

"You're just like all the rest," she said, "all that fancy lawyer talk."

Then I turned to the man sitting next to me. "If we take all the lawyers out and shoot them and AT&T decides to run their telephone poles across your front lawn and then through your bedroom, who would present your case in a condemnation proceeding?"

"I was only kidding," he said.

—Hating the Warriors, the Defenders of Freedom—

But many people in this country are not kidding. Most forget that the law, its fair interpretation, and its just enforcement have, from the beginning, been the business of lawyers. A nation without lawyers is a China, a North Korea. There is no need for lawyers in a totalitarian state. Lawyers starve in dictatorships. The court dockets are current in nations in which people have no rights. If people are without rights, there is nothing whatever to engage the judges. We had just as well hate the saints as to hate lawyers. When we hate lawyers, we hate Jefferson, Madison, Adams, Monroe, Hamilton, and Lincoln. I say, we ought not hate lawyers; we ought, instead, hate what some lawyers do.

—Training the Corporate Lawyer—

The problem, simply put, is that we are training lawyers to work for the corporate state in a corporate oligarchy, not to represent people in a democracy. We are training lawyers to represent the nonpeople, and worse, they are being trained with the people's tax money. That is something akin to training the enemy's soldiers. Indeed, America's law schools, utterly dominated by the American Bar Association, are in large part the training ground for the legal troops that will be sent against the people.

Let us take a closer look. The only entrance tests into our law schools are objective: first, the scholastic record of the student, and second, his or her ability to deliver a high score on the Law School Admissions Test (LSAT). That test tests what the testers can test. It does not test any of the qualities sought in lawyers qualified to represent people. The LSAT tests the ability of the candidate to play sophisticated word games. It tests the agility of his mind in certain narrow fields of mentation that have little to do with being a person. Indeed, when the LSAT supplemented undergraduate grades as a selecting tool, the LSAT delivered only 20 percent accuracy in law-school grade prediction, and it predicted graduation from law school only 5 percent of the time better than mere chance.

That the LSAT cannot predict either the successful student or lawyer has been known for many years. A study published in the legal journal *Law and the Social Order* in 1980 concluded, "There is no empirical evidence of a significant correlation between LSAT scores and probable 'success' in the practice of law." Former ABA president Chesterfield Smith admitted, "There is no authority suggesting that the LSAT can predict success," and even those who invented and administered the test have conceded that they "would not say that a low score on the LSAT would be an adequate basis for saying to a student, 'You'll never make it as a lawyer.'" But that is exactly what the law schools of America, directed by the ABA, say to those who are unable to kick up a high enough score on the computer-driven LSAT.

One day I decided to take the thing myself. A sample that students are given to practice on was handed to me by my son, who himself was practicing for the test. I sat down with pen in hand. I felt confident—arrogant, even. Why was so much fuss being raised over this little test? I thought of the hundreds of thousands of lawyers in this country who had passed it. Surely, somehow, I could at least approach their average intellectual powers.

I read the first question, and I puzzled over the multiple choices offered. I pondered. I reasoned. I backtracked. I went over the choices again. I thought of the ways the testers were likely trying to trick me. It was me against them. I read the question a third time. "Wait a minute, Dad," my son said. "Wait just a minute. I gotta time you. Start when I say go."

When my time was up, I hadn't finished the test. My head was swimming. I felt like my fat, out-of-shape brain had just run a marathon. My resulting score was far too low to make it into any law school! This is the experience of most candidates for law school, and they are required to take special courses to pass this thing. We are not selecting lawyers. We are teaching our young to pass a test that tests little. Hundreds of companies offer courses, none of them cheap, to assist the student in passing the LSAT. LSAT prep has become a multimillion-dollar business unto itself. We are lost. We no longer concern ourselves with the magnificence of the whole human mind. We are interested only in whether the brain can manage an obstacle course that leads nowhere and proves nothing.

If I were to ask, "What qualities do you wish your lawyer to possess?" you would likely answer, "I'd want my lawyer to be honest. I'd like him to care about me, to be sensitive to my pain, my fear, and my need for justice. I'd like him to be brave and relentless. I'd want him to be competent. I'd want him to be skilled in communicating with other human beings, because the successful practice of law and the successful trial of lawsuits amounts to nothing more than effective communication." And I would agree with you. A lawyer should possess all of the qualities you have just enumerated.

But having laid out the minimum requirements of a lawyer, we will find, to our horror, that our law schools, under the dictatorship of the American Bar Association, select their students based on none of these attributes. If the applicants have good grades, have no felony record, and have presented a high score on the LSAT, they are in. Welcome to the law. By 1979 the LSAT was required in all 178 of the nation's accredited law schools. I know of no exceptions today. Those we have selected to become our warriors for justice, our zealous advocates for the people, are those who possess the ability to play word games, who can ensnare, entangle, becloud, confound, confuse, and obfuscate better than their rivals. Given this criterion, Mother Teresa, with a low LSAT, would have been excluded, but Charles Manson, before his rampage in murder, would have been sought after by all the leading law schools, including Harvard and Yale.

—A Test That Excludes the Poor and Minorities—

Ralph Nader and Allen Nairn have researched the LSAT in depth and have found that it is as unrelated to the issues of social justice as catsup is to chocolate fudge. Peter J. Liacouras, former dean of Temple University Law School, says that the test sifts out ethnic minorities, and Nader and Nairn say the test tends to rank applicants according to how much their parents earn. As our law schools' reliance on the LSAT has increased, the number of black students in predominantly white schools has decreased, and the LSAT has been shown to exclude white ethnic minorities as well. Computers, not people, are selecting the lawyers of this country. When we engage a lawyer today, we know he has been kissed on both cheeks by a computer: first, the LSAT, a computer-driven test, and second, the Multistate Bar Examination, which is also a computer-driven test imposed on the profession by the ABA. As frightening as it may be, when we look into most lawyers' eyes it is likely that no human being looked into them at the time he was chosen for the profession.

—Training Lawyers for the Rich and Powerful—

Derek Bok, former president of Harvard University, has charged that the law schools of America are geared to supply new and exclusive talent for corporate firms that, in turn, deliver quality representation to the wealthy and the powerful. Bok further charged that the poor and the middle class find their access to the courts blocked by prohibitive costs and a bewildering array of rules and procedures. Bok went on to charge that our law schools have become "the refuge of able, ambitious college seniors who cannot think of anything else they want to do."

What Bok did not tell us, of course, is that the law schools are the profit centers of the universities. We are drowning in the wrong kinds of lawyers today in large part because it costs one-tenth as much to train a lawyer as it does a doctor. The universities can put one underpaid professor in the middle of an auditorium of two hundred or more students and collect hundreds of thousands of dollars in tuition from a single classroom.

John Hart Ely, former dean of Stanford Law School, said, "The students automatically assume from the moment that they're here that a job with a large corporate law firm is the brass ring." But the major law schools of the nation go right on selecting their students in the same old way, producing more of the same kinds of corporate servants they have, in large part, produced from their inception.

Judge Lois G. Forer, serving on the bench in Philadelphia, complained, "The aim of the law schools and their professors was, as it has been for decades, to train the 'brightest and the best' to staff the ever-expanding elite law firms that steadily raised their fees and symbiotically served their wealthy clients."

The writer Herbert Croly called it a "betrayed promise of America."

He argued that America's lawyers are no longer trusted to interpret and lead American constitutional democracy because they have abdicated their role in order to defend special interests instead. To fight for corporate profit. To steer great corporations over the people. To at last enslave the courts themselves to corporate power.

—They All Look Alike—

I think of the thousands of lawyers I have addressed across this land and the thousands of students I have encountered in the law schools. Something eerie has occurred. Their outside appearance reveals, of course, a wide variety of bodies and faces. But they look alike in a more dreadful aspect. They seem to *think* alike, *talk* alike, and *react* alike. They tend to be more mechanized in their thought processes than the population at large. They seem to be more immunized from experiencing the human condition, either in themselves or others. Although their journey into life ought to be a search for justice, they are often passive, rarely reflective; often timid, rarely scrappy; often cynical, rarely guileless; often predictable, rarely creative; often lethargic, rarely energetic; often dull, rarely exciting.

If you scour the home library of most lawyers, you will find little to read—some *Reader's Digest* books perhaps, several sets of the classics in their showy leather and gold bindings, their covers as stiff and unbroken as the day they came from the publisher. They may have read the latest Grisham. But they have likely never read *To Kill a Mockingbird*. They may have perused a law book or two they have dragged home out of desperation to meet a deadline. But they have never read the transcript of Clarence Darrow's Scopes trial.

—The Culture of Lawyers—

Among professionals, lawyers are the most uncultured of the lot. They would rather play a computer game than read a classic. They would rather watch *Wheel of Fortune* than paint. They would rather play golf than take a walk in the woods alone. They are a peculiar lot, often insulated from the forces of life itself, and although there are some great writers, poets, persons, communicators, musicians, and citizens among lawyers, there is also a ghastly paucity of the same.

But how can we expect more of such lawyers, these disadvantaged who are the mere siblings of the same mother—the computer—and who are excreted from the law schools as half man, half machine? What we behold here are members of a profession charged with saving us from despotism who are, instead, expert at droning pedantic legalisms and whose love is not for a living justice but for the dead—dead money.

—THE PATHETIC EDUCATION OF THE AMERICAN LAWYER—

And so now that we have these automatons admitted into our law schools—the kind who have excited the computer into some kind of orgasmic cybertizzy—how are they to be taught? And by whom? They are taught the law by others of their kind, the undertakers of the profession, the professors. Most law professors have never encountered an alive client, have never walked shaky-legged into a courtroom to defend the poor, the damned, or the maimed. Most are the kind who have never struggled to pay the rent and have never had to fight single-handedly some four-hundred-person law firm to get a little justice for a little person.

If we educated our surgeons as we do our trial lawyers . . . well, let us look in on such a scene. Imagine that a person with a brain tumor walks into a surgeon's office and, after an appropriate wait of several hours, is shown to a closet-size room with one chair and an examining table with intimidating full-color charts of brains and malignancies of every kind and character, the arteries in blue, the vessels, like thousands of hair roots, in red. Eventually, in comes the surgeon in his white smock, all serious, his nose wrinkling to hold up the thick glasses that continue to slide down his nose.

"How may I help you?" he asks.

"I'm told I have a brain tumor. I am looking for a surgeon. I was wondering if you would be able to operate on it for me."

"Of course," the doctor says with all due confidence. He points to a diploma in a gold-leafed frame that hangs on the wall. The paper contains an important-looking seal impressed in the lower left corner, and scrawled on it are a variety of illegible but official-looking signatures. "My diploma," he says.

"Yes, but have you done a lot of these?"

Silence. The doctor seems focused on his ever-sliding glasses. Finally he pushes them up with his thumb and says, "No."

"Have you ever done a brain surgery?"

"Well, no."

"But you would be willing to operate on me?"

"Of course."

Dumbfounded, the prospective patient asks, "Well, certainly you have done other operations. You've done an appendectomy?" he asks hopefully.

"No, I haven't," the doctor says impatiently.

"Well, how about a simple tonsillectomy?"

"No."

"*No?*"

"No."

"Well, certainly you were taught how to do these operations by professors who were expert at them."

"Well, no."

"*No?*"

"No. You see," the doctor at last attempts to explain, "our professors were the type who didn't want to get their hands bloody. That is why they became professors."

In this same way in today's law schools, our young, these future surgeons of the law, are trained as trial lawyers by professors, most of whom have never been in a courtroom. Most graduating lawyers have tried only a minor case or two in a clinic attached to the law school that serves as little more than an apology for no trial training at all.

I would rather have a nurse as a trial assistant than a lawyer fresh out of law school. The nurse has gone into her profession because she *cares* about people, not because she wants to gouge their money from them. She has been trained to *listen*. She can hear the patient, observe his pain, record it, and administer to his needs. Not so the young lawyer who has never learned to listen, to care, or to administer to his client.

In law school, I never saw a deed, never saw a contract, never saw a will, never met a client, never peered into a dark jail cell at a wretched prisoner. When I got out of law school, I went down to old Shorty Anderson's wool shed in Riverton, Wyoming, where the six-foot-long sacks of wool hung from the rafters and dripped the stench of wool grease as it melted in the heat of Shorty's potbellied stove. He was the justice of the peace, and he sat behind a card table next to the stove, the wool sacks hanging the full length of the shed behind him like rotting corpses in burlap. He pulled forms out of a box behind his desk and showed me how to fill them in so I could file my first justice of the peace case in his court—a claim for under twenty-five dollars. I was taught the *practice of law* by the likes of Shorty Anderson. I learned the law at the expense of my clients—one sad, painful case at a time.

And since those early days, things have not dramatically improved in our law schools. Worse than their lack of training, young lawyers emerge from law school void of creativity, heavy-headed and dull. Clarence Darrow said it: "The law is a bum profession. It is utterly devoid of idealism and almost poverty stricken as to any real ideas."

Although a few innovative professors struggle against the old ways, most still stumble blindly along the path laid out for them in 1870 by Christopher Columbus Langdell, dean of Harvard Law School, who left his irrevocable scar on legal education when he proclaimed, out of a brain fluttering on high, "What qualifies a person to teach law is not experience in the work of a lawyer's office, and not experience in dealing with men, nor experience in the trial or argument of cases, not experience in short, in using law, but experience in learning law." The law schools of the nation have been following his impotent, blind lead ever since.

Langdell was the father of the casebook method of teaching law that requires students to read mountains of cases, from which they are to extract the facts, the question in the case, and the holding of the court. That method consumes, more or less, three years of the student's time. The law it teaches could be learned in a fraction of the time, and any teacher could, in ten minutes, teach a reasonably intelligent eighth grader how to read a case in the Langdell method.

Langdell sought to endow the study of law with the dignity of a science. Said he, with utter authority, "It will scarcely be disputed that the law is one of the greatest and most difficult of sciences, and that it needs all of the light that the most enlightened seat of learning can throw upon it." He spoke nothing of justice. How could Langdell have known differently from his lofty view above the riffraff?

The law is not a science unless we wish science to become the embodiment of the day's whimsy and the reflection of the night's desire. *The law is a happening.* It cannot be studied as we study the physiology of a frog. It can only be experienced in the course of human lives. It is a dynamic search for justice, not a pedantic hymn tripping off the lips of stiff-collared professors.

Langdell, who likely would have withered in a courtroom like a rose in an oven, thought that "reading the law" in the office of a practicing lawyer, as was the education of Abraham Lincoln, should no longer be tolerated. "We must teach the student to think like lawyers," he cried. *To think like lawyers?* As if this mysterious cerebral exercise called the law would disqualify the lawyer from thinking like a human being!

—JUSTICE BE DAMNED—

The first concern of our law schools is not justice. In fact, in most classrooms, no student dare speak of justice. The student who objects to the ruling of a case on the grounds that it is "unjust" is often mocked by the professors and held up to the students as naïve and laughable. The words of Oliver Wendell Holmes have become immortalized in the law schools: "Do not speak to me of justice, young man. This is a court of law." Such bleakness in the judiciary is akin to the professor in medical school reproaching his students gathered about the patient on the operating table, "Do not speak to me about saving the life of this patient. This is a scientific operation!"

If we understand that to the species justice is often more important than food or shelter, that whole nations have laid down the lives of their sons for justice, that people will make all manner of sacrifice for it, then must we not begin to understand how crucial justice is to the human condition, and how poorly our lawyers are trained to fight for it? In an unjust world the cry for brave advocates for the people is heard across the land. The failure of lawyers to hear the cry, to listen to the anguish of a people seeking justice, is the principal reason people hold lawyers in such disdain.

But can we correct this student abuse? I call it abuse because it is as much an abuse to deprive young, principled people of their education as it is to slam the baby in the closet and lock the door forever.

Dream 24
New Warriors for the People

Let me tell you a story: We have proven that even in their mature years, lawyers can be saved, first as human beings and after that as warriors for the people. We are in our fifth year at our nonprofit Trial Lawyer's College (TLC), a pilot program we have organized and which we conduct every year at my ranch for training trial lawyers for the people.

I took the old cow barn and converted it to small stalls for sparse living quarters. No private baths. The attendees eat in the ranch cook house, do the dishes, and clean the latrines to remind them that they are no better than the people they fight for. Young men and women of all races who have demonstrated by their careers that they care about people are selected and invited, based not on their scholastic records, not on what law school they attended, not on who they know, not on their parentage or how much money they have, but on their record of striving for justice for the people. Corporate lawyers are not invited and cannot attend. Nor can prosecutors. Big-firm lawyers are not accepted. Only peoples' lawyers can come.

Most are poor single practitioners or come from two- or three-person firms or are public defenders. If these young people do not have the money to attend (and many do not), we somehow find the money for them.

The best trial lawyers in America are invited to attend as colleagues—"old warriors," we call them—to share with the young warriors what the old heads know and what they've learned though experience in the trial of lawsuits. The old warriors make their gifts of knowledge and experience without charge. The opportunity to share what they have learned with those who will follow them is a gift of immortality to the old warrior, for immortality is nothing more than the transfer of the best of our human experiences to the next generation.

The first step in the program at Trial Lawyer's College is to give the young warriors the opportunity to become human again. By the time they are out of law school, most humanity has been driven from them in the educational holocaust they have endured. Beginning in kindergarten, they have been forced to conform, to think as others think, to see things as others see them. The minds of students in this country are cast in molds of conventional thought so that by the time they emerge eighteen years later, they are merely predictable replacement parts for the larger machine. Those who have the most to offer are often discarded as incorrigible. Those who are the most creative often cannot endure the pain generated by academia's perpetual clubbing of the muse. Those who have ideals and high values, those who are motivated by the love of mankind and seek to better the human condition, are soon discouraged, and many drop by the wayside.

At our Trial Lawyer's College, both young warriors and old are given the opportunity to rediscover themselves. They are put through days of psychodrama by experienced psychologists. Just as important, they learn how to crawl into the hides of their clients, to experience their pain, to understand the witness on the witness stand, even to understand and care for their opponent. In the course of their training, they become the judge, and also feel how it is to be the juror.

Before the session is over, they have learned to sing again, for their voices are the principal instrument with which the songs of justice are sung. One cannot argue one's case for one's client with a one-stringed fiddle.

They paint. Lawyers painting? The act of striking the first stroke upon the canvas is akin to choosing the first word spoken in the courtroom before the jury. The picture must be painted for the jury. The last word must be chosen, the last stroke; the time to say no more must be recognized, knowing, as they learn with canvas and brush, that one stroke, one word too many, can ruin it all.

Many times I have had these bright young warriors come to me, weeping unashamedly over their canvas, for they have begun to realize that within them is something extraordinary that had been hidden from them, a spirit, a sense of self that was smothered from childhood.

These young warriors for the people are sent off into the wilderness alone to watch the sun rise and to answer simple questions: Who am I? What do I wish to do with my life? Gradually, very gradually, they become human beings again. And having learned to love themselves, they are more able to love their clients.

By the end of their experience at TLC, we have witnessed a miracle. Nearly every attendee has entered into the most sacred realm of human experience—that place I call personhood. They have learned to tell the truth, not only about their case but about themselves. They have learned the power of credibility. They have learned by repeated efforts in the makeshift courtrooms—some in the barn, some in the milk house—how to select a jury, how to make an effective opening statement, how to cross-examine, and how to deliver a winning final argument. There they learn how to fight for justice and to help the people realize that in America the law can still deliver justice and free the innocent.

The young warriors learn to trust—to trust themselves, to trust each other, and to trust juries. By the time the month in that isolated place without television or newspapers is over, they have learned more about the essential ingredients of trial lawyering than most lawyers learn in a lifetime. Then the miracles are tested outside in the real world. The miracles continue.

Case after case that could not be won before is now being won, cases against huge odds, against the corporate behemoths, against the Goliaths of government. Lawyers who had given up the practice of law as stale and meaningless have found new life. The testimonials bulge in the files.

—Kicking Over the Rotted Log—

As long ago as 1910, Woodrow Wilson was complaining about "lawyers who have been sucked into the maelstrom of the new business system of the country. They do not practice law. They do not handle the general, miscellaneous interests of society. They are not general counselors of right and obligation." He charged that corporate lawyers were to blame. "The country holds them largely responsible for it. It distrusts every corporate lawyer."

The distinguished scholar Jerold S. Auerbach observed that corporate lawyers were distrusted not because they were bad persons but because "corporate interests were ipso facto antithetical to social interests." Justice Louis D. Brandeis told his Harvard audience that "able lawyers have allowed themselves to become adjuncts of great corporations and have neglected their obligations to use their powers for the protection of the people." Today, Ralph Nader and Wesley J. Smith, in their courageous book *No Contest*, "kick over the rotted log our corporate-dominated legal system has become" to show how individual justice has been all but abandoned in America.

But the public knows. And as the public sees it, lawyers are to blame and lawyers are not trustworthy. Too few lawyers meet the expectations of their clients. But as deficient, even degenerate as many in the profession are, much of the blame does not rest with the individual practitioner. You cannot fault the doctor for the death of his patient when the doctor has been trained, say, to treat nearly all illnesses by bleeding his patient in order to release the offending demons. Legal training is nearly as far behind.

—Lawyers, Sick of the Law—

America's lawyers themselves know that something is tragically wrong. Disappointed, burned out, tired of billing pressures, sickened by the law and its meaningless machinery, 72 percent said in a recent survey that they enjoyed the law less than when they began practice, and 70 percent said that they would take advantage of an opportunity to change careers. Fifty-five percent said they didn't have enough time for themselves.

Sixty percent of recent disciplinary actions taken against lawyers in California and Oregon were blamed on chemical dependency or stress-related illnesses. The survey didn't inquire as to whether lawyers believed they were obtaining justice for the people, but I can think of no more deadly load to carry than the endless entanglements of the legal practice that goes nowhere, for no one, except to meet the billing quota of the attorney. Sadly, such has become irrelevant to justice.

—FREEING OUR LAWYERS, FREEING OURSELVES—

At last, we cannot be free until we free our lawyers. Until the people's advocates are trained to fight for us, we shall always be slaves. As long as our law schools, supported by our tax money, continue to disgorge hundreds of thousands of lawyers each year who have been inadequately and cheaply educated, the "best and brightest" of whom are scraped off the top by corporate America, we shall be never be freed.

As long as our law schools are dominated by academic drones, we shall never train fighters for the people. As long as we cling to the pathetic past in the education of our warriors, we shall remain forever enslaved in the future. And as long as we hate our warriors, distrust them and defile them, we shall remain at the mercy of the master. And as long as our lawyers listen only to the crinkle of dollars in their ears, the people's cry for help will never be heard.

TWENTY-FIVE

·•·

Judges, the Master's Henchmen

————— ·•· —————

Scarcely any political question arises in the United States that is not resolved, sooner or later, into a judicial question.
—ALEXIS DE TOCQUEVILLE,
DEMOCRACY IN AMERICA, 1835

—A COUNCIL OF KINGS—

America has been betrayed by her judges. Generation after generation of those to whom we have entrusted the critical ingredient of democracy, our liberty, have betrayed us. Although they have been granted only the power to interpret the law, in truth they make it.

—THE YARD LIGHT IN THE PRISON—

This Constitution, this remarkable instrument that we have cherished as the beacon of liberty, has become instead the yard light in the prison. The principal bedeviling force has been the unlimited power of a Supreme Court peopled by judges who represent not the powerless many but the powerful few. Jefferson saw the danger from the outset. A lawyer himself, he distrusted judges. Here is what he said:

It has long, however, been my opinion . . . that the germ of dissolution of our federal government is in the constitution of the federal judiciary; an irresponsible body working like gravity by night and by day, gaining a little today and a little tomorrow, and advancing its noiseless step like a thief over the field of jurisdiction, until all shall be usurped from the States, and the government of all consolidated into one. To this I am opposed; because when all government, domestic and foreign, in little as in great things, shall be drawn to Washington as the center of all power, it will render powerless the checks provided of one government on another, and will become as venal and oppressive as the government from which we separated.

—How the Judiciary Fathered the Corporate Master—

By the time of the Constitution, our countrymen had already endured over a hundred years of corporate domination. The East India Company, the king's corporation chartered in 1600 to carry on the business of the throne, maintained its own army, conducted its private wars, and eventually opened up the opium trade with China. And the Hudson's Bay Company, another corporation, exploited the Indians and denuded large portions of the nation of its fur-bearing animals.

It was the East India Company that forced cheap government-subsidized tea on the colonists, leading inexorably to the explosion of the Boston Tea Party, the preface to the American Revolution. Suffice it to say, our Founding Fathers saw the corporate form as a weapon of enslavement wielded against them by a tyrant king and, above all, sought to protect themselves against the rise of corporate power in America.

Yet the regenerating powers of the corporate hydra are nearly inconceivable. By 1791, the federal government itself had already organized the Bank of the United States, a corporation, and in 1816, corporations were again threatening the vision of the framers. In that year, Thomas Jefferson said, "I hope we shall crush in its birth the aristocracy of our moneyed corporations which dare already challenge our government to a trial of strength, and bid defiance to the laws of our country."

Then the courts took over. In 1819, Chief Justice John Marshall, in the celebrated case of *McCulloch* v. *Maryland*, upheld the right of the federal government to form corporations under its "implied powers" for governmental or quasi-governmental purposes. And in 1886, as John

Adams had predicted, the American grand experiment in democracy suffered what would prove to be a fatal blow when in the now infamous *Santa Clara* v. *Southern Pacific Railroad* case the United States Supreme Court ruled that the fictional person—the corporation—should have the *same rights as a living person* and was entitled to the same protections of the Fourteenth Amendment.

The Supreme Court, endowing the corporate fiction with life, held that the states were no longer permitted to withhold from the corporation its life, liberty, or property without due process of law. Corporations with power exceeding many of the states—indeed, with economies larger than those of many sovereign nations—were thereafter protected by the Constitution to the same degree as living persons. To put things in historical perspective, in 1776, Virginia had 493,000 inhabitants. By 1976, General Motors already had 681,000 employees. Ours is a nation of nation-states, for corporations have, in substantial ways, replaced the concept of statehood, and they enjoy rights under the Constitution that even the states do not.

Corporations with no loyalty to the United States, with no soul, corporations that could not be imprisoned for their crimes or executed for their murders, corporations who were to become the owners of presidents and Congress itself, were now given the same rights as the citizen under the Constitution. But, as we have seen, the duties of good citizenship were not concurrently imposed upon the corporation.

The *Santa Clara* decision stretched the Constitution until its very fabric tore. It gave to the corporate-behemoth the right to compete constitutionally with the citizen-ant. Sixty years later, Justice William O. Douglas would write, "There was no history, logic or reason given to support that view." But the *Santa Clara* case became the dreary dirge by which the new king, the corporate state, was crowned.

—THE POPULAR PASTIME OF CONSTITUTION WHITTLING—

From the earliest times, the United States Supreme Court began its constitution whittling. In 1819, Chief Justice John Marshall made the first deep thrust into the sovereign rights of the state. In the famed *Dartmouth College* case, the court held that the Constitution prohibited

New Hampshire from revoking a charter granted to the college in 1769 by King George III. The court's attack on the sovereignty of the states outraged many. Protest pamphlets flooded the country. Thomas Earle, a nineteenth-century pamphleteer, wrote, "It is an aristocracy and despotism to have a body of officers [the judges] whose decisions are, for a long time, beyond the control of the people."

David Henshaw, a Massachusetts legislator, said it more purposely: "Sure I am that, if the American people acquiesce in the principles laid down in this case, the Supreme Court will have effected what the whole power of the British Empire, after eight years of bloody conflict, failed to achieve against our fathers."

Following the Civil War, these judges, always carefully chosen as the faithful voice of power, gave certain corporations the power of eminent domain—the right to take the property of citizens with minimum compensation. Often, when corporate interests were involved, they eliminated jury trials, and by modern times, except in criminal cases, they eliminated the jury trial altogether, leaving only the empty *appearance* of a jury trial to placate the people.

—CAPONIZING THE AMERICAN JURY—

The judicial scheme of eliminating the jury but leaving it on display for all to see in the courtroom has been one of the remarkable magical tricks in the macabre history of the judiciary. By permitting juries to assemble to hear the cases and seemingly decide them, but stripping juries of their actual power, the courts have left the people believing their sacred jury is intact when, in fact, so far as cases against the corporate king are concerned, the jury is often powerless.

Today, in civil cases, juries are dutifully called to hear the evidence and return their verdicts. But ultimately, juries do not decide such cases. These are cases in which injured citizens, the sexually harassed, and those who have been discriminated against seek justice. Aside from those between warring corporate interests, these are cases of widows and orphans, of cripples and paupers, of the defrauded and wasted who come pleading to the court for justice. They are usually cases of the ordinary citizen, "the little guy" against the corporate leviathan: claims by workers against the corporate employer, the corporate manufacturer, the corporate banks, and the omnipresent insurance companies whose secret presence dominates the courts today.

In such cases, the juries return their verdicts, and the people believe they have been heard by their peers. But at all levels the judges give the juries' verdicts only as much weight as the judges, in their sole discretion, deem appropriate, which depends on the judge and, too often, to whom the judge is beholden for his appointment, or upon whom the judge depends for his continued occupancy of the bench.

In America, trial by jury has become another myth. In the trial itself, the jury is permitted to hear only the evidence the judge will allow. And although the proper function of a judge is to eliminate from the trial evidence what is unreliable or unfairly prejudicial, it is the judge himself who shapes the trial. Like the baker, he decides what ingredients will be used to make the cake—and if the sugar is omitted, we simply don't have much of a cake. In this country, cases are as much decided by who the judge is as by what the evidence is.

But the selection of the evidence is not the sole control exercised by the judge over the jury. Before they are seated, all jurors must raise their right hand and swear or affirm to follow the law as given to them by the judge, and jurors who will not agree to follow the instructions of the court are disqualified from sitting on any jury. Often jurors must obediently follow the judge's instructions whether the jurors agree that the instructions are just or not. I have seen jurors emerge from the jury room, their eyes filled with tears because they were jammed into moral conflict by a judge who instructed them, under their oath, to apply a law the jurors felt unjust.

Juries today, especially on the civil side of the law where corporate money is usually at stake, are often mere figureheads whose most predominant function is to perpetuate the myth that we enjoy a jury system in this country. Instead of looking to the jury for ultimate justice, the injured citizen must first obtain the jury's verdict before he can face the *real* jury, the appeals court, where are often seated the master's own jury, the appellate judges, who always possess the power to substitute their judgment for that of the jury.

The Founders believed in juries and held judges in high suspicion.

Understanding that justice does not come in one size and one shape but must be tailored to fit the person and the situation, jurors were given the power to nullify the law and to view it as merely a guide-line to justice. If the individual is the keystone to democracy, then individual justice must be delivered as well, a justice tailor-made for the case.

America's founders saw jurors as the protectors of the individual from the tyrannical yoke of unjust rule. John Adams said in 1771 that it was not only the right of the juror but his *duty* "to find the verdict according to his own best understanding, judgment and conscience, though in opposition to the direction of the court." Even the conservative Alexander Hamilton, who stood for the commercial interests of the new nation, stated in 1804 that the jurors in a criminal case were duty-bound to acquit, despite the instructions of the judge, "if exercising their judgment with discretion and honesty they have a clear conviction that the charge of the court is wrong."

John Jay, the first chief justice of the U.S. Supreme Court, told a jury, "Gentlemen, you have a right to determine the law as well as the facts in controversy." Thomas Jefferson described the jury's function thusly: "If the question relates to any point of public liberty, or if it be one of those in which the judges may be suspected of bias, the jury undertakes to decide both law and fact."

—NULLIFYING THE JURY'S RIGHT TO NULLIFY INJUSTICE—

The right to *jury nullification* was intended as the statement of the Founders decrying the absolutism of the king's rule. But the courts would soon take away the people's right when justice required it to nullify the law. In 1895, in the case of *Aparf and Hanse* v. *United States,* the Supreme Court amputated the right leg of the people's liberty by terminating the power of federal juries to nullify the law. Since then, nearly every state has followed suit.

Today, the jury follows the law not as justice conceives it but as the judge dictates it. Except for an acquittal in a criminal case, today, if the judge does not agree with the verdict rendered, the judge may nullify the jury's decision altogether. Moreover, judges may non-suit injured people, throwing their cases out of court before a jury can even hear them, or instead of setting the verdict aside, the judge may, after the jury returns its verdict, reduce the verdict or alter its terms to suit him.

This is not to argue that judges ought not be empowered to set aside the occasional obvious miscarriage of justice that might occur in their courts, or that appellate courts ought not, as a collective mind, cautiously review the proceedings below, for a system in which both judges and juries are dedicated to the search for justice is the most powerful system of all. But too often judges have come to usurp their power and abuse their function, with the result that judges, not juries, decide our cases.

—JEFFERSON WAS RIGHT—

At the end of the day, Jefferson saw the fatal flaw—"that the germ of dissolution of our federal government is in the constitution of the federal judiciary; an irresponsible body . . ."

Our courts make the law. Judges hold the power to affirm or veto every piece of legislation that the people's representatives might pass. Yet the judges remain above it, and despite their decisions and their indifference to the great wrongs suffered by many, they cannot be removed for their judgments. And even though their decisions may prove to be as stupid as the blitherings of high-perched idiots, those who practice before them, under the penalty of contempt, are not permitted to criticize. They are the high council of kings in America, thrones, robes, pomp, and all. Each has his own fiefdom, his own supreme domain. Some are more mighty than others, but the high courts can deprive the citizen of his rights, his property, and his life without having seen the person, read his case, or heard his plea. And one could as easily flip a coin as predict with any accuracy the justice that would dribble from the mouths of any given bank of judges on any given day in America.

And when judges of the United States Supreme Court cannot read the same law in the same way on the same day from the same book, but split in almost every case along party lines, can we still credibly argue that this is a court of law and not an elitist body politic?

—THE FALSE LIGHT OF GREAT JUDGES—

To be sure, we have been gifted with many great and brave judges who have struggled vainly to deliver justice to the people. I think of Judge Learned Hand and Justice William O. Douglas. I think of Justice Rose Bird of California, who chose to be expelled by the voters rather than renounce her abhorrence of the death penalty. I think of Frank Theis on the federal bench in Wichita, who stood firm against all corporate pressures in the trial of Karen Silkwood. I think of Harl Haas of Portland, Oregon, who found a better way to deal with drug addicts and street criminals, and Judge Miles Lord, who, in open court, called the corporate manufacturers of the Dalkon Shield to task for their immorality. I think of Judge Robert R. Rose, to whom this book is dedicated, one of the greatest human beings who ever graced the face of this earth.

I know many great judges who distinguish the judiciary with an uprightness of purpose and a passion for duty and who stand for the best sentiments of America. I have seen their troubled eyes as they tugged against the tether-stake of the law, often as helpless to deliver justice to the deserving as the people's advocates before them.

But the great judges of this country often do us little service, for although they are the few shining lights, we focus on them believing, as is our wont, that our judiciary is as they. The great judges of this country have become false symbols. Instead we should hoist on high for all to see those other rascals who populate the courts of this nation and who deprive the people of the smallest measure of justice.

—THE LUST FOR POWER—

Judges, like any politician, seek the bench for only two reasons: to serve the people, or to serve themselves. After over forty years in this country's courtrooms, I regret to report that for every judge who would, no matter the obstacles, stay the course for justice for the people, there are hundreds who will turn their heads with little more concern than having swatted a fly. Too many judges, usually in a reflection of the power structure that selected them, suscribe to the notion that what's good for business will be justice for the people.

Judges' pay is not phenomenal. Most, in truth, would not take a money bribe, and in that sense most are honest. But in the same way that those who seek public office do so because they crave power, judges become judges because they need to judge others. Grateful exceptions noted, many need to be fawned over and to exert power over the helpless. Always they need to be right. As a group, they are the most insecure, frightened, self-hating men (and, today, a few women) I have encountered outside of the penitentiary, where prison guards run the judges a close second.

The lust for power rests on a foundation not of strength but of weakness. It is, as Erich Fromm explains, "the expression of the inability of the individual self to stand alone and live. It is the desperate attempt to gain secondary strength where genuine strength is lacking." The truly potent person does not require power to dominate others, and thus lacks all lust for it. "Power," says Fromm, "in the sense of domination, is the perversion of competency, just as sexual sadism is the perversion of sexual love."

We know that the individual who is heavily soaked in sadism may consciously believe that he is motivated by his sense of duty. He may even cloak his sadistic drives so that he appears on the surface as a person who exists without them. Yet Fromm says that "any close analysis of his behavior, his fantasies, dreams, and gestures would show the sadistic impulses operating in deeper layers of his personality." Fromm sees such persons as revealing what he calls the "authoritarian character."

The authoritarian personality described by Fromm habitually finds its way to the benches of America. This is not news to any lawyer who practices much before the courts. What I say is simply not often said by lawyers, since we must appear before these judges, and indeed, if not distinguished for their service to mankind, they are renowned for their long memories and vindictive hearts. If we could earn the confidence of veteran trial lawyers and persuade them to speak to us in candor, we would find them in agreement—that although America is blessed with many good judges who struggle to deliver justice, overall our judges fail to fulfill the expectations we have for the judiciary.

—THE BRAWL IN THE LIFEBOAT—

Nor, I must admit, do most judges respect most lawyers. Most judges disdain most lawyers, and although their aversion is often well deserved, some judges needlessly and without cause go out of their way to embarrass lawyers, to cause them pain, work, and worry. Too many do whatever they may to exert their power over lawyers, to disrupt their lives and cost them and their clients unnecessary expense in time and money. Despite that they are often justified in their belief that lawyers are incompetent, many judges forget that they were once lawyers—and, most often, mediocre lawyers at that.

In theory, lawyers are officers of the court. That means that the judge and the lawyers in the case, acting together, have the responsibility of rendering justice. But is that not impossible when the team of judge and lawyers despise, distrust, and disrespect each other? Is justice not improbable when the judge is neurotically motivated to exercise his power over lawyers and litigants alike, and the lawyers are motivated to take part in the process only to gain wealth? Too often judges and lawyers relate to one another, albeit with all external decorum and propriety, like brawling ruffians in a lifeboat.

—A CASE IN COURT—

Consider for a moment this typical case: A husband and father is run over and killed by a drunk. The drunk is insured by a major insurance company. His wife and children sue for the loss of their loved one, for being deprived of his earnings that supported them, for the doctor and hospital bills incurred before he died, for the cost of his funeral and burial, and for the family's "loss of care, comfort, advice, and society," as the law, in its stifled sentiments refers to the ripping apart of the family from the death of the husband and parent. Variations of this case are filed every year in our courts by the thousands. Because the family is without funds to hire a lawyer, a personal-injury lawyer agrees to represent the family on a contingency fee, the lawyer earning a percentage of what he recovers for the family.

Now in comes the insurance company with its bevy of lawyers to defend the drunk. The company hires the best and, win or lose, pays them by the hour. These lawyers take the depositions—the sworn testimony—of all of the family's witnesses, including the wife and children themselves. The company's lawyers hire experts on, say, the Breathalyzer test to testify that it was unreliable and that the drunk was not under the influence of alcohol. Or the company lawyers hire reconstruction experts to say that, whether he was drunk or not, the accident took place on the drunk's side of the road. The company lawyers hire doctors who claim that the dead man may have died for reasons other than his injuries—perhaps the negligence of a doctor intervened—and the company lawyers hire psychologists to testify that the family was not such a close-knit group after all and that the father's loss to the family was minimal, perhaps even a benefit. At last the company lawyers hire an economist who will show that the family's loss of the father's income, whatever it was, is reducible to much smaller numbers than the family demands.

In the meantime, the lawyer for the family may hire many of his own experts to testify to the same issues. He, too, takes the depositions of the drunk's witnesses and advances thousands of dollars in deposition costs. Before the case comes to trial, the insurance company lawyer will ask the judge to throw out the case. Sometimes the case has no merit and should be dismissed. But more often, an insensitive or impatient judge, once an insurance company lawyer with an insurance company bias will throw out a just case before the jury has had an opportunity to hear it. The family's only remedy then is to appeal to yet more judges who may lean in the same direction.

If the family is lucky in its draw of the judge and its choice of a lawyer, perhaps the case will be set for trial. Sometimes motions and pretrial proceedings can extend over months or years. At times cases are old enough to go to school before they get to a jury. Judges go on vacation. Judges are busy. Other cases that are considered to be of greater urgency may preempt the family's case. Attorneys find ways to delay the case. Sometimes a judge will sit on the decision of a simple motion for months, even years. Lawyers spar. Often the injured party gives up and settles the case for an unjust amount. The misery goes on and on as justice remains stuck in the corner.

By the time the day of trial arrives, only a small portion of the testimony available will go to the jury, and usually the amount of the family's claim will be pared down to match the legal boundaries set by hostile legislatures or by the judges themselves. Caps on jury awards to injured people have been adopted in many states. Perhaps the judge's rulings will be fair. Perhaps not. But always, the law requires that the parties, by omission, lie to the jury. The parties on both sides of the case are bound by law never to divulge or even intimate to the jury that the drunk, who is sitting in the courtroom in his shabby suit and who looks poor and pathetic, will *not* have to pay the verdict the jury returns—his insurance company will.

No attorney can suggest the truth to the jury—that one of the most powerful corporations in the world sits behind the drunk, hires the best lawyers money can buy, pays his court costs, provides him his witnesses, and will pay the final judgment in the case. The fact that an insurance company is the real party, the nonliving corporate party hiding behind the face of a live human being, remains the secret held from the jury in nearly every case.

Now suppose that after all of the mountains of pretrial paper have been filed and the arguments made, after months and years have elapsed since the case was originally filed, the judge has finally allowed the case to be submitted to the jury. These lawyers for the companies know how to talk to juries. They are usually the ones with the open, honest faces. They are usually reasonable-sounding men and women who appear to be the most decent, considerate kind. And the poor drunk, who wasn't drunk, they argue, and was on his own side of the road when the accident took place—this poor man who sits here in his rags and with his sad face—ought not be held responsible and penalized for the rest of his life—not on the flimsy evidence in this case.

The skillful company lawyers argue on. They remind the jury of the law that the judge has given the jurors that says the jurors cannot be governed by sympathy. "And remember," the company lawyer will say with a small, kind smile, "you folks took an oath to follow the law."

But even when the jury returns a just verdict for the family, it can mean little. It is merely the ticket the family must first obtain in order to get to the *real jury*—the appellate judges. And who is this new set of judges the family must face? Had their kind been drawn as jurors at the trial, the family would have thrown most of them off the case for their bias. But the family cannot take part in choosing this jury of judges who will now hear the family's case when the insurance company appeals. The rule is always gilded with exceptions, of course, but the appellate judges of the nation at both the state and federal levels have often been chosen by special interests, by politicians—usually, in short, by corporate power.

Now that the family's case is in the court of appeals, what will be the fate of the jury's verdict? This new jury of judges has never seen the family and never will. This judicial jury has never looked into the eyes of the wife or seen the agony of the children. These judges will take the lawyers' briefs, which have been written in flat, unemotional legalese, and even then the judges may not read them. No one can make judges read briefs. Indeed, lawyers know and judges know that some judges never open a brief. In many cases their clerks, often young, wrinkle-free children fresh out of law school, read the briefs, after which they brief the judges on the briefs.

Now the judges will hear the arguments of counsel. But often the case will be put on an abbreviated docket so that the lawyers have only fifteen minutes to argue—only fifteen minutes about a decision that must last a widow and her children their lifetimes! Sometimes the judges do not listen, not even for fifteen minutes. They may be thinking of their golf game. They may be thinking of the argument they should have made to their wives at the breakfast table. They may be in dreamland. No one can make these judges listen. But one should not blame the judges entirely. One must credit them with extreme endurance, facing, as they often do, the deadly boring presentations made by many lawyers.

After the arguments, the judges will retire to their cloaking room, disrobe, and then kick back and decide the case. Politics sometimes take over. One judge may vote one way in one case if another will vote another way in another. They will likely never look at a law book—that is the work of clerks. They will not decide the case according to the black-letter law because, more than likely, there is law on both sides of the question. In the end, each judge will vote for a result that reflects his individual philosophy of justice, religion, politics, economics, and human behavior.

Next, one of the judges will be assigned by the chief judge to write the majority decision. The majority may have altered the jury's verdict or voted to throw the case out altogether. On the other hand, the majority may have affirmed the verdict, especially if it went against the family. But these judges have the absolute power to do as they please, the jury be damned. When the judges want the jury's verdict to stand, they will cite the jury as the ultimate authority. They will even say they cannot alter the jury's verdict so long as there is substantial evidence to support it. But if the judges wish to set the verdict aside, they can do so on endless grounds—that the trial judge erred in the evidence or the law, or that there was no substantial evidence upon which the jury could have based its decision, to mention the most common reasons offered. And after the appellate court is finished with the case, in some states there is an appeal to yet a higher court.

Be that as it may, the jury no longer retains the power to deliver justice to the people. Instead, the jury's verdict has become a hurdle that must first be jumped by the injured party before the injured party reaches the appeals court, where he must then jump though a new set of judicial hoops in his nearly endless and, too often, futile pursuit of justice.

—How the Kings Ascend—

Who are these judges, and how do they ascend to the bench to glare down, to pass their judgments on man and beast and child and property? Some are elected, of course, and some are appointed for life. In larger cities, the people rarely have any idea who the judges are who run for election. They have never met them, never heard of them. They are often part of a party's ticket, and the voters, loyal to the party, go down the ticket checking off the names. The candidates got on the ticket by doing party work, by currying favor, by making their contributions. In some states, judges run on a nonpartisan ticket. But they are usually partisan nevertheless.

Whenever judges are elected, money is frequently involved. Campaigns must be run—advertising, billboards, yard signs, television. It costs money to win an election. Who pays it? Big-firm lawyers pay. Big-time plaintiffs' lawyers pay. Businesses pay. And the payback comes in the judge's decisions. Nothing overt, mind you. Nothing illegal. It's just the way the judge happens to see the law. Bessy Lou Jerguson, a clerk at a grocery chain, injured carrying loads too heavy for her frame and and now trying to get the company to pay her worker's compensation, doesn't know the judge. Never contributed. Nor did her lawyer. But her employer did—that sort of thing. Nobody cries about it much. It is part of the system, the subtle *way of things*. If the trial judge doesn't follow the law, well, Bessy can always appeal it—to other judges she doesn't know, either.

On the other hand, the judge on the federal bench is appointed for life. One would think that would make the federal judge untouchable. But he was already touched before his appointment. He was likely a corporate lawyer to begin with, or a prosecutor. Usually he was not one passionately inclined toward people, one with a record of fighting for the underdog. Those kind rarely get to the federal bench. The typical federal judge may not have tried very many cases at all. Instead, he was likely a member of the party in power at the time of his appointment. His best qualifications for office were his political connections, having demonstrated long before he was considered a candidate that his heart was in sync with the power structure that sponsored him.

A recent profile of President Bill Clinton's nominees for judicial appointment consisted of twenty-five men and women whose average net worth was $1,798,670. But only 13 percent of Clinton's appointees were millionaires, compared to 32.5 percent of Bush's, 21.4 percent of Reagan's, and 3.9 percent of Carter's. Of the twenty-five awaiting confirmation by the Senate, Clinton's nominees own nearly $22 million in listed securities. Among the stocks most favored were Merck, IBM, Philip Morris, RJR Nabisco, Ford, Coca-Cola, General Electric, AT&T, and Nike. And these twenty-five awaiting appointment have paid their dues to the Democratic National Committee, having handed over a total of $79,910 to that bastion of virtue and another $10,250 to Clinton's reelection fund.

Ed Rendell, mayor of Philadelphia and husband of Clinton nominee Marjorie Rendell, raised $42.5 million for the Democratic National Committee in 1996. He gave an additional $170,000 from his political action committee. And we are to accept his assurance that there was no quid pro quo so far as his wife's chances at a judgeship are concerned?

Oliver Wendell Holmes and many others have debunked the presumption that judges, despite the method of their selection, would faithfully apply existing rules of common justice in deciding cases. The politicians who appoint them for these lifetime jobs know better. The judges know better, too, and so do we.

Yet occasionally the candidate who takes the bench wearing one stripe ends up wearing another. Such a judge was Chief Justice Earl Warren, who led far-reaching judicial and social reform during his reign. The son of a car repairman for the Southern Pacific Railroad, he never forgot where he came from. Eisenhower, who had chosen him to be his conservative legacy to the nation, was to later claim that his appointment of Warren was "the biggest damn fool mistake" he ever made. Anthony Lewis wrote in *The New York Times,* "It is a delicious irony that the appointment of Chief Justice Warren may go down in history as the single most important act of Eisenhower's presidency."

Considering the unpredictability of the judiciary, the clean bright spots that shine through the fog still occasionally give hope. When we are about to give up on the judicial system, we are provided *Brown* v. *Board of Education, Roe* v. *Wade, Miranda,* and other landmark cases that preserve the rights of the people guaranteed under the Constitution. In the end, a minority of great judges have saved the nation from ultimate tyranny, and because of them, many people still innocently invest their faith in the justice system.

—JUDGES ON THE FOOTBALL FIELD—

It is clear that we must invent a better way to select our judges. Football referees are charged with seeing that the rules of the game are enforced and that both sides have a fair shot at winning. They perform on the football field the approximate function of the judge in a jury trial. But what if we choose our referees in the National Football League in the same manner that we choose our judges? What if the Dallas Cowboys were given the power to appoint the referees that would judge their games, and the appointment would be for life? I predict there would be rioting in the streets and the people would lose all faith in the game and abandon it.

On the other hand, suppose that the referees were elected rather than appointed. Can't we see it now? The little signs stuck in the front lawns of the people: ELECT GEORGE SMITH REFEREE—HE'LL GIVE YOU AN HONEST CALL. And then we discover that the Dallas Cowboys have paid for those little signs, his billboards, and his radio and television advertisements. What then? And what if the referee, in a tight call during the Super Bowl, fearing he will not be reelected, throws the call to the side with the most votes?

In America, with minor modifications, these are the two methods by which our judges, judicial whips in hand, ascend to the bench. Surely there is a better method of choosing them.

—PREDICTING THE TYRANT—

But to begin with: How can we predict who will emerge as a good judge? Ask any lawyer who practices before numerous judges. The poor choices made in the selection of our judges are manifold, painful, even tragic, and usually last us a lifetime. We have already seen that those who seek judgeships ought to be disqualified the moment they drop their hat in the ring, because they *need* to be judges, not to serve a people desperate for justice, but to serve their own psyches, which crave power.

The ancient Chinese in those great early dynasties never permitted their rulers to seek power. *They* sought their rulers. Plato spoke of this phenomenon in *The Republic*. "Whereas the truth is that the State in which the rulers are most reluctant to govern is always the best and most quietly governed, and the State in which they are the most eager, the worst."

—THE FAILED AMERICAN BAR ASSOCIATION—

Even if we could scrutinize our judicial candidates in a better way, it would still be impossible to make any sound predictions about which candidate would serve the people wisely and out of a benevolent heart. The American Bar Association has attempted such measures. Its Standing Committee on the Federal Judiciary, which passes judgment on all nominees to the federal bench, has from its birth been composed of lawyers who were said to be the "best and the brightest" of that Anglo-Saxon elitist bar. More than half the committee's membership came from the very corporate law firms that have perennially held the reins of the bar. Few if any of its members have specialized in the defense of those charged with crimes, or have practiced family law. We would not let the corporate-dominated American Bar Association choose our jurors. Why would we give that master's organ the power to approve our judges?

DREAM 25
JUDGES FOR THE PEOPLE

The nature of judging a vast and diverse people demands a more random method of selecting our judges. I say we must draft those who will serve us in much the same way that we draft juries. We would not select juries to sit for life. We would not select jurors from those who run to the courthouse waiving their placards, crying to be put on a case. On the contrary, one of the questions I often ask a prospective juror is whether he or she would like to serve, and if so, why? When the answer is, "I want to sit on this case because I think it is my duty to do so," I shy away from the juror. Loosely translated, that answer too often means, "I think it is my duty to convict your client with all due haste and see him hung." What a better chance one's client has for justice with a juror who says, "I'd rather not sit here. It makes me uncomfortable to pass judgment on others."

But how do we draft our judges, and from what source? In the same fashion that jurors are drafted, let us draft our judges from a pool composed of competent trial lawyers of good repute. I say trial lawyers because judges must be persons familiar with the law and expert in the procedures of the court. Again, such a pool will more fairly reflect the population as a whole. It will comprise more women, more minorities, more lawyers for the poor, and more lawyers who represent the people than those who presently occupy our benches. An appointments clerk will simply punch a few keys on a computer, and up will come the name of the lawyer who is to serve as judge on that case.

Already I hear the screaming from my brethren of the bar: "We are too busy to interrupt our important work to serve as a judge on some silly case!" But to the persons involved, the case may be as important as life itself. And every citizen chosen as a juror whose work and life has also been involuntarily disrupted must make a contribution of his or her time to the system. Lawyers expect ordinary citizens, whenever called, to trot right down to the courthouse and go through the abusive process of being selected or rejected as jurors in a case. I should think lawyers who make their living by the trial of cases ought themselves give something back to the system. Besides, they will be paid a reasonable stipend for their service, and when they have sat on the case to which they have been assigned (or a series of such cases), they will be released from such "judge duty" and returned to their practices.

When the cases are appealed, we will draw a panel of appellate judges from a pool of the more seasoned trial lawyers who have previously served as trial judges. That panel of judges will hear a calendar of cases, and then they, too, will be released to return to their practices. Under this process, court calendars will *always be current* because we will draft as many judges as necessary to keep them up to date. I should think that the very prospect of enjoying prompt justice rather than waiting years for lethargic or overworked judges to hear our cases would argue eloquently for the proposal. And drafting judges will be cheap. We will not be stuck with hundreds of millions for judicial salaries, benefits, retirement, expenses, clerks, functionaries, and other costs. When a lawyer is so chosen, he or she will hear the case, perform the service, make the decision, and go home when the case is over.

To be sure, we will, by the luck of the draw, get a bad judge now and then. But today, only rarely do practitioners rejoice in the judges assigned to their cases. And under the proposed system, when we get a bad judge, we will not be stuck with him for the rest of his natural life. Moreover, those judges who sentence men to die, who wrest babies from their mothers and seem to delight in dumping a plethora of miseries over the hides of the people, appear to thrive on it. Bad judges live approximately forever. Under the proposed system, we need live with a bad judge for but a few cases. And we will have a right of appeal to a panel of judges who have not climbed a neurotic ladder to the bench where they hold office beholden to politics, money, and power.

Lawyers who have in this way served as judges will be better lawyers. And judges who must return to the law, to plow the fields of practice, will be better lawyers. Plato expressed this same idea in *The Republic*:

> *The business of the founders of the State . . . must ascend until they arrive at the good; but when they have ascended and seen enough we must not allow them to do as they now do. I mean they must be made to descend again among the prisoners in the den, and partake of their labors and honors.*

Slaves can never be free if those who pass judgment on them are the mere minions of their masters. Slaves can never be free when the judges themselves have become the masters. The judiciary was envisioned as a safeguard from tyranny. It was designed to balance against the power of the executive and the legislative branches. Instead, it has become its own kingdom, vying always with the other branches of government for more power, and has often become the seedbed of tyranny itself.

The Founders saw judges as guides who would lead us through a forest of laws to the other side, where the light of justice shone through. Instead, too often our judges have led us into deeper jungles, where the light of justice can never penetrate.

To be free, we must free ourselves of the judges. Such is one of my dreams for justice in America.

TWENTY-SIX

Free at Last

I have a dream that one day, on the red hills of Georgia, the sons of former slaves and the sons of former slave owners will be able to sit down together at the table of brotherhood.

—MARTIN LUTHER KING, JR., 1963

—DARWINISM IN THE CITADEL—

In America, a sort of Darwinian capitalism has been set upon the land, an idea generously embraced by the New Master and supported by the religion of Free Enterprise. It is the notion that the fittest survive, that the inferior serve the strong. Such a scheme ignores the better seeds of our nation, remembering, as we do, John Winthrop, who in 1630 exhorted his flock that "every man afford his help to another in every want or distress . . . and that he perform this out of the same affection which makes him careful of his own good."

We have forsaken the idea that the strong do not possess the right to exploit the weak simply by virtue of their strength. We have forgotten that by reason of their strength, the strong bear the greater duty to protect the weak, for in any just society all must enjoy the same opportunity to realize their potential and an equal right to enjoy the fruits of their uniqueness. I do not speak of a socialism of wealth. I speak of a socialism of opportunity.

The prevailing vision in America reveals not a state in which the people are free, but one where the powerful have license to exploit the frail and the unfortunate. That vision is supported all along the class hierarchy, as in the jungle where the hunter stalks the lion, the lion devours the anteater, and the anteater gobbles the ants. As we have observed, we laud the scheme—as long as we are not the ants. Such a hierarchy, of course, permits the New Master to enslave us all—from the CEOs to the ditch diggers, from the born rich to the wretched homeless sleeping on grates.

We remember, of course, that this same hierarchy dragged into civil war the South's poor whites, the great majority of whom were non-slave owners who gave up their lives by the hundreds of thousands because they claimed a position on the ladder one step above the black slave. To the poor white man in the South, that lowly rung became as valuable as life itself. The fear of being cast to the bottom permits such hierarchies to exist and, at last, enslaves all who cling to the ladder.

Today, the individual is cast into the arena to fight for his survival, while above the carnage the power structure is already safely ensconced. In that arena, the individual is now offered his most revered right as an American: the opportunity to trammel over the bodies of the fallen as he seeks a higher rung on the ladder for himself. A subtle, sophisticated internal war rages among the people, leaving those at the top securely in place while the focus of those below is diverted from their oppression as they grapple in the frenzied free-for-all. So long as Darwinian capitalism is the name of the economic game, we shall be a locked-in nation of hurt and hate, of fear and distrust, of alienation and loneliness—and of slavery.

—The Threat of Fascism in America—

The exploitation of the weak as a legitimate activity of capitalism has always been a perilous venture. It creates a fertile climate for the flourishing of fascism, itself a political philosophy that lauds the enslavement of the weak. The distinction between democracy and fascism is that in the former the elevation of the individual is the goal of a legitimate government, while in the latter the individual is made subordinate to the glory of the state. In fascism, the individual found expression for himself in the collective Aryan, and although the individual forfeited his rights to the state, he was, as a member of the regime, elevated to a higher rung on the ladder by the persecution of Jews. In *Mein Kampf,* Adolf Hitler argued that primitive man "certainly depended less on the tamed animal, but rather on the use of inferior people." And Hitler never fought the power of the German industrialists. Instead, he enlisted them and perched them on the highest rung of his ladder of hate and racism.

Hitler's intent, of course, was to rule the world. He believed that Germany's dominance of the world would end in a peace founded by the "victorious sword of a people of overlords which put the world into the *service of a higher culture.*" Hitler proclaimed that nations that permitted the races to intermarry were committing "a sin against the will of eternal Providence." Such words might as well have escaped the lips of many an antebellum preacher and indeed exemplify the primary doctrine of today's Aryan Nations, the skinheads, and the budding culture of far-right fundamentalists.

It is into this dark Darwinian milieu that we have begun our latest foray and from which we must immediately turn back. The fascist state, prepared as always to reassert itself in America, is strongly supported by many tentacles and thoughtless proxies grown out of the imperial nature of the economic system itself. And, as in the fascist state, the attack is perpetually focused against those least able to defend themselves.

Although much of the philosophy of the fascist state is hidden from the ear by the muting of political correctness, minorities are, as in the Third Reich, still judged as inferior. Such organizations as the Aryan Nations and the Ku Klux Klan are brazen conspirators who continue to repress man's divine mission to enjoy the fruits of his uniqueness. The question we are loath to address, however, is whether fascism is likely to take hold in America. The idea seems beyond the pale. Yet startling similarities between the seedbed from which the poison weed of Nazism was sprouted and conditions prevalent in America today cannot be ignored.

Erich Fromm observed that the Nazi takeover in Germany was possible because of a tiredness, a resignation of the people. He wrote of a sense of alienation—that man's most dreaded state is his feeling of not belonging to the larger group—and he mentioned that the new generation of Germans were attracted to a leadership that hated the weak and lauded the strong.

After the First World War, the middle class in Germany declined, and in the Depression of 1929, it was the hardest hit. The kaiser was the subject of public ridicule. No leader in which the people could place their trust stood tall. The family was shattered with the demise of the old middle-class morality, and the young did as they pleased with or without the approval of their parents. The vast majority of the population felt insignificant and powerless, and had long ago concluded that democracy did not work.

Fromm observed, "Although Nazism proved to be economically detrimental to all other classes, it fostered the interests of the most powerful groups of German industrialists." And as Fromm saw it, Nazism never embraced any genuine set of economic or political principles other than "radical opportunism." The principal justification for Nazism's domination of other people was "for their own good," an idea we have repeatedly encountered from the introduction of the first slaves in America to the current trickle-down theory of economics that lauds the concentration of economic power in the megacorporation in exchange for the jobs it provides the workers.

Nazism was bullyism at its pinnacle. Hitler never attacked the established strong. Instead, his attack, as well as Mussolini's, was always against those who could not defend themselves.

In our own times, in our anguish of separation and our disgust with the system, we, too, have been invited to embrace the philosophy of the far right, which offers to serve us through its fanatical persecution of minorities and its pitiless view of all human beings who occupy a place in the hierarchy below. A new fascism promises security from the terror of crime. All that is required is that we take away the criminals' rights—which, of course, are our own. Out of our desperation and fear we begin to feel a sense of security from the new totalitarian state. Already we sense an implied rejection of democracy, a distrust of the legal system and juries, and a hatred of those who fight for our rights—the lawyers.

—Wars, the Product of Testicles—

I have expressed the hope over and over that the freeing of us, the New American Slaves, might be brought about without a revolution of blood and death. Wars are fought by the ignorant. Wars are the product of men's testicles and their greed. Wars are often fought to preserve bad ideas. Wars are the criminal acts of a society. Wars distinguish human beings as the most inhumane of all creatures on the face of the earth. Even vultures do not wage wars against their own species.

I say birds have more sense than men. Birds conduct their wars by singing their enemies out of their territory. I should hope, therefore, that the revolution will be conducted without war. For if war is the only means by which a revolution to free us can be accomplished, then we have become slaves to our most despicable trait.

—The Dimming of the Shining Light—

I have been critical of the Founding Fathers, those slave owners who demanded freedom for themselves but denied it to a whole race of people, to women, and to the poor. Although I have been critical of the Founders, I revere them for their dreams, for their daring to follow them, for their bravery to launch the great new experiment called democracy. Although enslaved themselves by their own economic goals—which, indeed, drove the Revolution—they nevertheless furnished us with a paradigm—of men who had a vision by which they sought to achieve their liberty.

Because they had dreams, the Founding Fathers were able to shine a light that would begin to illuminate a darkened world. Their dreams had never been tested. No model of the democracy they envisioned had ever existed. They were mostly young men, their dreams tempered by the wisdom of Franklin and the practical knowledge of Jefferson. They did not shy away from the risk. The idea of freedom so utterly permeated their plan that a sublime purity percolated through their deliberations and a sort of innocent resolution impelled their actions. And what they have bequeathed, of course, is not a free nation, not liberty and justice for all, not a nation without slaves, not a nation where all men are created equal. What they have left us are the blessed tools to free ourselves.

But the Founders could not have freed themselves had they not recognized that they were the subjects of King George III. Without a king against whom to rebel, the rebellion could not have occurred. Without an acute awareness of their servitude, the American Revolution could not have given birth to a nation. A pervasive sense of bondage is a prerequisite of every slave uprising. And in that respect, the work of the Founders was made easier by the king, for the colonists did not suffer endless propaganda from a master that washed away at their brains and left them sopped in the myth of liberty. The king saw the colonists as his subjects. The king treated them as his subjects. He demanded of them his due, and when his demands became intolerable, the Revolution was born.

But as we have seen, the problem today in America is more subtle and immensely more difficult. Most modern American slaves do not believe themselves slaves. Most are insulted at the suggestion of it. We have been taught that we are free, and have accepted such teaching in the place of freedom. And the lesson is constantly reinforced with liturgy and dogma. Our children mouth the fantasy daily at their schools when they pledge allegiance to the flag that symbolizes "liberty and justice for all." Our people sing the hymns that squeeze at our hearts when we proclaim that our star-spangled banner still waves "o'er the land of the free and the home of the brave." We have been conditioned, like Pavlov's dogs, to drool patriotic sentiments whenever criticism of our system is heard.

As we have seen, we have elevated the notion of free enterprise to a religion, and without deep questions, we have accepted it with all of its cruelty. We have grown to embrace the corporate-governmental master as part of the landscape, like mountains that cannot be moved. Having no means by which to test the efficacy of the propaganda fed to us as our daily diet, we accept it as true. Although our system provides more freedom than any in the world, we are willing to remain enslaved in this more benevolent system of slavery than to carefully consider the extent of our actual slavery.

We are a people who demand prescriptions: Tell us how to achieve a better life. Tell us how to lose weight. Tell us how to get rich. Tell us how to better organize our lives. And, yes, tell us how to become free. But prescriptions are meaningless if, before we follow the advice of the guru, we do not realize we are unhappy, fat, poor, disorganized, or enslaved. Prescriptions for freedom become so much empty rhetoric as long as we believe we are already free. One wonders what the consequences might be if tomorrow an entire nation awakened to clearly and accurately perceive our condition in servitude. What if all of us, as we shaved or put on our lipstick, said to ourselves in the mirror, "You have been fooled. You are not free. You are a slave." And what if we believed it?

—A Look Back—

I have spent much of this effort in exposing the enslaving institution and attaching it to its precursor, the slavery of the old South. It is not that free enterprise is a bad system; it is that, in the hands of the corporate oligarchy, it is used badly. It is not that corporations as such are evil; it is that megacorporations have become the woof and government the warp of the cloth that today composes the corporate power center, the stifling shroud that has been thrown over the people and that smothers the breath of freedom from us.

I do not argue that the spoils of the universe should be shared equally. I only argue that each of us should have an equal chance to explore his or her own universe and to exploit not the helpless, not our neighbors, but the unique treasures we discover in ourselves.

—Whose Duty?—

The duty to restore liberty to the people is a universal duty. It does not belong to the mystical *them*. When we see a person bleeding to death in a wrecked automobile along the road, the duty to save the occupant does not belong to the mystical *them*. When we witness a bully beating up on a child, the duty to save the child does not belong to the mystical *them*. By having been given life, we have the duty to preserve it. By having been given the gift of liberty, we have the duty to join in the fight for those who do not possess it.

The duty is best served by enlightenment, not blood; by patience, not anger; by love, not aggression; by a persistent giving, not violence. In the end, freedom, no matter the means by which it is given birth, will always prevail. Still, the history of the species is one of paradox in action. The species enslaves itself, but as we have seen, both master and slave are bound one to the other. And once enslaved, the species struggles eternally to be free.

—THE ROAD OUT—

The road out is not an easy one. Nearly four hundred years have elapsed since the first slave ship landed in Jamestown in 1619. That began our descent into this deep abyss, where the sun reaches the bottom only part of the day. The climb out cannot be accomplished overnight. And many do not wish to climb out. Many will fight to stay. Many will revile those who begin the journey. The way out is threatening to many and not clear to most. But already we are awakening.

Already we see the signs. As I have written these words, I have shared my observations with many. And most, in some way, admit they are aware of their servitude. I ask, "Are you a slave?" And the person nods. Some say they are slaves to the system, some say they are slaves to the corporation they work for. Some say they are slaves to the government, others say they are slaves to themselves. But no matter to whom, they are enslaved just the same.

A friend wrote: "You once told me that when I work for a corporation I am property—something to be used to wipe the grease off the company machinery, and when they are through with me, they will throw me out. That has just happened to me. What shall I do?"

I wrote back, "Congratulations. This is the best day of your life. The road ahead will be frightening, but, oh, to be free—to own *yourself!*"

Most have felt the rough walls of the slave quarters and the whip of the master laid with psychic accuracy on the tender parts of human hope. But the people are awakening, looking around, wondering if they are alone. They are searching for their tribal brothers and sisters, the tribal family from whom they have been separated these many years, yes, these lifetimes.

—Tomorrow, a Garden in Bloom—

Soon neighbors will again learn to speak to one another, to listen, to hear, and to care, and gradually a new trust will take root, a trust that will enrich the new community. Already small villages within the larger are organizing themselves. Out of the crumble of the inner city, new communities are being born. A growing number of the middle class has begun to shun the suburbs and to reestablish the village in the heart of the wreckage. According to the U.S. Census Bureau, the trend is nationwide. New small communities are becoming the flowers of a new free America, and one day their blooms will blend as the rose garden of a new nation.

Dream 26
The Dream of Dreams

In my dream, in place of the deadly cities, new villages within the cities have been born. They emerge as gardens of hope, of children laughing. I see them, the families there, the families working together and free.

In my dream, a new value has taken over in the village. The madness is diminishing. To work for money alone has been rejected as against life. To see money as God—that madness is gone. To see the possession of dead money as success, to trade human life for it—that madness is gone. The people are beginning to grow back their eyes. They are seeing. They see that chains cannot be dissolved by *things*. Chains cannot be broken by crawling into the new car, the new boat. Chains cannot be eliminated by wearing the new stylish pants. That insanity is gone. To swear fealty to the corporate nothing, to declare loyalty to that which cannot be loyal in return—that madness, too, is gone.

Great rivers have their source from tiny springs. In similar small ways, my dream has begun to emerge as reality. We are beginning to understand that trust of one another is the seed stock of a free people. We are awakening to the fact that our neighbors are vastly good, that the beginning of the tribe is next door, that there are wisdom and power in the village, and we can trust them. Today we are witnessing a happening. The happening is the gradual awakening of America. We see we have been like children who traipse though the woods, believing whatever we have been told to believe. But we are coming of age. And we are emerging from the woods.

Already we are taking steps to stop the corporate ownership of our Congress and our presidents. We are on the verge of stopping the bribery. And we will stop it not with violence but with laws, plain laws. The people will demand it, and they will never rest until it is done. What is left of the honor of the media will survive. Many decent editors true to their sacred task will never rest until it is done. And if the courts shall bow to our corporate masters and throw out our plain laws, we shall find other ways. For we are awakening to the sound of drums. They are *our* drums.

The Weapons of Revolution

The music of freedom comes to us when we rattle the bars. We have learned that we can free ourselves and, after ourselves, our neighbors. We know *the feel of freedom* even as the invisible whips are laid on our backs, for the whips free us and enslave the master. And the whips are our weapons.

We have learned to question. We no longer believe simply because we have been taught to believe. Nor do we disbelieve, because cynicism enslaves as well. We are open like lilies in the morning, and we question. We question, because questioning gives us new eyes. The great question mark—that has become a powerful weapon for freedom.

Not all of the people will arise. The old plow horse never tests the fences or balks in the traces. The revolution will be led by the few. Our Founding Fathers were the few. The few will show the many the way. So it is in all revolutions.

The New Tribe

When we have taken back our Congress and our presidency, the rest will follow. We shall begin to govern from our small villages. We shall set our schools to work in educating our children. We shall educate them with love, and teach them to question. We shall teach them that the first knowledge is the knowledge of the self. Spontaneity will become the sacred religion of the schools, and all that inhibits and intimidates, that turns precious creative minds into automatons, will be heretical. No longer will the goal of the schools be to create identical replacement parts for the master's machinery; rather, it will be to acknowledge the towering uniqueness of every child. And the children shall be free.

The New American Slaves
Corporations shall become the New American Slaves. Corporations shall be governed by the people. Corporations, although fictions, are but machines to serve the people, and they will become weapons of freedom.

Corporations will become tools to support the village, a place where free people can work, a place where people can discover themselves and grow, a place they can come to, but also a place they are free to leave. The corporation shall have a conscience because the people will own their government, and the People's New Congress will have installed a conscience into the rib cage of the corporation.

A New Voice for the People
In my dream, the airways have been returned to the people and the voice of the master has been muted. How pleasant to hear the music of caring, the violence gone because we no longer retain a need for it. How we rejoice to hear the voices of many people questioning, always questioning *the way of things*, looking, always looking, always striving for the better way, for beauty and for light.

The Dream Beyond Dreaming
I dream the dream beyond dreaming—of a land where every child has a roof over his head, every child enough food. I think of a land that has put its priorities in order—where people come before profit (though profit is part of it); a land where the general welfare of the people comes before the maintenance of a giant war machine that can bully the world. But defense of our liberty is part of it. I dream of a land where the earth and the people become compatible once more, a land where the people and the earth live in harmony.

Ideas are the greatest of all the tools for freedom.

The Long Trek

We have already begun the long trek to liberty. We have been on the march for freedom from the beginning. We began it when we spoke out against the first injustice. We began it when we saw the uniqueness in ourselves and the decency in our neighbor.

We have been on the march, and the master knows it. The master is helpless against the people, for to the same extent that the master was created by the people, so, too, can the master become the tool of the people. Even in our bonds, the master is our slave, for *the master is dependent upon us*. Our knowledge of that is the great weapon we wield. Freedom is in our hands, and the master trembles.

In its desperation to retain its power, the master spews the phlegm of false arguments over us. It steps up its threats. It clutches its dead money for security. It grabs at the poor for even more power. But the master knows that the ultimate power has always been in the people, and the master knows that despite how it washes at the brain cells of the people, it cannot change the human gene that lusts for freedom. The freedom gene is in us, and *that* the master knows.

Free as Brothers and Sisters

I dream that racism will no longer separate us. We have seen racism's ugly progeny, the great American holocaust against the black slave and the guilt and hate of it that divides us still. But white men have enslaved white men as well.

I think of the white men who have fought for the black man. I think of John Quincy Adams struggling against the slave-holding majority in Congress until his old stiff body and his quivery voice gave out. I think of William Lloyd Garrison and John Brown, who risked it all for the cause of black people in bondage. I think of the uncounted nameless men and women who risked their lives operating the Underground Railroad, which transported slaves to freedom. And I think of the hundreds of thousands who lost their lives in the great Civil War.

I think of the black men who have fought for the liberty of all people, black and white. I think of the countless slaves who fought valiantly in the Civil War alongside their white brothers. I remember the black soldiers in our wars of freedom whose blood was as dear as the white man's, and who bled along with their white brothers for this freedom.

I think of our civil rights leaders, of Martin Luther King, Jr., who have shown us the way, black and white together.

Yet, these enlightened generations later, the racial misery in the nation still brings anguish to millions. Our ghettos, our concrete swamps, are brimming with those who have escaped the hand of the New Master. Our streets are lined with those who have been disenfranchised, white and black, the Hispanic, the homeless, those suffering in wretched poverty, the hungry children. Such are the shameful living symbols of a system gone awry. They mock our failure. They rage at our hypocrisy. We are despised, not for their suffering but for our turned backs, our blank eyes. They charge us with having abandoned the human race because our love of money mattered more than our love of justice, more than our love of liberty.

The racial issues divide us, and the New Master laughs. It always laughs when there is dissension in the slave quarters. It laughs because in conflict the slaves cannot rise up and free themselves. It laughs when it sees us, the New American Slaves, hurl our anger against one another like sled dogs that rip and tear at their fellows in the traces but pull obediently for the driver whenever he snaps his whip over their heads.

There can be no legitimate racial issue in this country, not while there seethes the perennial issue of slavery, for slavery comes in every color.

We long for true leaders. And leaders will appear. They will be chosen, but not by the color of their skin. One cannot choose the best fiddle player by his complexion. One cannot choose the great poets by the color of their hides. The idea of complexion as a reflection of the soul reflects the ultimate stupidity.

Still, we must beware, for the racial trap is ever ready to ensnare whenever we choose leaders by the color of their skin rather than by the architecture of their souls.

Perhaps a black person will lead us out, for his were the fathers in chains. His were the mothers sold for breeding. Must the black man not know more about slavery—both his and ours? And should the black leader appear who can lead us to the Promised Land, we must be ready to join hands, for hands of all colors joined together are the extension of the same soul.

"FREE AT LAST! FREE AT LAST!
THANK GOD ALMIGHTY,
WE ARE FREE AT LAST!"

That is my dream of dreams. "Thank God Almighty, we are free at last!"

It was the dream of the black slaves. It was the dream of the Pilgrims in tall hats. It was the dream of the Plains Indians, long ago slaughtered with the buffalo and imprisoned on reservations. It is the dream of our children. It is the eternal dream of the species.

And it is our dream, we, the New American Slaves; we, the new Indians who have thrown down the beads and the trinkets and picked up the weapons of freedom, for at last we have empowered ourselves, and at last *we have overcome*.

That is my dream of dreams.

NOTES
◆·◆

—PART I—

Chapter 1

Howard Zinn provided the description of the slave ships, the statistics as to the number of slaves that had been transported to America by 1800, and the quotation of Madison concerning his profit per slave, in his *A People's History of the United States* (New York: Harper & Row, 1980), pp. 28, 29, 33.

The numbers of American soldiers who lost their lives in the Civil War, is from the herein often quoted magnificent work of James M. McPherson, *Battle Cry of Freedom: The Civil War Era* (New York and Oxford: Oxford University Press, 1988), p. 854.

The speech of John Winthrop on the flagship *Arbella* was quoted in Perry Miller, *The American Puritans: Their Prose and Poetry* (New York: Columbia University Press Morningside Edition, 1982), pp. 78–84.

John Brown's ". . . let it be done" is from a report of Brown's speech quoted in the *New York Herald,* Nov. 3, 1859, printed in Oswald Garrison Villard, *John Brown, 1800–1859: A Biography Fifty Years After* (Boston, 1910), pp. 498–99, and reported by McPherson in *Battle Cry of Freedom,* p. 209.

That by 1776 slavery was practiced in all thirteen colonies and the statistics quoted in that regard are from William Lee Miller's powerful and important story, *Arguing About Slavery: The Great Battle in the United States Congress* (New York: Alfred A. Knopf, 1996), p. 16. See also Miller at p. 13 for the facts establishing the early domination of the government by slave masters; p. 11 for the statistic that by 1835 nearly half of the states had economies dependent on slavery; p. 10 for the estimation of the number of slaves in the country by 1836 and their annual increase, as then cited by James Henry Hammond, a congressman from South Carolina; and p. 10 for Lincoln's quoted story about the two preachers.

The estimations of the number of slaves held in Virginia in 1700 and again by 1763 are from Zinn, *A People's History of the United States,* p. 32.

The observations of Julian Niemcewicz concerning the living conditions of Washington's slaves and the description of Jefferson's slave quarters are from Julius Lester, *To Be a Slave* (New York: The Dial Press, 1968), p. 63.

The quotes from the Lincoln-Douglas debates are from McPherson, *Battle Cry of Freedom,* pp. 184, 185, 187.

The quotation attributed to Washington and the provisions of his will by which he ordered his slaves freed are from Richard Brookhiser, *Founding Father: Rediscovering George Washington* (New York: The Free Press, 1996), pp. 182, 183.

Chapter 2

The story of Queen Elizabeth, John Hawkins, and the Puritans is from *The People's Chronology 1987–1996* contained in Microsoft corporation's *Bookshelf 98,* "The People's Chronology," licensed from Henry Holt and Company, Inc. Copyright © 1995, 1996 by James Trager.

The story of Lavinia Bell is a true story first recounted in the Montreal *Gazette,* Jan. 31, 1861, and later retold in James W. Blassingame, *Slave Testimony: Two Centuries of Letters, Speeches, Interviews, and Autobiographies* (Louisiana State University, 1977).

The advertisements reprinted in the *Liberator* came from Henrietta Buckmaster, *Let My People Go: The Story of the Underground Railroad and the Growth of the Abolition Movement* (Columbia, South Carolina: University of South Carolina Press, 1992), p. 49.

The true story of Old Charley is recounted in *Bullwhip Days: The Slaves Remember,* edited by James Mellon (New York: Avon Books, 1988), pp. 103–114.

Chapter 3

Henry David Thoreau's quotation is from "On the Duty of Civil Disobedience," 1849.

The fate of John Walter of AT&T was reported in a story by Steve Rosenbush, *USA Today,* July 18, 1997.

Chapter 4

The story of Mary Reynolds, the old slave, is a true story reported in Mellon, *Bullwhip Days,* pp. 15–23.

Chapter 5

The quotes about slavery providing cradle-to-grave security, that slavery was "a great moral, social and political blessing," that all respectable systems of civilization were founded in slavery, and John Calhoun's assertion that slavery "is a positive good" are all from McPherson, *Battle Cry of Freedom,* p. 56, as are Douglas's quotes about "thick-lipped blacks" and "Free love and free niggers will surely elect old Abe," pp. 128, 224.

The quote from the Texas Methodist weekly about the South's fair daughters being forced "into the embrace of buck negroes for wives" is from McPherson, *Battle Cry of Freedom,* p. 229. That the North intended to "free the Negroes and force amalgamation between them and the children of the poor men of the South" is also from McPherson, as are the quotations concerning abolition preachers who will "be at hand to consummate the marriage of your daughters to black husbands" and the "hellish lust of the Negro," all on p. 243.

Georgia's Governor Joseph Brown's claim that, among other things, slavery "is the poor man's best government and that he belongs to the only true aristocracy, the race of white men," is from McPherson, p. 244. The George Fitzhugh quote is from p. 196.

The 1858 argument of James Hammond of South Carolina that in all social systems there must be a class to do the menial duties, and his criticism of the North's wage slaves are from McPherson, p. 196.

The statement of Thomas B. Labreque, chief executive of Chase Manhattan Bank, is from N. R. Kleinfield, "The Downsizing of America," *The New York Times,* March 4, 1996.

Calhoun's oratory on slavery, claiming that the African race had never had it so good and that the South was being slandered and insulted is from Miller, *Arguing About Slavery,* pp. 122–33.

The quote from the pre–Civil War Southerner who thought the South was becoming morbidly sensitive on anything pertaining to the "dear nigger" is from James O. Breeden, *Advice Among Masters: The*

Ideal in Slave Management in the Old South (Westport, Conn., and London: Greenwood Press, 1980), p. 330.

Chapter 6

My discussion of virtue, commonweal, and equality is drawn from Mc-Pherson, *Battle Cry of Freedom,* Ch. 1.

The statement of the condition of workers in Boston, the report to the American Medical Association on worker conditions, the quote from the Cochee Manufacturing Company, and the statistic on the number of persons in prison for debt in Boston are from Ralph Korngold, *Two Friends of Man* (Boston: Little Brown and Company, 1950), p. 63.

The New York Times poll showing that 19 million people suffered a crisis from a lost job in their family and how downsizing has touched nearly every American is from Louis Uchitelle and N. R. Kleinfield, "The Downsizing of America," *The New York Times,* March 3, 1996.

The statistics concerning the reemployment of workers who lost their jobs from 1993 to 1995 are from an op-ed piece by Ward Morehouse and David Dembo, *The New York Times,* Oct. 20, 1996.

The discussion and statistics concerning the loss of jobs in America and their replacement with lesser paying jobs with poorer benefits is from Uchitelle and Kleinfield, "The Downsizing of America."

The quotation concerning the loss of jobs in the years since Reagan was elected is from Ellizabeth Kolbert and Adam Clymer, "The Downsizing of America," *The New York Times,* March 8, 1996.

The statistic for the loss of wages by unskilled workers between 1980 and 1996 is from a story by Peter Passell, *The New York Times,* June 14, 1998.

The number of people who this past year have given up looking for a job is a statistic from the U.S. Labor Department reported by Kevin Phillips, "The Forum," *USA Today,* Feb. 5, 1997.

That 36.4 million people in this country live in poverty is from Michael Gartner's column in *USA Today,* Oct. 1, 1996.

The statistic that 25 million people—19 percent of the workforce—were out of work or underemployed is from an article by John E. Schwarz, *The New York Times,* Oct. 12, 1997.

The percentage of the national income shared between the rich and the poor and the statistics supporting my contention that the poor are getting poorer and that the American middle class is a myth are from Paul Krugman's article in *Mother Jones,* Nov./Dec. 1996.

That hunger and homelessness increased in 1996 for the twelfth straight year, and that the mayors of the twenty-nine major cities of the nation predict that cuts in welfare will exacerbate the problem are from a story by Richard Wolf in *USA Today,* December 14, 1996.

That retraining does not provide a better job at a better wage is shown by Donald L. Barlett and James B. Steele in their remarkable series first published in *The Philadelphia Inquirer* and republished in *The Denver Post,* Sept. 22, 1996. Their several stories and statistics quoted are from their Sept. 22, 1996, article.

The slaves' description of a day's work in the cotton fields and their quotas are from Julius Lester, *To Be a Slave* (New York: Scholastic, 1984), pp. 70, 71.

Juliet B. Schor's quotation is from her insightful book *The Overworked American: The Unexpected Decline of Leisure* (New York: Basic Books, 1991), p. 5.

The statistics on the typical CEO's pay at 150 times the average manufacturing employee's are from Paul Krugman's article, "The Spiral of Inequality," *Mother Jones,* Nov./Dec. 1996, as are his quotes.

The details of Michael Eisner's salary, the skyrocketing salaries of American CEOs as reported in *Industry Week,* and the other statistics and quotations as well as the statistics about the nation's supervisors' pay are from David M. Gordon's important book *Fat and Mean: The Corporate Squeeze of Working Americans and the Myth of Managerial "Downsizing"* (New York: The Free Press, 1996), pp. 34–36.

Chapter 7

The quote about 250 million tires is from a review of Jane Holtz Kay, *Asphalt Nation: How the Automobile Took Over America, and How We Can Take It Back, The New York Times Book Review,* July 20, 1997.

The statistics concerning our incarceration rates compared to other nations is from an article by MR Franks, "Slavery Returns to the USA," *New Law Journal,* Dec. 19, 1997, p. 1843.

The quote of the slave master treating Negroes as they treat their horses is found in Breeden, *Advice Among Masters*, p. 49.

As to the rising productivity of the American worker and the statistics comparing American workers' productivity to those in Germany and Japan, see Schor, *The Overworked American*, p. 2.

David M. Gordon's statement concerning the vast majority of Americans who can barely make ends meet is from his book *Fat and Mean*, p. 2.

The story about Georgina Cheng-Canindin and her arbitration is from an article by Roy Furchgott, *The New York Times*, July 20, 1997.

As to the claim that Nike uses child labor in Third World countries, see Del Jones's story in *USA Today*, June 6, 1996.

The story of Ford and General Motors doing deals in China is from *USA Today*, Oct. 23, 1997.

Julius Lester's quotation is from *To Be a Slave*, p. 74.

Chapter 8

The story of Nat Turner is from Henrietta Buckmaster, *Let My People Go*, pp. 52–54.

Wendell Phillip's quote is from Korngold, *Two Friends of Man*, p. 366.

The American Medical Association statistics about disputes that started at home and carried over into workplace violence, the number of children that died from child abuse and neglect, and the number of senior citizens that suffered some form of abuse are from an article by Doug Levy in *USA Today*, June 12, 1996.

—PART II—

Chapter 11

The report of the study of the Agricultural Society of Union District of South Carolina on providing slaves with religion is from Breeden, *Advice Among Masters*, pp. 237, 238, as is the slave owner's statement about the great civilizer, cowhide, p. 330. The statement that slavery was ordained in heaven is found at p. 16.

Frederick Douglass's letter to his former master is from *Letters of a*

Nation: A Collection of Extraordinary American Letters, edited by Andrew Carroll (Kodansha, 1997), pp. 93–101.

The Susan Boggs quote is from American Freedmen's Inquiry Commission Interviews, 1863, reported in Blassingame, *Slave Testimony,*
pp. 419–21.

The quotes concerning the attitude of the church toward slavery
came from Robert W. Fogel and Stanley L. Engerman, *Time on the
Cross: The Economics of American Negro Slavery* (Boston: Little Brown
and Company, 1947).

The claim that the Vatican helped large numbers of Nazis escape is
from Mark Aarons and John Loftus, *Unholy Trinity: The Vatican, the
Nazis, and Soviet Intelligence* (New York: St. Martin's Press, 1998).

George Baer's statement was reported by Edward S. Herman, *Corporate Control, Corporate Power* (New York: Cambridge University
Press, 1981).

The Ludlow massacre story can be found in Richard O. Boyer and
Herbert M. Morais, *Labor's Untold Story,* 3rd ed. (United Electrical
Workers, 1982).

The quote from Archbishop Hughes was reported by McPherson,
Battle Cry of Freedom, p. 507.

Henry Ford's statements are from John Naisbitt and Patricia Abur-
dene, *Re-Inventing the Corporation: Transforming Your Job and Your
Company for the New Information Society* (New York: Warner Books,
1985), and David Halberstam, *The Reckoning* (New York: William Mor-
row, 1986).

Chapter 12

Erich Fromm's theory that the anxiety of predestination is responsible
for modern man's compulsion to activity is discussed in his *Escape from
Freedom* (Henry Holt and Company, 1965), pp. 39–102.

Smahalla's statement that his young men will never work is from
T. C. McLuhan, *Touch the Earth* (New York: Promontory Press, 1971),
p. 56.

Chapter 15

The quote of Assistant Secretary of War Dana that the bravery of the
black union soldiers "completely revolutionized the sentiment of the

army with regard to the employment of negro troops" is from McPherson, *Battle Cry of Freedom*, p. 634, as is the story of the 54th Regiment, p. 565.

Lincoln's writing to the Democrats concerning the Emancipation Proclamation is from McPherson, p. 687.

Chapter 16
The quote from a master concerning the machinery-like aspect of managing his slaves is from Breeden, *Advice Among Masters*, p. 31, as is the statement that the slave should never exercise his will, p. 30. The slave master's view of security is from pp. 8, 9.

The quote from John Farrell concerning a corporation not owing anyone a career is from N. R. Kleinfield, "The Downsizing of America, *The New York Times*, March 4, 1996.

The plantation owners' concern that the workers, if required to exceed their quota, might stampede to the swamps is from Fredrick Law Olmsted, *The Cotton Kingdom: A Traveller's Observations on Cotton and Slavery in the American Slave States* (New York: McGraw Hill, 1984), p. 193.

Robert Reich's suggestion for tax incentives to corporations who, in summary, treat their employees fairly is from Kolbert and Clymer, "Downsizing America," *The New York Times*, March 8, 1996.

Chapter 17
The statistics on Bill Gates are from *The Nation*, Oct. 4, 1997, p. 20, and the statistic about 358 billionaires and the statistics following are from *The Nation*, Oct. 13, 1997.

—PART III—

Overture
The statement of Samuel May is found in Ralph Korngold, *Two Friends of Man*, p. 81.

Chapter 18
The statistics on the campaign donations made by major corporations are from "Reforming Campaign Financing," *USA Today*, Dec. 12, 1996.

The quote from *USA Today* about soft money raised in 1997 is from an editorial, Feb. 26, 1998.

Pat Choate's statements and the statistics concerning the power of foreign campaign contributions are from his article that appeared in *USA Today,* Dec. 5, 1996.

The statement of David Rice about how the rich who hold the slaves also make the laws is from Ira Berlin, *Slaves Without Masters: The Free Negro in the Antebellum South* (New York: Vintage Books, 1976), p. 85.

How D'Amato raises money and the reference to the "giant sucking sound" is from an article by Leslie Wayne, *The New York Times,* Oct. 13, 1996.

About Clinton's early advertising blitz, Thomas Ferguson's study, and the naïve lamentation in the *Philadelphia Inquirer* is from Thomas Ferguson, "Bill's Big Backers," *Mother Jones,* Nov./Dec. 1996.

The facts on Ralph Nader's campaign were set out in Norman Solomon's column in *The Arizona Republic,* Nov. 18, 1996.

Dick Morris's reports about the reelection of President Clinton are from his book, *Behind the Oval Office: Winning the Presidency in the Nineties* (New York: Random House, 1997).

Henrik Ibsen's complaint that the people are never right is from his play *An Enemy of the People,* Act 4.

Chapter 19

Joseph Davies's letter is quoted in *Stalin,* edited by Thomas H. Rigby (Englewood Cliffs, N.J.: Prentice-Hall, 1966), Pt. 2, Ch. 4.

Calvin's belief that God damned even the pious man is found in Fromm, *Escape from Freedom,* p. 86.

Chapter 20

The story of Coleman McCarthy of *The Washington Post* is from an article by Norman Solomon in the *Minneapolis Star Tribune,* Jan. 10, 1997.

The Norman Lewis Corwin quote is in his book *Trivializing America* (Secaucus, N.J.: Lyle Stuart, 1983).

The figures on the record box office of Beavis and Butt-head are from an article by Rick Taylor, *USA Today,* Dec. 23, 1996.

Ford's sponsorship of a *Murphy Brown* episode is from *USA Today,* Oct. 23, 1997.

Chapter 21

The John Swinton quote is offered by Jack McLamb, *Aid and Abet Police Report,* Phoenix, Ariz.

The Cronkite quote is from his article in *Censored: The News That Didn't Make the News—and Why, 1996* (New York: Seven Stories Press, 1996), edited by Carl Jensen and Project Censored, p. 27.

That General Electric has the largest stock value in the world was reported in *USA Today,* Feb. 21, 1997.

The statistics concerning the recent concentration of the ownership of America's media in a few large corporations and the opinion that General Electric and Westinghouse are the Coke and Pepsi of nuclear power are from *Censored, 1996,* pp. 36–40, as are the facts concerning 153 corporate welfare programs that exceed by three times the amount paid for human welfare, at pp. 53–55. The statistic concerning the conservative *Reader's Digest* is from p. 40.

The story of the fate of Jim Hightower and Robert Sam Anson after their criticism of Disney is set out in *EXTRA! Update,* the bimonthly newsletter of FAIR, Dec. 1995.

That *60 Minutes* pulled a former tobacco company executive interview on advice of its attorneys is found at *Censored, 1996,* p. 44, as is the statement by Carl Jensen, p. 8. Walter Cronkite's quote about the networks thinking of their pocketbooks rather than the people's right to know is from *Censored, 1996,* p. 44.

The statement by Don Hewitt concerning the news as entertainment is from a story by Peter Johnson, *USA Today,* Oct. 9, 1997.

How Procter & Gamble canceled its advertising on the station carrying boycotters' ads is from William Greider's brave book *Who Will Tell the People: The Betrayal of American Democracy* (New York: Simon and Schuster, 1992), p. 174.

Newt Gingrich's advice to corporations concerning advertising boycotts is from an interview of Jeff Cohen, executive director of FAIR, entitled, "Media Monopolies: Corporate Merger Mania," interviewed by David Barsamian, Boulder, Col., Sept. 8, 1995. Jeff Cohen's quotation concerning public television moving further and further to the right is also from this interview.

The quote from *Advice Among Masters* about how masters should keep their slaves from communicating with abolitionists is from p. 332.

Bill Moyers's statements concerning his inability to air controversial views and S. L. Harrison's statement that programs on public television were regularly previewed by underwriters are drawn from Harrison's article "Prime Time Pablum, How Politics and Corporate Influence Keep Public TV Harmless," *The Washington Monthly,* Jan. 1986.

Chapter 22

The story of John Quincy Adams's defense against a motion of censure for presenting petitions against slavery is from Miller, *Arguing About Slavery,* pp. 436, 437.

Chapter 23

The story on the Prudential fraud case by Christine Dugas appeared in *USA Today,* Sept. 25, 1996.

The report on Burger King and child labor appeared in *USA Today,* Nov. 19, 1992.

That Laboratory Corporation of America Holdings paid $182 million to resolve allegations that it submitted false claims for lab tests was reported in *Corporate Crime Reporter,* Nov. 25, 1996.

The statement about employing labor in poverty-stricken Haiti by J. C. Penney, K mart, and Disney is from an article by Tom Squitieri, *USA Today,* June 12, 1996.

The numbers establishing the misconduct of large corporations in the ten years preceding his study is from the work of Amitai Etzioni, professor of sociology at George Washington University, as reported by Saul W. Gellerman in his article "Why 'Good' Managers Made Bad Ethical Choices," *Harvard Business Review,* July/Aug. 1986.

Marshall Clinard and Peter Yeager undertook a massive study for the Law Enforcement Assistance Administration of various criminal administrative actions brought by 25 federal agencies against the 477 largest publically owned manufacturing companies in the United States. See their book *Corporate Crime* (New York, Free Press, 1980). These statistics, along with those in *Fortune* magazine, are contained in an article by William J. Maakestad, "State v. Ford Motor Company: Constitutional, Utilitarian and Moral Perspectives," 27 *St. L.UL.J* 857. See also Gerry Spence, *With Justice for None: Destroying an American Myth* (New York: Times Books, 1989), notes to Ch. 10, pp. 346, 347.

For the story of the Silkwood case see Gerry Spence and Anthony Polk, *Gunning for Justice* (Garden City, New York: Doubleday & Company, 1982).

The statement of Governor Henry Hubbard is from Richard L. Grossman and Frank T. Adams, *Taking Care of Business* (Charter, Ink, Red Sun Press, 1993), p. 10, as is the reference to the *Terrett* case, p. 11.

The statistics on General Electric are from *USA Today,* Feb. 1997; see also "Money Talks: The Mother Jones 400," *Mother Jones,* May/ June, 1997.

The story about National Cash Register is from a story by Sara Rimer, "The Downsizing of America," *The New York Times,* March 6, 1996.

Chapter 24

The statistics and quotes concerning the LSAT are from an article entitled "Startling Admissions," by Ralph Nader and Allan Nairn, which appeared in *Student Lawyer,* March 1980. Peter J. Liacouras's conclusions are from his article "Toward a Fair and Sensible Policy for Professional School Admission," *Cross Reference,* Vol. 1, No. 2.

Harvard's Dean Bork's quotations as well as the quotation from John Hart Ely are from *The New York Times Magazine,* May 22, 1983.

Judge Lois G. Forer's quote is from her book *Money and Justice: Who Owns the Courts?* (New York: W. W. Norton & Company, 1984).

Herbert Croly's quotation is from his book *The Promise of American Life* (Cambridge: Harvard University Press, 1965).

Christopher Columbus Langdell's quotes are found in Arthur E. Sutherland's *The Law at Harvard: A History of Ideas and Men, 1817–1967* (Cambridge: Harvard University Press, 1967).

The statements of Auerbach, Wilson, and Brandeis were gathered by Jerold S. Auerbach in his prize-winning book, *Unequal Justice: Lawyers and Social Change in Modern America* (New York: Oxford University Press, 1976).

The story about burned-out lawyers and their desire for another profession and the statistics showing alcohol and drugs as the basis of disciplinary action are from a story by Judith Schroer, *USA Today,* Oct. 7, 1993.

Ralph Nader and Wesley J. Smith's powerful and honest book is *No Contest: Corporate Lawyers and the Perversion of Justice in America* (New York: Random House, 1996).

Chapter 25

The quotes of Thomas Earle and David Henshaw are from Grossman and Adams, *Taking Care of Business,* p. 11.

The quotations of Jay, Adams, and Hamilton were gathered by Jon M. Van Dyke in his article "The Jury as a Political Institution," *The Center Magazine,* Vol. III, No, 2, March 1970.

The profile of Bill Clinton's nominees is from an article by Richard Willing, *USA Today,* March 17, 1997.

Chapter 26

The Winthrop quote is from Miller, *The American Puritans,* p. 80.

Hitler's quote is from *Mein Kampf* (New York: Reynal & Hitchcock, 1940), p. 405.

Erich Fromm's discussion of the roots and psychology of Nazism and his quotation are from his *Escape from Freedom,* p. 205ff.

ACKNOWLEDGMENTS

If this book provides insight, hope, and direction to the people of America, as has been my motivation for its writing, they may thank my editor, Robert Weil. His tireless attention and enduring devotion to this work have been as a father to a child. Without him this book would not exist.

I have been richly rewarded by Peter Lampack's friendship. His contributions have extended far beyond the duties of a literary agent. His counsel, caring, and encouragement have been indispensable to this endeavor and to me, for which I am deeply grateful.

I thank John Sargent, the powerful young leader of St. Martin's, for his faith in me, and for his wise and available guidance and assistance throughout the entire process of bringing this book to fruition.

I am grateful for the relentlessly intelligent assistance of my copy editor, Beth Pearson, and for the work of Richard E. Nichols who performed much of the background investigation for Part I, and whose suggestions from time to time have been so valuable to me.

The sacrifice of any author's spouse to his work should be forbidden. Yet, like a squalling child demanding undue attention, his work often inserts itself into the marriage. I thank my darling, Imaging, for providing me safe and happy places to think and to write and for her cheerful endurance of this intruder into the household. But more, I thank her for her constant encouragement and her good sense, which are reflected in every page.

A book that is not read becomes merely the self-indulgence of the writer shouting his piece into the void. I therefore thank the many good and devoted people of the St. Martin's sales and marketing force for their efforts in selling this book so that I shall have been saved, at last, from the tragic waste of transferring one's intended gift onto unread pages.

—GERRY SPENCE
Jackson Hole, Wyoming

INDEX

·—•—·

ABOUT THE AUTHOR

Gerry Spence was born and educated in the small towns of Wyoming, where he has practiced law for over forty-five years. He has spent his lifetime representing the poor, the injured, the forgotten, and the damned against what he calls "the New Slave Master," mammoth corporations and mammoth government. He has tried many nationally known cases, including the murder defense of Randy Weaver at Ruby Ridge, the Karen Silkwood case, the case against *Penthouse* magazine for Miss Wyoming, and other important criminal and civil trials. He is the founder of the Trial Lawyer's College, which has established a revolutionary method of training lawyers for the people. He is a well-known television commentator, and continues to practice law from his office in Jackson Hole.

Spence is also the author of eight previous books, including the bestseller *How to Argue and Win Every Time, From Freedom to Slavery, O.J.: The Last Word,* and *The Making of a Country Lawyer.* The author is also a noted painter, poet, and photographer.